CHARACTER ABOVE ALL

Ten Presidents
from
FDR to George Bush

Edited by
ROBERT A. WILSON

A TOUCHSTONE BOOK
Published by Simon & Schuster

TOUCHSTONE
Rockefeller Center
1230 Avenue of the Americas
New York, NY 10020

First Touchstone Edition 1997
TOUCHSTONE and colophon are registered
trademarks of Simon & Schuster Inc.
Designed by Edith Fowler
Manufactured in the United States of America

10 9 8 7 6 5 4 3 2 1

The Library of Congress has cataloged the
Simon & Schuster edition as follows:
Character above all : ten presidents from FDR to
George Bush / edited by Robert A. Wilson.
        p.   cm.
    1. Presidents—United States—History—
20th century.   2. United States—Politics and
government—1933–1945.   3. United States—
Politics and government—1945–1989.
4. United States—Politics and government—
1989–1993.   I. Wilson, Robert A., 1941–   .
E176.1.C485   1996
973.9′092′2—dc20   95-44827   CIP
ISBN 0-684-81411-0
ISBN 0-684-82709-3 (Pbk)

Grateful acknowledgment is made for permission to
reprint the following previously published material:
"John Brown's Body" by Stephen Vincent Benét.
Copyright 1927–1928 by Stephen Vincent Benét.
Copyright renewed © 1955–1956 by Rosemary
Carr Benét. All rights reserved. Reprinted by per-
mission of Brandt & Brandt Literary Agents, Inc.

FOR MY SISTER, BETH FLOOR.

AND SPECIAL THANKS TO:

Raymond Nasher for providing this initiative its crucial impetus. His character reflects the ideals of the nation's oldest public school, Boston Latin, from which he graduated and whose history he honors by the life he leads.

Bernard Rapoport for his unfailing generosity of spirit and the example of his full-time citizenship.

Carl Yeckel for his support at the very beginning.

Tom Luce, once again, for his counsel and insight, which always leave good ideas intact, only stronger and more viable.

CONTENTS

———

PREFACE

THIS BOOK was conceived as an act of defiance. Against the consultants and campaign managers who feel we'd rather read a good bumper sticker than a good book, who believe it's their business, not ours, to elect candidates, who think we are consumed by self-interest.

What we needed was a way to focus more on the character of those seeking to reach the height of American political ambition. My thought was to provide a forum for us to learn from men and women of distinction who had studied and reflected upon the lives and character of past presidents. The insights of these historians, biographers, and journalists could energize and elevate the nation's political discourse by focusing attention on presidential character and its impact on the creation of trust and leadership. That was the idea.

The first person I contacted to help was the Pulitzer Prize–

winning Truman biographer, David McCullough. The friendship and intelligence and energy he always brings to bear made the critical difference. He believed in the importance of the initiative, and his three words, "Count me in," helped me persuade the other extraordinary people to join up: Doris Kearns Goodwin, Stephen Ambrose, Richard Reeves, Tom Wicker, James Cannon, Hendrik Hertzberg, Peggy Noonan, Robert Dallek, and Michael Beschloss. We were on our way.

There would be three components. The first was the book of essays in your hands, covering the sixty years from 1932 through 1992, FDR through George Bush. Ten presidents, half of whom had had assassination attempts made on their lives, one of which succeeded. I was lucky enough to have Esther Newberg as my agent and she presented the idea to publishers. Within a week Simon & Schuster's distinguished editor Alice Mayhew committed to the book.

There would also be lectures on the subject, broadcast nationally by C-Span, delivered by the team of ten. For our venue we selected the LBJ School of Public Affairs at the University of Texas, Austin, because its dean, Max Sherman, believed so strongly and enthusiastically in our effort. And finally, MacNeil-Lehrer Productions committed to coproduce a special in early 1996 on our subject, which now had a title, *Character Above All*.

Somewhere in a Raymond Carver story a character asks, "We started out such good people. What happened to us?" Maybe we started letting other people do for us what we should do for ourselves. Our political process does reflect us, as do our politicians. If we pay only superficial, limited attention to that process, why should we expect any more than we have, to be better off than we are? If we don't think the media is focused sufficiently enough on the complexity of character, we should find a way to focus on it ourselves. If the media wants to zero in only on the campaigns—whose TV spots do what to whom, who's up, who's down, who's looking for love in all the wrong places—let them.

This is our country, we are its citizens, and it's up to us to shoulder the responsibilities of citizenship our nation confers. Being informed, carefully and deeply informed, is one of them. Understanding the depth of character of a presidential candidate is another. To that end I hope this book will help.

—ROBERT A. WILSON

FRANKLIN D. ROOSEVELT

1933–1945

---

by

Doris Kearns Goodwin

"I'LL TELL YOU," Franklin Roosevelt once told a friend during the toughest years of his presidency, "at night when I lay my head on my pillow, and it is often pretty late, and I think of the things that have come before me during the day and the decisions that I have made, I say to myself—well, I have done the best I could, and turn over and go to sleep." With this simple story, Roosevelt provides the key to understanding the essence of his presidency, for no factor was more important to his leadership than his absolute confidence in himself and in the American people.

"There's something that he's got," White House aide Harry Hopkins once told Labor Secretary Frances Perkins. "It seems unreasonable at times, but he falls back on something that gives him complete assurance that everything is going to be all right." This inner well of serenity, historian Arthur Schlesinger once observed, proved to be an unending source of spiritual refreshment for Roosevelt.

In tracing the roots of this sublime confidence, biographers are invariably drawn to Hyde Park, to the boyhood home which remained for the man a powerful source of strength all the days of his life. "All that is in me goes back to the Hudson," Roosevelt liked to say, meaning not simply the peaceful, slow-moving river and the big, comfortable clapboard house but the ambience of boundless devotion that encompassed him as a child. As the adored only son of a young mother and an aging patriarch, Roosevelt grew up in an atmosphere where affection and respect were plentiful, where the discipline was fair and loving, and the opportunity for self-expression abundant. From his position of primacy in his family home, he seemed to develop what Sigmund Freud has called "the feeling of a conqueror, that confidence of success that often induces real success." The sense of being loved wholeheartedly by his parents taught him to trust that the world was basically a friendly and agreeable place.

Man's identity, Erik Erikson observed, is not fixed; it continually evolves through different phases of life. Some experiences induce growth in character; others provoke regression. From childhood through adulthood, most of Roosevelt's experiences—from his being taken everywhere by his parents when he was a child to his enrollment at Groton, Harvard, and Columbia Law, from his appointment as Assistant Secretary of the Navy to his nomination by the Democrats as Vice President at the young age of thirty-seven—confirmed his innate confidence in himself and in his world. But ironically, perhaps no experience stretched Roosevelt more, both intellectually and emotionally, than his bout with polio, which left him, at the age of thirty-nine, paralyzed from the waist down. This was what Eleanor Roosevelt later called his "trial by fire."

"I think," Eleanor observed, "probably the thing that took most courage in his life was his mastery and his meeting of polio. I never heard him complain." And though anyone remembering how athletic and strong he had been as a young man could not fail to realize what a terrific battle must have gone on within him, "he just accepted it as one of those things that was given you as discipline in life." After his struggle with polio, he seemed less arrogant, less smug, less superficial, more focused, more complex, more interesting. "There had been a plowing up of his nature," Frances Perkins commented. "The man emerged completely warm-hearted, with new humility of spirit and a firmer understanding of philosophical concepts." He had always taken great pleasure in people, but now they became what one historian has called "his vital links to life." Far more intensely than before, he reached out to know them, to understand them, to pick up their emotions, to put himself into their shoes. No longer belonging to his old world in the same way, he came to empathize with the poor and the underprivileged, with people to whom fate had dealt a difficult hand.

What is more, Roosevelt had a remarkable capacity to transmit his internal strength to others, to allow, as White House counsel Sam Rosenman observed, the men and women who came to Washington during the New Deal "to begin to feel it and take part in it, to rejoice in it—and to return it tenfold by their own confidence." Frances Perkins claimed that "his capacity to inspire and encourage those around him to do tough, confused and practically impossible jobs was without dispute." Like everyone else, she said, she "came away from an interview with the president feeling better not because he had solved any problems," but because he had somehow made her feel more cheerful, more determined, stronger than she had felt when she went into the room. "I have never known a man who gave one a greater sense of security," Eleanor said. "I never heard him say there was a problem that he thought it was impossible for human beings to solve."

So it was in 1933, when in the midst of the worst days of the Depression, that the new President was able to communicate his own strength and assurance to a badly frightened people. In his first inaugural, *Collier's* magazine reported, the new President did not delude himself as to the difficulties that lay before him, and yet he was serenely confident as to the ultimate outcome. "That speech," historian James MacGregor Burns wrote later, "was more than a speech—it was an act that loosened a tidal wave of support behind the new administration." By this single speech, Rosenman marveled, Roosevelt accomplished one of the most significant achievements of his presidency: "the renewal of the courage and hope and faith of the American people." Within days of the inauguration, historian William Leuchtenburg noted, "the spirit of the country seemed markedly changed, a feeling of hope had been reborn." Thousands of telegrams poured into the White House expressing faith in the new President.

"We have a leader," one headline exclaimed. "Roosevelt stiffened people's spines to face hardship," historian Garry Wills observed, "and even when the hardship did not go away, people drew strength from the very cock of his head, the angle of his cigarette holder, the trademark grin that was a semaphore of hope."

Seven years later, in 1940, when Nazi Germany conquered Western Europe, Roosevelt's serenity and strength were precisely the qualities called for as America faced a second national crisis even more frightening than the first. The situation could not have been more perilous. With German armies sweeping with unparalleled speed through Belgium, Holland, and France, the United States stood eighteenth in military power, behind Holland, behind Switzerland—moving to seventeenth only when Holland surrendered to Germany. There were only 500,000 men in the U. S. Army compared to more than 6 million men under arms in Germany. Years of depression and isolationism had depleted America's military might to the point where the United States possessed almost no modern planes or tanks or guns. Yet, even in these grimmest days, Roosevelt had no doubt that once the dormant energies of democracy were mobilized, the United States would fully meet the Nazi threat. He was absolutely convinced that the uncoerced energies of democracy would prove more than a match for the totalitarian regimes. One of Sam Rosenman's most vivid recollections was seeing Roosevelt's top military advisers—General George Marshall, Admiral Ernest King, and General Henry Arnold—as they left the Oval Office after their daily consultation with the President, "and I always remember their calm, determined, fighting faces; and I always felt certain that a great deal of that calm confidence and firm determination were reflections of the spirit of the man whom they had just left."

And once again, Roosevelt was able to communicate his faith beyond Washington to the American people at large, helping to energize the massive shift to a wartime economy, the construction of hundreds of new factories, the migration of millions of citizens to the cities and towns where the new factories were built, and the creation of new public-private partnerships between business and government which produced planes, ships, tanks, guns, and ammunition in such unimaginable quantities that by 1942, America was outproducing not only the Axis powers but all the Allied powers together, providing weapons and supplies to its Allies in all the corners of the world. Though the way a president communicates his own strengths to the entire nation remains partly a mystery, there is no doubt that Roosevelt created the national climate that made this unmatched productivity possible.

CLOSELY LINKED to Roosevelt's confidence was his willingness to try everything. He never seemed to lose his faith that the right solution to a vexing problem would eventually turn up. When he made up his mind to do something, Eleanor said, he did it to the best of his ability, but if it went sour, he simply started in all over again and did something else. He never spent time repining. "He recognized the difficulties and often said that, while he did not know the answer, he was completely confident that there *was* an answer and that one had to try until one either found it for himself or got it from someone else."

"I have no expectation of making a hit every time I come to bat," Roosevelt liked to say. "What I seek is the highest possible batting average." His mind was almost always flexible and hospitable to new ideas, the writer John Gunther once observed. "He was one of those persons with the good luck to grow up slowly." Until the end of his days, he was always fresh, youthful in mind and receptive to experiment. "Remember," Eleanor once told a friend,

17

"the nicest men in the world are those who always keep something of the little boy in them." That, she emphasized, was Franklin's strength.

During the Depression Roosevelt tried one economic cure after another—heavy spending, public works, direct relief, the NRA Codes, the Blue Eagle campaigns, regulation of industry, restrictions on spending. "He understood," Garry Wills noted, "the importance of psychology—the people have to have the courage to keep seeking a cure, no matter what the cure is. Those who wanted ideological consistency or even policy coherence, were rightly exasperated with Roosevelt. He switched economic plans as often as he changed treatments for polio." And while the New Deal did not overcome the Depression—it took the war to fully mobilize the economy—the multiplicity of government programs kept the people going, and in the process preserved the system of democracy at a time when so many other countries in similar despair were turning to fascism or communism.

To overcome opposition to the New Deal programs in the old-line bureaucracies, Roosevelt created a host of new emergency agencies. "We have new and complex problems," he explained. "Why not establish a new agency to take over the new duty rather than saddle it on an old institution?" He deliberately confused spheres of authority and reinforced the confusion by appointing people of clashing attitudes and temperaments to the competing positions. The costs of this competitive system were borne most heavily by the cabinet members, none of whom were ever completely certain of where they stood. The perpetual competition was so nerve-wracking at times that everyone's performance was hampered. "He has never been a good administrator and the consequence of this has made service under him as a Cabinet officer difficult," War Secretary Henry Stimson lamented. Treasury Secretary Henry Morgenthau agreed. "The thing FDR prided himself the most about," Morgenthau remarked, "was 'I have a happy ship.' But he never had a happy ship."

But so long as his administrative system produced energy,

ideas, and momentum in the country at large, where he rightly believed it really mattered, he was willing to let it be confused at the top. At the same time, the system kept the reins of power in Roosevelt's hands, allowing him to employ all the resources he had developed as a child against the tensions at home brought about by his father's illness and his mother's domineering nature: secrecy, manipulation, charm, negotiation, avoidance, and control. A lesser man, a man of smaller ego would have sought greater concentration of control, more rigid lines of responsibility and authority. But Roosevelt never felt that he or his leadership was threatened by multiplicity and confusion. Supremely confident in his own ability to exert mastery over a multitude of men and institutions, he could let the horses run, never doubting his ability to rein them in if they became uncontrollable.

To be sure, with all this experimentation, he could and did make mistakes and he was forced at times to go back on promises he had made. But he met defeat with serenity and simply moved on, and it never seemed to diminish his confidence nor to damage his image among the people. A case in point revolved around an unfortunate speech that he made in Pittsburgh at the end of the 1932 campaign in which he rashly promised that he would slash government expenditures in order to balance the budget. Once he got into office, however, Roosevelt found that state relief programs and private charity, however preferable, could not fulfill the needs of a people sunk in depression, and he deliberately unbalanced the budget even further to meet these needs. "If starvation and dire need on the part of any of our citizens make necessary the appropriation of additional funds which would keep the budget out of balance," he explained, "I shall not hesitate to tell the American people the full truth and ask them to authorize the expenditures of that additional amount." His explanation held for several years, but when the 1936 campaign got under way, he came under relentless attack for breaking his original pledge.

His first response was to meet the attack with humor. At one strategy session, he roared with laughter at the suggestion that his best line of defense was to categorically deny he was ever in Pittsburgh. But after puzzling over his predicament for a while, he came up with a brilliant rationale for having promised something which he could not deliver. "Governments can err, presidents do make mistakes," he told the cheering audience at the 1936 Democratic Convention, "but the immortal Dante tells us that divine justice weighs the sins of the cold-blooded and the sins of the warmhearted in different scales. Better the occasional faults of a government that lives in a spirit of charity than the constant omissions of a government frozen in the ice of its own indifference."

Nor was he afraid to scrap an idea—or an agency—that had outlived its usefulness. When wartime mobilization brought the country toward full employment, New Deal work programs were no longer needed. The President's beloved Civilian Conservation Corps was the first to go; the Works Progress Administration and the National Youth Administration followed. While some New Dealers, including Eleanor, found the demolition of the old agencies difficult to watch, Roosevelt accepted the need for change. In a celebrated press conference on December 28, 1943, he let it be known that he wished the press would no longer use the term "New Deal" to describe his administration, for the times had changed and there was no longer a need for the New Deal. He wished, he said, to substitute "Dr. Win the War" for old "Doc New Deal."

Moreover, the same man who was regarded as the enemy of big business, who vowed to master the forces of organized wealth, was to become capitalism's greatest benefactor. Under Roosevelt's wartime leadership, the government entered into what must be considered the most productive partnership with private enterprise in the history of the country. As soon as the war broke out, Roosevelt recognized that his hostile relations with the business community had to be improved. Without the cooperation of private industry, the massive production effort needed to catch up to Nazi Germany would never get off the ground. While the Congress could provide the money, it could not build the planes, design the tanks, or assemble the weapons. So Roosevelt brought prominent businessmen into the government, exempted business from anti-trust laws, allowed business to write off the full cost of investments, and sanctioned new cost-plus, fixed-fee contracts which allowed business to defray all costs essential to the execution of defense contracts and guaranteed generous profits. Business flourished under his leadership, reaching unprecedented heights of productivity and laying the foundation for postwar prosperity. In an era when totalitarian dictatorship seemed to be a masterpiece of organization, Roosevelt put his faith in the unorganized momentum of democratic capitalism.

But Roosevelt always thought in terms of human beings rather than in abstract concepts, and as a result, he refused to forge his new partnership with business at the expense of labor. In calling for a massive mobilization effort in 1940, he insisted that "there be no breakdown or cancellation of any of the great social gains which we have made." While businessmen argued for a suspension of New Deal regulations that bore on labor, working conditions, and minimum wages on the ground that such legislation restricted speedy mobilization, Roosevelt took the opposite tack. There was nothing in the emergency he said, to justify lowering the standards of employment, reducing the minimum wage, making workers toil longer hours without due compensation, or breaking down the old age pensions. On the contrary, he maintained: "While our navy and our airplanes and our guns may be our first lines of defense, it is still clear that way down at the bottom, underlying them all, giving them strength, sustenance and power, are the spirit and morale of a free people."

THROUGH THE TURMOIL of the worst days of both the Depression and the war another central quality of Roosevelt's character came into play: his capacity to relax, to cast off his worries, to enjoy himself in the company of his friends and associates. It was this capacity that allowed him to replenish his energies to face the struggles of the following day. Every night Roosevelt followed an extraordinary ritual. He went into his second-floor study, lined with tall mahogany bookcases and stuffed with books, for a cocktail hour to which he invited his friends and associates with the strict rule that no one could talk about serious subjects. Begun during Roosevelt's years in Albany, the cocktail hour soon became an institution in Roosevelt's official family, a time for reviewing events in an informal atmosphere, a time for swapping the best day's laughs. For a few relaxing moments, no more was said of politics or war; instead, the conversation turned to subjects of lighter weight—to gossip, movies, sports, funny stories and reminiscences.

"I never knew anyone," Eleanor's friend Lorena Hickok said, "who had a better sense of humor than Franklin Roosevelt. He was also an unmerciful tease and when he laughed, you could hear him all over the house." Even during serious discussions, Sam Rosenman noted, those working with him were never afraid to interrupt and tell him a funny story or a joke. For some reason, the writer John Steinbeck made Roosevelt laugh. "To the end of his life," Steinbeck recalled, "when occasionally he felt sad and burdened, he used to ask me to come in. We would talk for half an hour and I remember how he would rock in his chair behind his littered desk and I can still hear the roars of laughter."

Beyond the relaxation provided by the cocktail hour, Roosevelt was able to lose himself in hard-fought poker games, rounds of solitaire, movies—preferably mysteries and adventure tales—and long fishing trips. Indeed, on one of his fishing trips, a ten-day sail under the healing Caribbean sun in the middle of the winter, he came up with the idea of lend-lease, the creative idea that broke the logjam on Capitol Hill by suggesting that the United States send weapons to Britain without charge and then after the war be repaid in kind rather than in dollars. "You rarely find a professional politician," White House speechwriter Robert Sherwood joked, "who would make the mistake of being caught in the act of creating an original idea!" And he could spend hours at a time, with his magnifying glass in his hands, arranging and rearranging his beloved stamps. On a weekend trip to Shangri-la (now Camp David), Winston Churchill marveled at Roosevelt's complete absorption in his stamps. Sitting by his side, Churchill watched "with much interest as he stuck them in, each in its proper place and so forgot the cares of State."

But no activity provided greater relaxation than returning to his boyhood home at Hyde Park. Nearly two hundred times during his presidency, Roosevelt journeyed to Hyde Park, where, once he got into his familiar bed, he was able, to the astonishment of his associates, to sleep for twelve or fourteen hours at a stretch. This capacity to relax so totally, which few politicians possess, allowed him to replenish his strength continually, so much so that the burdens of the presidency rarely overwhelmed him. Unlike most of his fellow presidents, he did not gradually deteriorate year by year. Until his last year in office, when his heart began to fail him, he looked as vigorous and vibrant as he had at the start of his presidency. "On none of his predecessors has the office left so few marks as on Mr. Roosevelt," *New York Times* reporter Anne O'Hare McCormick observed. To be sure, he was a little grayer and a little heavier by the middle of his third term, but nothing had shaken his steady self-assurance. On the contrary, McCormick noted, he is "more at ease in all circumstances, more at home in his position, than any leader of his time. His nerves are stronger, his temper cooler and more even. If he worries, he gives no sign of it."

ONE PSYCHIC STRENGTH led to another. Roosevelt's internal confidence freed up energies that allowed him to be unusually receptive to the needs of other people, both the individuals he encountered on a daily basis and the mass of the American people as a whole. Eleanor once said that he made people feel that he was deeply interested in their lives and their families, for he encouraged them to talk about themselves and he always listened with deep attention. This capacity shaped his presidency from the very beginning. During his first days and weeks in office, he made the majority of the people feel that their president cared deeply about them, that he understood their concerns and would somehow protect them from harm. And as the months passed and the New Deal programs began to take root in the country, he received thousands of letters from families thanking him for saving their homes, for finding them a job, for allowing their children to stay in school. In the Denver freight yards, William Leuchtenburg notes, a message in chalk was written on the side of a boxcar: "Roosevelt is my friend."

He had, the British philosopher Isaiah Berlin suggested, an exceptionally sensitive awareness, conscious or subconscious, of the desires, the hopes, the fears, the loves, the hatreds of the human beings who composed his democracy. This uncanny awareness, Berlin argued, was the source of Roosevelt's genius. It was almost as if the inner currents and tremors of human society were registering themselves within his nervous system with a kind of seismological accuracy.

Where this knowledge came from remains partly a mystery. As a child, his mother claimed, Roosevelt was remarkably intuitive, able to anticipate the desires of his parents even before he was told what to do, able to sense the complex emotions in his family when his father became an invalid. From the moment of his father's heart attack when Franklin was only eight, the boy's innate desire to please was amplified by the fear that if he gave his parents any trouble, he might further damage his father's health. His mother took pride in the fact that she never had to be strict with her son merely for the sake of being strict. His instincts were so finely tuned that he never seemed to require that kind of handling.

Then, too, his bout with polio undoubtedly increased his awareness of what other people were thinking and doing. Determined to put others at ease with his disability, to ensure that no one pitied him, not even for a single instant, he instinctively assessed every new situation and figured out how best to preserve his dignity and pride. The actor Gregory Peck recalled waiting at a harbor when he was a boy to catch his first glimpse of the President. Like most Americans, Peck had no idea that Roosevelt was a paraplegic. While he knew that Roosevelt had had polio when he was younger, he had no understanding of the full extent of his disability, no idea that he had to call for his valet every morning to help him get out of bed. Because there was an unspoken code of honor on the part of the press never to photograph the President looking crippled, never to show him helpless, never to show him on his crutches or in his wheelchair, most people simply assumed that the polio had left him a bit lame but that he could still walk on his own power.

So when the young Gregory Peck stood on the dock that day and saw Roosevelt being carried off the boat like a child, he was so stunned that he started to cry. But then, Peck recalled, Roosevelt instantly put everyone at ease. As soon as he was placed in his chair, he put his hat on his head, placed his cigarette holder in his mouth, waved to the crowd and smiled his dazzling smile, and suddenly, Peck said, "I started clapping and everything was fine. He seemed with every gesture to be saying, 'I'm not pitying myself, so why should you worry about me?' "

Roosevelt's manipulation of other people's reactions to his disability perfectly prepared him, Garry Wills suggests, to be an actor in the best sense of the word. As he learned to transform pity into admiration, he learned to "feign a welcome to unwanted constituents' attentions, cooperate with despised party allies, wax indignant at politically chosen targets. This is not the work of inferior politicians, but of the masters."

BUT ROOSEVELT would be the first to admit that beyond his own intuition and his experience with polio, his extraordinary understanding of the American people came as a result of his wife Eleanor's remarkable ramblings around the country. For she was, as he said over and over again after his polio, his eyes and his ears. Traveling tens of thousands of miles each year through every section of the nation—through the coal mines of Appalachia, the migrant labor camps of California, the ghettos of Detroit and Chicago, and the flatlands of the Middle West—Eleanor served as a voice for people who did not have a voice of their own, for blacks and women, for struggling laborers and the unemployed, for migrant workers and tenant farmers. "She really tried to get to know what their problems were by doing," Morgenthau's daughter Joan Hirschhorn said. "She really went to their homes; she really tried to understand at a gut level what they were experiencing in a way that very few people did."

The Roosevelt partnership is all the more remarkable when one realizes that Eleanor's deep-rooted insecurity and shyness stood in direct contrast to her husband's confidence and charm. "You couldn't find," Eleanor's daughter, Anna Boettiger, once said, "two such different people as Mother and Father." Whereas Franklin had "too much security and too much love," Eleanor seemed forever starved for love and affection, never having received from either her alcoholic father or her self-absorbed mother the affirmation she so desperately craved. Through most of her childhood, Eleanor felt herself to be an outsider in her own family, believing that her beautiful mother was fatally disappointed in her only daughter's lack of a pretty face. Indeed, the presiding memory of Eleanor's childhood is standing outside the parlor in the late afternoons while her mother sat by the fire inside, looking elegant but unapproachable to the little girl who worried that she would render the lovely scene ugly by simply entering the room. For the rest of her life, Eleanor was unable to shake the haunted feeling that she was an outsider—a feeling powerfully reinforced by her discovery in 1918, after twelve years of marriage, that Franklin was having an affair with a young woman named Lucy Mercer. When Eleanor came upon a packet of love letters that Lucy had written to her husband, she said that the bottom dropped out of her world. She immediately offered him a divorce, but after long conversations and a solemn pledge on Franklin's part that he would never see Lucy again, Eleanor agreed to stay with her husband.

From that moment on, the marriage was fundamentally reconstituted, for Eleanor was able to do something few married women at that time could do—find genuine fulfillment and self-expression outside the home. She became involved in teaching and in settlement house work. She joined a group of women reformers who taught her that she had a series of talents she had never known she had before—for public speaking, for organizing, for articulating a cause. Gradually, she developed an increasing confidence in her ability to understand and express the needs of others, particularly those who fell outside the system of power and influence. Not surprisingly, the little girl who had always felt herself to be an outsider in her small family circle felt a special affinity toward defenseless children, immigrants, minorities, and the poor.

Eleanor's budding political activism assumed a new dimension when Franklin got polio and had to spend weeks and months at a time in Warm Springs, Georgia, trying desperately and ultimately unsuccessfully to walk on his own power again. During these long sojourns away from home, he needed Eleanor to keep his political ambitions alive by going from one meeting to another in New York, which she did so effectively that he was able to return in 1928 just in time to run for governor. And then, when he became President, her travels on his behalf multiplied. During the worst years of the Depression, Eleanor traveled nearly two hundred days a year, visiting with southern blacks and migrant workers, inspecting Civilian Conservation Corps camps and National Youth Administration projects, absorbing an unprecedented knowledge that allowed her to determine which of her husband's programs were working or failing, wasteful or underfunded. And when she returned, in contrast to the filtered accounts that deferential subordinates too often provide their superiors, she was brutally honest in telling Franklin what she had seen, giving him the base of knowledge he needed to alter his programs or change his approach.

They made an extraordinary team. She was less devious, less patient, more uncompromisingly moral; he possessed a more practical understanding of how to get things done, a more finely tuned feeling for the American people, a greater flexibility of mind and heart. There was a game called "point to point" that Eleanor played at the house of her uncle Teddy Roosevelt when she was young. The game called for running straight from one point to another even if you had to climb over a house or swim a stream or go through a neighbor's living room. "It was often very rough," Eleanor told her grandson Curtis Roosevelt, "and many children didn't make it, for it required steadfast determination, even bullheadedness to get to the goal," but it was something Eleanor always remembered. And it was reflected in her own political style years later when, in contrast to her husband's tendency to move sideways and backwards before moving forward, Eleanor consistently displayed what Franklin once described as "a backbone that didn't bend."

But the war threatened the partnership that had worked so well during the Depression years, for suddenly the President was spending more and more time with businessmen, conservatives, military men, and southern congressmen, and Eleanor felt she was losing her partner, and in losing her partner, she felt she was losing herself. She cycled into one of her periodic depressions and came out of it only when she became convinced that there was still a critical fight to be fought, and that was to make the war a vehicle for social reform, to ensure that when the soldiers came home, they would find a country more socially just than the one they had left behind. It meant that she had to become an agitator, often working at cross-purposes with her husband because his central focus was on winning the war. It meant being relentless and pushy at times, but underneath Franklin's occasional exasperation with his wife, he understood that most of what she was pushing him to do needed to be done, and his presidency was immeasurably enriched as a result.

Nowhere was Eleanor's influence on her husband greater than on civil rights. At the start of the war, blacks were openly discriminated against in both the war factories and the armed forces, but by the end, through the combination of Eleanor's insistent agitation and the power of the budding civil rights movement, millions of blacks were working at all skill levels in the factories and serving as pilots, radiomen, and officers in the Army and the Navy. Throughout the war, Eleanor successfully argued that a fully productive work force required everyone's talents, blacks and women alike; and if the women were to work in the factories, their children required day care. She played a central role in securing government funds for day care centers and in getting local cities and towns to provide after-school programs, takeout foods, and community laundries. As a result of these measures, the absentee rate dropped and productivity soared.

To be sure, Eleanor provoked widespread criticism, particularly in the South, for being so far ahead of her time on civil rights. Can't you muzzle that wife of yours, Roosevelt was frequently asked, or at the very least chain her up? A consistent refrain in the President's mail suggested that he must be somewhat emasculated by having such a strong and independent wife. Do you have lace on your panties for allowing your wife to speak out so much? one critic asked. But Roosevelt was so confident in his own strength that he never feared that a strong woman would make him look weak. Moreover, he recognized that Eleanor's temperament and travels alike had brought her into closer sympathy and contact with whole segments of the population that he needed to understand and represent.

BUT IF ROOSEVELT's receptivity to others, aided in large part by his wife, was a central factor in his leadership, it is important to understand that his was not a passive receptivity. He received impressions and absorbed the feelings of others in order to act, to lead, to educate, to shape public opinion. His strength came in leading the people step by step, never getting too far ahead of them, but always moving them forward little by little, toward the goals he had defined for the nation. And in shaping public opinion, Roosevelt proved to be an exceptional teacher. He understood that communicating his decisions to the people so that they understood why he was doing something was as important as making the right decision in the first place. And in all his contacts with the media, he understood the importance of maintaining at all times the dignity of his office.

Though he was accessible to the press, more than any previous president—twice a week, year after year, he opened his doors to reporters in wide-ranging press conferences—it was always on his terms, in the setting of the Oval Office, with the flags and the presidential seals behind him, with the understanding that they could quote him directly only if permission were granted. Roosevelt's very first press conference, held on March 8, 1933, at a terrible moment in America's national life, had set the tone. The banks were closed, a third of the labor force was idle, and the country's confidence was at its lowest ebb. Yet, again and again, in the course of the thirty-five minutes, the President managed to elicit vigorous laughter from the newspapermen, projecting a mood of fearlessness and hope that they proceeded to carry to hundreds of cities and towns across the country. "He was informal, communicative, gay," William Leuchtenburg wrote. "When he evaded a question it was done frankly. He was thoroughly at ease. He made no effort to conceal his pleasure in the give and take of the situation." Indeed, so overwhelmed were the reporters by the warmth and frankness of the President's attitude, in contrast to the stiffness of his predecessors who demanded written questions in advance, that when the meeting ended, they broke into spontaneous applause.

With his celebrated "fireside chats," Roosevelt understood the importance of rationing his appearances to make each one a dramatic event for the country. In the twelve years of his presidency, he delivered fewer than thirty fireside chats, averaging only two or three a year. For each speech, he put in an average of four or five days' preparation, working and reworking drafts, rehearsing again and again in front of his staff, revising various parts so that the emotional impact could be strengthened. The hard work paid off: listener polls suggested that more than two or three times as many people listened to each of his fireside chats as listened to the most popular radio shows at that time—Jack Benny, Amos 'n' Andy, Bob Hope, Fibber McGee. Relaxed in a basement room in the White House, he developed a simple and direct conversational style. In his mind, he could picture people sitting in their living rooms and kitchens listening to him, and he was able to connect with them as he talked.

His first fireside chat explained the complex banking crisis in such direct and simple terms that the people did not panic when he announced that he had closed the banks and would reopen them on a gradual basis. He used concrete illustrations and everyday analogies to make his arguments. The next three talks focused on the currency situation, the New Deal program, and the National Recovery Act. Almost every speech called on some aspect of American history, a memory of the days of the Revolution, the westward migration, the Civil War, the great immigration. "The sense of history in a political leader," Archibald MacLeish noted, "is a sense of the past as the past has meaning for the future, and Roosevelt's sense of history and of the American tradition was very strong indeed."

Perhaps his most effective address was the so-called map speech, delivered in February 1942 at a low ebb of the war. In the week before the speech, he asked everyone to get a map so they could follow with him the course of the war in the Pacific. That week there was a run on maps all over the country. On the night of the broadcast, nearly 80 percent of the home audience sat listening to their President, their maps spread before them, as he patiently explained how each battle in the various arenas halfway around the world fit into the larger picture. The American people, he warned, must be prepared to suffer more losses before the situation turned. With such frank talk, Sam Rosenman later observed, "there was no such thing as a 'credibility gap' in the White House. But he never for a moment betrayed the slightest doubt that victory would come in the long run; for he never felt any doubt." Indeed, he was absolutely certain, he promised, that the tide would turn, for he trusted in democracy and in the people, and he knew that just as George Washington had suffered defeats and limited supplies in the winters at Valley Forge but ultimately triumphed, so would the Allied forces.

The speech was so effective that before the night had ended, hundreds of letters and telegrams poured into the White House, telling him that the only way to sustain morale was for him to go on the radio every day. But Roosevelt understood intuitively that if he tried to replicate his talks too often, they would lose their rallying power. "The one thing I dread," he wrote at the time, "is that my talks should be so frequent as to lose their effectiveness."

ABOVE ALL, in shaping public opinion, Roosevelt possessed a magnificent sense of timing. He understood when to invoke the prestige of the presidency and when to hold it in reserve. "I am like a cat," he once said, "I make a good stroke and then I relax." He was always careful, James MacGregor Burns noted, "not to confront his political opponents when they were mobilizing; after waiting for the crest of the opposition effort to subside, he acted quickly." Nowhere was this sense of timing more critical than in the first days after his inauguration, when he instinctively understood the importance of acting boldly and quickly to create a sense of momentum that would transform the mood of the people across the nation and then serve as a foundation for everything else he wanted to do from that point on.

And then again, in 1940, his timing was impeccable as he brought an isolationist people along to a greater and greater commitment to the Allied cause through a brilliant series of small steps. In the spring of 1940, for instance, he let the anguished reaction to the Nazi invasion of Western Europe build before he addressed a joint session of Congress on May 16 and challenged the American people to begin the mobilization process. He let a citizens' group take the lead on the draft in the summer of 1940 while he focused on making the destroyer deal with Britain. Then, when it looked as though the draft would be defeated, he delivered a strong endorsement that carried the bill through. Three months later, he sat quietly for days aboard the *Tuscaloosa* after receiving Churchill's urgent plea for help with Britain's financial crisis until he suddenly emerged with the lend-lease idea. Then, perfectly sensing exactly how far the public was willing to go at that moment, he successfully sold lend-lease to the Congress and the country as America's best alternative to war. And these examples could be multiplied by a dozen more.

Moreover, Roosevelt's sensitivity to public opinion did not paralyze him from making difficult decisions that he believed had to be made for the well-being of the country despite the current state of feeling at the time. "Boldness," John Gunther suggested, "probably had some roots in the fact that his father was a very old man; consequently, he grew up with little fear of authority." As commander-in-chief, he picked a first-class military team—Marshall, King, Arnold, Admiral William Leahy—and gave them wide latitude to run the war. But at critical junctures, against the advice of these trusted advisers and the sentiments of the people, he had the courage to force action. In the spring and summer of 1940, he insisted on giving all aid to Britain short of war, though isolationism was still the most potent attitude across the land and though his military chiefs warned him he was jeopardizing U.S. security by sending limited weapons and planes to a country sure to be defeated by Germany. The following year, he brought Russia under the lend-lease umbrella though his advisers believed Russia had no chance of holding out against the German invaders. And he personally made the controversial decision to invade North Africa in 1942, which General Eisenhower considered a serious mistake at the time but later agreed was the right thing to do. "Above all," Isaiah Berlin concluded, "he was absolutely fearless. He was one of the few statesmen in the twentieth century or any other century who seemed to have no fear of the future."

To BE SURE, Roosevelt's sensitive antennae produced occasional problems. His techniques and ways of dealing with the world were so deeply rooted in his character and his nature that alteration proved impossible, even when those techniques proved counterproductive. So skillful was he in sensing what people wanted him to say that he often made visitors feel he was agreeing with what they were saying when he really didn't agree at all. He gave people, Eleanor later admitted, false impressions at times. "Perhaps in the long run," one disillusioned aide said, "fewer friends would have been lost by bluntness than by the misunderstandings that arose from his charming, engaging ambiguity." Moreover, so desirous was he of making other people like him that he was unable to fire anyone—neither the drunken valet who was supposed to help him out of his bed into the bathroom every morning nor the Germanic housekeeper at the White House who refused to prepare for him the foods he loved, insisting that she knew what was best for him. With more serious consequences, he delayed firing his isolationist Secretary of War, Henry Woodring, for months and months, until the German conquest of Western Europe finally forced his hand. His real weakness, Eleanor observed—and it came out of a strength, really, she said—was that he had great sympathy for people and great understanding, and he couldn't bear to be disagreeable, and he couldn't bring himself to do the unkind thing that had to be done until he got angry. This weakness was a chief source of the disorderliness of the Roosevelt administration, of his double dealing and his tendency to procrastinate.

At times, Roosevelt seemed to enjoy deception and dissimulation for its own sake. His desire to keep the levers of control in his own hands led on occasion to manipulation and lack of candor, to frustration and disappointment on the part of those who worked with him. "He enjoyed being tricky," Gunther noted, and possessed an almost childish love of secrecy. The roots of this deviousness, like the roots of his equanimity, can be traced to his boyhood at Hyde Park. The very closeness with his mother that helped produce his amazing self-confidence also produced a continuing battle for autonomy, for space in which he could be an individual in his own right, pursuing his separate wishes and goals. In order to escape his mother's potentially suffocating love, he developed the habit of telling her only what she needed to know, even at times of deceiving her. "The effort to become his own man without wounding his mother," historian Geoffrey Ward suggests, "fostered in him much of the guile and easy charm, love of secrecy and skill at maneuver he brought to the White House." The pattern of concealing his genuine feelings while appearing to be open and accessible made it difficult for all those who worked with him to know where they really stood. "Nearly all around him," his aide

Raymond Moley lamented, "had the chilling fear that he regarded them as indispensable."

Roosevelt's ego—the source of his greatest strength—was also a source of troubling weakness, for it prevented him in both 1940 and 1944 from grooming a successor. Though he always meant to develop somebody, Frances Perkins observed, he never quite got around to it, and as a result, he effectively paralyzed the political process with everyone waiting for him to decide whether he would run for an unprecedented third or fourth term. "Perhaps he was working at cross-purposes with himself," Perkins added. For, at bottom, "he obviously did like being president. It was a full time occupation for all of his energies and talents and anybody is happy and content when fully functioning." Journalist W. M. Kiplinger agreed, suggesting that Roosevelt fed on applause. "He does his best when he is in the center of the limelight, and when he hears the cheers of the public. Then he is warmed and he rises to heights." Put in less sympathetic terms, Moley suggested that Roosevelt had begun to feel that he was the only possible man to lead the country. "I think he began to feel that way more and more the longer he stayed in office."

One must also concede the failures of perception and the failures of vision that led to his abortive Supreme Court packing scheme, which Harry Truman later blamed on "that growing ego of his, which probably wasn't too minuscule to start with," his ill-conceived purge of conservatives in the 1938 by-election, his forcible relocation of the Japanese-Americans, and the lack of a more decisive response to the extermination of the European Jews. Totally focused on winning the war, Roosevelt mistakenly accepted the specious argument that the incarceration of the Japanese-Americans was a military necessity. In so doing, he deprived tens of thousands of men, women, and children of Japanese descent of their civil liberties and trampled on values that he himself cherished. Similarly, his intensity of focus on winning the war as the best means of rescuing the Jews blinded him to a series of steps that could have been taken, such as bombing the train tracks to the concentration camps or even bombing the camps themselves. Though the results that might have been expected from these actions were far from certain, they would have put him on the right side of one of the most important issues in history.

BUT IN THE END, Roosevelt's strengths far outweighed his weaknesses. Despite confusions and conflicts, clashing interests and disparate goals, labor strikes and riots, he somehow kept the American people together during the two greatest crises of the twentieth century, the Great Depression and World War II, creating the national climate that allowed the country to move forward. He was able to fit the smallest details and the most varied impressions into a coherent pattern. "He would have flashes of almost clairvoyant knowledge and understanding of a terrific variety of matters that didn't seem to have any particular relationship to each other," Perkins marveled. There were times when it seemed that he could truly see it all—the relationship of the federal government to the states and to the people, the relationship of the home front to the war front, of the factories to the soldiers, of speeches to morale, of war aims to the shape of the peace to come. "The fact that one thing relates to another," historian Eric Larrabee concluded, "was not merely a condition of his thinking but its guiding principle—and this enabled him not only to perceive the war as a whole but to convey that perception of it to his constituency."

"Oh, we all know he could be exasperating," Harry Hopkins once said, "and he could seem to be temporizing and delaying, and he'd get us all worked up when he thought he was making too many concessions to expediency. But all of that was in the little things—the unimportant things. But in the big things—all the things that were of real, permanent importance, he never let the people down." Through the whole of Franklin's career, Eleanor commented, there was never any deviation from his original objective to help make life better for the average man, woman, and child. "A thousand and one means were used, difficulties arose, changes took place, but his objective always was the motive for whatever had to be done." He always cast his vote for life, Arthur Schlesinger wrote, for action, for forward motion, for the future. His response to the magnificent emptiness of the Grand Canyon was typical. "It looks dead," he said. "I like my green trees at Hyde Park much better—they are alive and growing." It was this vitality, this fundamental belief in the future, that won Roosevelt the love and confidence of his fellow citizens, making him the only President to be elected four times to the White House.

THE WORLD has turned many times since Roosevelt was first elected. He would surely be among the first to agree that the very different conditions and problems of the day demand fresh approaches, a new imagination, innovative policies. In that sense, there can be no objection to "dismantling the New Deal," as if one can dismantle what was intended as an ongoing experiment, itself a continuation of what George Washington called the "Great Experiment" that is America. But Roosevelt would not agree with any abandonment of the great principles that guided his efforts, could not agree without denying his own beliefs, the meaning of his life and of his leadership—the American pursuit of justice, which requires a commitment to the well-being of every citizen. Under Roosevelt's leadership, the rich stayed rich, but the poor got richer and became the great middle class. Under his leadership, almost every hitherto oppressed segment of the American people made large advances toward fair treatment and equal opportunity— blacks, women, laborers, impoverished tenant farmers. For that objective was not a changeable policy, but the fixed purpose of all policy.

If it was often difficult to identify exactly which policies Franklin Roosevelt stood for, no one could ever doubt which side he was on in the unending conflict between interests that is the underlying theme of democratic life. Certainly the people he led had no doubt. When he died, on April 12, 1945, there was an outpouring of emotion then unequaled in American history. As his funeral train slowly made its way from Warm Springs, Georgia, to Washington, thousands gathered to say goodbye. They stood in clusters, heads bowed, openly weeping. "They came from the fields and the farms," one reporter wrote, "from hamlets and crossroads and in the cities they thronged by the thousands to stare with humble reverence and awe." Merriman Smith noted that "men stood with their arms around the shoulders of their wives and mothers. Men and women openly wept."

The *New York Times* editorialized that "men will thank God on their knees a hundred years from now, that FDR was in the White House. . . . Gone is the fresh and spontaneous interest which this man took, as naturally as he breathed air, in the troubles and hardships and the disappointments and hopes of little men and humble people." Musician Woody Guthrie sang, "The world was lucky to see him born." And in every continent of the globe multitudes agreed. One is justified in wondering who among the leaders of today will earn such tribute.

HARRY S. TRUMAN
1945–1953

by
David McCullough

HARRY TRUMAN was President of the United States for not quite eight years. Looking back now we see him standing there in the presidential line, all of five foot nine, in a double-breasted suit, between two heroic figures of the century, Franklin Delano Roosevelt and Dwight D. Eisenhower. It's hard to convey today the feeling Americans had about General Eisenhower, the aura of the man, after World War II. He was charismatic, truly, if anyone ever was. Truman was not like that, not glamorous, not photogenic. And from the April afternoon when Truman took office, following the death of Franklin Roosevelt, he would feel the long shadow of Roosevelt, the most colossal figure in the White House in this century. He had none of Roosevelt's gifts—no beautiful speaking voice, no inherited wealth or social standing, no connections. He is the only president of our century who never went to college, and along with his clipped Missouri twang and eyeglasses thick as the bottom of a Coke bottle, he had a middlewestern plainness of manner that, at first glance, made him seem "ordinary."

He had arrived first in Washington in the 1930s as a senator notable mainly for his background in the notorious Pendergast machine of Kansas City. He was of Scotch-Irish descent, and like many of Scotch-Irish descent—and I know something of this from my own background—he could be narrow, clannish, short-tempered, stubborn to a fault. But he could also be intensely loyal and courageous. And deeply patriotic. He was one of us, Americans said, just as they also said, "To err is Truman."

He was back in the news again after the Republican sweep in November 1994, the first such Republican triumph since 1946, and so naturally comparisons were drawn. Like Bill Clinton, Truman had been humiliated in his mid-term election of 1946, treated with open scorn and belittlement by Republicans, and seldom defended by his fellow Democrats. He was written off.

But how Truman responded is extremely interesting and bears directly on our subject, character in the presidency. It was as if he had been liberated from the shadow of Roosevelt. "I'm doing as I damn please for the next two years and to hell with all of them," he told his wife, Bess. And what's so remarkable and fascinating is that the next two years were the best of Truman's presidency. The years 1947 and 1948 contained most of the landmark achievements of his time in office: the first civil rights message ever sent to Congress, his executive order to end segregation in the armed forces, the Truman Doctrine, the recognition of Israel, the Berlin Airlift, and the Marshall Plan, which saved Western Europe from economic and political ruin and stands today as one of the great American achievements of the century.

He showed again and again that he understood the office, how the government works, and that he understood himself. He knew who he was, he liked who he was. He liked Harry Truman. He enjoyed being Harry Truman. He was grounded, as is said. He stressed, "I tried never to forget who I was, where I came from, and where I would go back to." And again and again, as I hope I will be able to demonstrate, he could reach down inside himself and come up with something very good and strong. He is the seemingly ordinary American who when put to the test, rises to the occasion and does the extraordinary.

Now by saying he knew himself and understood himself and liked himself, I don't mean vanity or conceit. I'm talking about self-respect, self-understanding. To an exceptional degree, power never went to his head, nor did he ever grow cynical, for all the time he spent in Washington. He was never inclined to irony or to grappling with abstract thoughts. He read a great deal, enjoyed good bourbon—Wild Turkey preferably—he was a good listener. His physical, mental, and emotional stamina were phenomenal. . . . There's much to be seen about people in how they stand, how they walk. Look at the photographs of Harry Truman, the newsreels—backbone American.

In the spring of 1945, the new untested President of the United States sat in the Oval Office. Across the desk, in the visitor's chair, sat a grim-looking old friend, Sam Rayburn, the Speaker of the House. They were alone in the room, just the two of them, and they were, in many ways, two of a kind. Rayburn knew he could talk straight from the shoulder to Truman, who had been in office only a few days.

"You have got many great hazards and one of them is in this White House. I've been watching this thing a long time," Rayburn began. "I've seen people in the White House try to build a fence around the White House and keep the very people away from the president that he should see. That is one of your hazards, the special interests and the sycophants who will stand in the rain a week to see you and will treat you like a king. They'll come sliding in and tell you you're the greatest man alive. But you know, and I know, you ain't."

Truman knew he wasn't Hercules, he knew he wasn't a glamour boy, he knew he didn't have—and this is so important—the capacity to move the country with words, with eloquence. He had none of the inspirational magic of his predecessor. If Roosevelt was Prospero, Truman was Horatio.

Character Above All is the title of this book, and character counts in the presidency more than any other single quality. It is more important than how much the President knows of foreign policy or economics, or even about politics. When the chips are down—and the chips are nearly always down in the presidency—how do you decide? Which way do you go? What kind of courage is called upon? Talking of his hero Andrew Jackson, Truman once said, it takes one kind of courage to face a duelist, but it's nothing like the courage it takes to tell a friend, no.

In making his decision to recognize Israel, Truman had to tell the man he admired above all others, no—but more on that shortly.

TRUMAN HAD SEEN a lot of life long before he came to Washington. He was born in 1884. He was a full-grown, mature, nearly middle-aged man by the time of the Great War, as his generation called World War I, which was the real dividing line between the nineteenth and the twentieth centuries and the turning point in his life. Everything changed in the period after World War I, which in retrospect may be seen as the first, hideous installment of a two-part world catastrophe. Even the same characters—Hitler, Churchill, Roosevelt, Truman, MacArthur, Marshall—reappear in World War II. Growing up in Victorian middle America, Truman came to maturity with much of the outlook, good and bad, of that very different time.

At heart he remained a nineteenth-century man. He never liked air-conditioning, hated talking by telephone. (And thank goodness, for he wrote letters instead, thousands as time went on, and as a result it is possible to get inside his life, to know what he thought and felt, in a way rarely possible with public figures, and presidents in particular.) He disliked Daylight Saving Time and time zones. (He liked wearing two watches, one set on Eastern Standard Time, the other on Missouri time, "real time," as he called it.)

He was also a farmer, a real farmer let it be remembered, not a photo opportunity or a gentleman farmer like FDR or Tom Dewey. With his father, he *worked* on the farm, facing all the perils

of bad weather, failing crops, insect plagues, and debt. Truman &
Son, of Grandview, Missouri, were never out of debt. He was there
for eleven years, until he went off to war in 1917, and as he used to
say, "It takes a lot of pride to run a farm." Certainly on a family
farm, you don't "do your own thing." Let down your end and the
whole enterprise may fall. And every morning there's your father at
the foot of the stairs at five-thirty, no matter the weather, no matter
the season, telling you it's time to be up and at it.

There was no running water on the Truman farm, no electric-
ity. When his mother had to have an emergency appendectomy,
she was operated on by a country doctor on the kitchen table, and
it was young Harry who stood beside her through all of it holding
the lantern.

He was, as his pal Harry Vaughan, once said, "one tough
son-of-a-bitch of a man. . . . And that," said Vaughan, "was part of
the secret of understanding him." He could take it. He had been
through so much. There's an old line, "Courage is having done it
before."

It's been often said that Truman was poorly prepared for the
presidency. He came to office not knowing any of the foreign policy
establishment in Washington. He had no friends on Wall Street,
no powerful financial backers, no intellectual "brain trust." When
Winston Churchill came to Washington in the early 1940s and
busied himself meeting everybody of known influence, no one suggested he look up the junior senator from Missouri.

But Truman had experienced as wide a range of American life
as had any president, and in that sense he was well prepared. He
had grown up in a small town when the small town was the essence
of American life. He'd been on the farm all those years, and he'd
gone to war. And the war was the crucible. Captain Harry Truman
returned from France in 1919 having led an artillery battery
through the horrific Battle of the Argonne and having discovered
two vitally important things about himself. First, that he had courage, plain physical courage. Until then he had never been in a fight
in his life. He was the little boy forbidden by his mother to play in

roughhouse games because of his glasses. He was a bookworm—a sissy, as he said himself later on, using the dreaded word. But in France he'd found he could more than hold his own in the face of the horrors of battle and, second, that he was good at leading people. He liked it and he had learned that courage is contagious. If the leader shows courage, others get the idea.

Often he was scared to death. One of the most endearing of his many letters to Bess was written after his first time under fire in France, to tell her how terrified he was. It happened at night in the rain in the Vosges Mountains. The Germans had opened fire with a withering artillery barrage. Truman and his green troops thought it could be the start of a gas attack and rushed about trying frantically not only to get their own gas masks on, but to get masks on the horses as well. And then they panicked, ran. Truman, thrown by his horse, had been nearly crushed when the horse fell on him. Out from under, seeing the others all running, he just stood there, locked in place, and called them back using every form of profanity he'd ever heard. And back they came. This was no Douglas MacArthur strutting the edge of a trench to inspire the troops. This was a man who carried extra eyeglasses in every pocket because without glasses he was nearly blind. He had memorized the eye chart in order to get into the Army. And there he was in the sudden hell of artillery shells exploding all around, shouting, shaming his men back to do what they were supposed to do.

Now flash forward to a night thirty years later, in 1948, at the Democratic National Convention in Philadelphia, when Democrats on the left and Democrats on the right had been doing everything possible to get rid of President Harry Truman for another candidate. The Dixiecrats had marched out of the convention. The liberals, who had tried to draft General Eisenhower, were down in the dumps as never before, convinced, after Truman was nominated, that all was lost. Truman was kept waiting backstage hour after hour. It was not until nearly two in the morning that he came on stage to accept the nomination. That was the year when the conventions were covered by television for the first time and the huge lights made even worse the summer furnace of Philadelphia. The crowd was drenched in perspiration, exhausted. For all the speeches there had been, nobody had said a word about winning.

Truman, in a white linen suit, walked out into the floodlights and did just what he did in the Vosges Mountains. He gave them hell. He told them, in effect, to soldier up—and that they were going to win. It was astounding. He brought the whole hall to its feet. He brought them up cheering. Old hand reporters, even the most diehard liberals who had so little hope for him, agreed it was one of the greatest moments they had ever witnessed in American politics.

So there we have it, courage, determination, call it as you will. Dean Acheson, his Secretary of State, much later, searching for a way to describe the effect Truman could have on those around him, and why they felt as they did about him, quoted the lines from Shakespeare's *Henry V*, when King Henry—King Harry—walks among the terrified, dispirited troops the night before the Battle of Agincourt:

> *. . . every wretch, pining and pale before,*
> *Beholding him, plucks comfort from his looks. . . .*
> *His liberal eye doth give to every one . . .*
> *A little touch of Harry in the night.*

Acheson was remembering one of the darkest times of the Truman years, when unexpectedly 260,000 Chinese Communist troops came storming into the Korean War. Through it all, as Acheson and others saw at close hand, Truman never lost confidence, never lost his essential good cheer, never lost his fundamental civility and decency toward those who worked with him. He was never known to dress down a subordinate. "Give 'em hell, Harry" never gave anybody hell behind the scenes, on the job.

His decision to go into Korea in June 1950 was the most difficult of his presidency, he said. And he felt it was the most important decision of his presidency—more difficult and important than the decision to use the atomic bomb, because he feared he might be taking the country into another still more horrible world war, a nuclear war. Yet at the time, it was a very popular decision, a point often forgotten. The country was waiting for the President to say we would go to the rescue of the South Koreans, who were being overrun by the Communist North Korean blitzkrieg. The lesson of Munich weighed heavily on everyone. In Congress, the President had strong support on both sides of the aisle, at the start at least. He was applauded by the press across the country. It was only later that summer of 1950 when the war went so sour that it became "Truman's War."

But you see, there was no corollary between popularity and the ease or difficulty of the decision. His most popular decision was, for him, his most difficult decision, while his least popular decision was, he said, not difficult at all. That was the firing of General Douglas MacArthur, by far the most unpopular, controversial act of his presidency. Attacked by all sides, torn to shreds in editorials and by radio commentators, a potent force then as today, Truman went on with his work as usual, just riding it out. He seemed to have a sort of inner gyroscope for such times. Those around him wondered how it was possible. He said he was sure that in the long run the country would judge him to have done the right thing. Besides, he had only done his duty. The Constitution stated clearly that there will be civilian control over the military and he had taken an oath to uphold the Constitution. "It wasn't difficult for me at all," he insisted.

TRUMAN'S PROFOUND SENSE of history was an important part of his makeup. He believed every president should know American history at the least, and world history, ideally. A president with a sense of history is less prone to hubris. He knows he is but one link in a long chain going all the way back to the first president and that presumably will extend far into the future. He knows he has only a limited time in office and that history will be the final judge of his performance. What he does must stand the test of time. If he is blasted by the press, if his polls are plummeting as Truman's did during the Korean War, these are not the first concerns. What matters—or ought to matter—is what's best for the country and the world in the long run.

Truman probably understood the history of the presidency as well as or better than any president of this century with the exception of Woodrow Wilson, and in his first years in the White House he felt acutely the presence of his predecessors. He was sure the White House was haunted. This was before restoration of the old place, when it creaked and groaned at night with the change of temperature. Sometimes doors would fly open on their own. Alone at night, his family back in Missouri, he would walk the upstairs halls, poke about in closets, wind the clocks. He imagined his predecessors arguing over how this fellow Truman was doing so far.

His reputation seems to grow and will, I believe, continue to grow for the reason that he not only faced difficult decisions and faced them squarely, if not always correctly, but that the decisions were so often unprecedented. There were no prior examples to go by. In his first months in office, he made more difficult and far-reaching decisions than any president in our history, including Franklin Roosevelt and Abraham Lincoln. This much belittled, supposed backwater political hack, who seemed to have none or certainly very few of the requisite qualities for high office, turned out to do an extremely good job. And it is quite mistaken to imagine that nobody saw this at the time. Many did, and the closer they were to him, the more clearly they saw. Churchill, Marshall, and especially, I would say, Acheson, who was about as different from Harry Truman in background and manner as anyone could be. Acheson once remarked that he had great respect for Franklin Roosevelt, but that he reserved his love for another president, meaning Harry Truman. Acheson didn't much like Roosevelt, I suspect, because Roosevelt was condescending toward him. I imagine that if Acheson were to tolerate condescension, it would have to be Acheson being condescending toward someone else.

In the course of more than one hundred interviews for my biography of Truman, I found no one who had worked with him, no one who was on the White House staff, or the White House domestic staff, or his Secret Service detail, who did not like him. He knew everybody by name on the White House staff and in the mansion itself. He knew all the Secret Service people by name. He knew all about their families—and this wasn't just a politician's trick. If he could have picked his own father, one former Secret Service man told me, it would have been Truman.

John Gunther, in a wonderful interview with Truman when Truman was Vice President, asked him what he was most interested in. "People," Truman said without hesitation.

He had a further quality, also greatly needed in the presidency: a healthy, resilient sense of humor. He loved especially the intrinsic humor of politics, the good stories of politics. Campaigning in Texas by train in 1948, he had nothing but blue skies and huge, warm crowds everywhere he stopped. It was the first time a Democratic candidate for President had ever come to Texas to campaign. That had never been necessary before. The reason now was his civil rights program, which was anything but popular in Texas. There had been warnings even of serious trouble if ever he were to show his face in Texas. But his reception was good-natured and approving the whole way across the state and Truman loved every moment. It was probably his happiest time of the whole 1948 whistle-stop odyssey. On board the train were Sam Rayburn and young Lyndon Johnson, who was running for the Senate, as well as Governor Beaufort Jester, who had earlier called Truman's civil rights program a stab in the back.

But all that was forgotten in the warmth of the days and the warmth of the crowds, and at the last stop, Rayburn's home town of Bonham, Rayburn invited the President to come by his little house on the highway, outside of town. When the motorcade arrived, hundreds of people were on the front lawn. Rayburn told them to form a line and he would see they met the President. The Secret Service immediately objected, saying they had no identifications for anyone. Rayburn was furious. He knew every man, woman, and child on that lawn, he said, and could vouch for each and every one. So the line started for the house where Governor Jester offered greetings at the door and the President, a surreptitious bourbon within reach, shook hands with "the customers," as he called them. All was going well until Rayburn, who never took his eye off the line, shouted, "Shut the door, Beaufort, they're coming through twice."

Yet for all that it is mistaken to picture Harry Truman as just a down-home politician of the old stamp. The Harry Truman of Merle Miller's *Plain Speaking*, or of the play *Give-em Hell, Harry*, is entertaining and picturesque, but that wasn't the man who was President of the United States. He wasn't just some kind of cosmic hick.

NOW HE DID MAKE MISTAKES. He was not without flaw. He could be intemperate, profane, touchy, too quick with simplistic answers. In private conversation, he could use racial and religious slurs, old habits of the mouth. In many ways his part of Missouri was more like the Old South than the Middle West, and he grew up among people who in so-called polite society commonly used words like "nigger" and "coon."

Yet here is the man who initiated the first civil rights message ever and ordered the armed services desegregated. And let's remember, that was in 1948, long before Martin Luther King, Jr., or *Brown v. Board of Education*, the landmark Supreme Court decision on the desegregation of schools, or the civil rights movement. When friends and advisers warned him that he was certain to lose the election in 1948 if he persisted with his civil rights program, he said if he lost for that, it would be for a good cause. Principle mattered more than his own political hide. His courage was the courage of his convictions.

Truman's greatest single mistake was the loyalty oath program, requiring a so-called loyalty check of every federal employee. It was uncalled for, expensive, it contributed substantially to the mounting bureaucracy of Washington and damaged the reputations and lives of numbers of people who should never have had any such thing happen to them. He did it on the advice that it was good politics. He let his better nature be overcome by that argument. It was thought such a move could head off the rising right-wing cry of Communists in government, the McCarthy craze then in its early stages. But it didn't work. It was shameful.

His Supreme Court appointments weren't particularly distinguished. His seizure of the steel industry during the Korean War to avert a nationwide strike was high-handed and rightly judged unconstitutional, though his motives were understandable. We were at war and a prolonged shutdown of production of steel threatened the very lives of our fighting forces in Korea.

He himself thought one of his worst mistakes was to have allowed the pell-mell demobilization that followed World War II. Almost overnight American military might had all but vanished. When we intervened in Korea, we had little to fight with, except for the atomic bomb. That Truman refused to use the atomic bomb in Korea, despite tremendous pressure from General MacArthur and others, stands as one of his most important decisions and one for which he has been given little credit.

The idea that Harry Truman made the decision to use the bomb against Japan and then went upstairs and went to sleep is an unfortunate myth for which he is largely accountable. I think he gave that impression because he came from a time and place in America where you were not supposed to talk about your troubles. "How are you?" "I'm fine." You might be dying of some terrible disease—"I'm fine. And you?" He refused ever to talk of the weight of the decision except to say that he made it and that it was his responsibility.

He dropped the atomic bomb on Japan to end the war. Was it right? Was it wrong? I think he saw it as necessary. It is so very important to understand the atmosphere of the moment, the atmosphere in which the decision was made. We were at war. Moreover, we were suffering increasingly heavier casualties the closer we came to Japan. In Europe we had just endured horrendous losses at the hands of the supposedly defeated German army. There were 76,000 American casualties at the Battle of the Bulge, one of the most costly battles ever fought by Americans. Then came the bloodbath of Okinawa, with a toll greater than anyone in Washington had foreseen, some 40,000 American casualties before it was over, and the Japanese were certain to fight with still greater ferocity when we invaded the home islands.

It must also be understood that by then we were sending massive, devastating B-29 raids against Japan on a routine basis. The slaughter was extreme—20,000, 40,000 lives at a blow. The raid on Tokyo on March 10, 1945, may have taken 100,000 lives.

When Robert Oppenheimer, director of the project that developed the bomb, was asked how many casualties might result from use of the bomb, presuming it worked, he said perhaps as many as 20,000. Now suppose you are the President and you know these horrible raids you are sending against Japan are killing as much as twice or three times that number, and that possibly one bomb delivered by one plane might, if it worked, have the effect of shocking the enemy into surrendering and all the slaughter could stop. An invasion of Japan would become unnecessary. Thousands of American lives would be saved. And imagine also that no one among your top advisers is telling you not to use the bomb.

The President—the commander-in-chief—gave the order. The war ended.

WITH THE RETURN of peace, Truman's political troubles began. The year 1946 was particularly rough. He seemed hopelessly ineffectual. He seemed to be trying to please everybody at once, willing to say to almost anybody whatever they most wanted to hear. He wasn't at all like the Harry Truman I've been describing. He had never wanted the job and for some time appeared willing to give it up as soon as possible. He tried twice to get General Eisenhower to agree to run as a Democrat in the next election, saying he would gladly step aside. According to one account, he even offered to run as Vice President with Ike at the head of the ticket. But then after the setback in the '46 congressional elections, he became a different man.

Fire-in-the-belly for presidential glory was never part of his nature. He wasn't in the job to enlarge his estimate of himself. He didn't need that. He didn't need the limelight or fawning people around him in order to feel good about being Harry Truman.

On that note, it is interesting to see whom he did choose to have around him, as a measure of his character. There were Omar Bradley and Matthew Ridgway at the Pentagon, Eisenhower at the head of NATO. George C. Marshall served as Secretary of State and later as Secretary of Defense. There were Dean Acheson, Averell Harriman, Robert Lovett, George Kennan, Chip Bohlen, David Lilienthal, James Forrestal, Sam Rosenman, Clark Clifford—the list is long and very impressive. That most of them had more distinguished backgrounds than he, if they were taller, handsomer, it seemed to bother him not at all. When it was suggested to him that General Marshall as Secretary of State might lead people to think Marshall would make a better president, Truman's response was that yes, of course, Marshall would make a better president, but that he, Harry Truman, was President and he wanted the best people possible around him.

As no president since Theodore Roosevelt, Truman had a way of saying things that was so much his own, and I would like to quote some of them:

"I wonder how far Moses would have gone, if he had taken a poll in Egypt."

"God doesn't give a damn about pomp and circumstance."

"There are more prima donnas in Washington than in all the opera companies."

He is also frequently quoted as having said, "If you want a friend in Washington, buy a dog," and, "If you want to live like a Republican, vote Democratic." I doubt he said the first, but the second does sound like him.

"The object and its accomplishment is my philosophy," he said. Let me say that again. "The object and its accomplishment is my philosophy." And no president ever worked harder in office. At times, a little discouraged, he would say, "All the President is, is a glorified public relations man who spends his time flattering, kissing and kicking people to get them to do what they are supposed to do anyway."

WHERE WERE his strengths and his weaknesses in conflict? In interviews with those who knew him, I would ask what they believed to have been the President's major flaw. Almost always they would say he was too loyal to too many people to whom he should not have been so loyal—not as President. They were thinking mainly of the cronies—people like Harry Vaughan. Or remembering when Boss Tom Pendergast died and Vice President Harry Truman commandeered an Air Force bomber and flew to Kansas City for the funeral. "You don't forget a friend," was Truman's answer to the press.

Tom Pendergast had made Truman, and the Pendergast machine, though colorful and not without redeeming virtues, was pretty unsavory altogether.

But Truman was also, let us understand, the product of the smoke-filled room in more than just the Kansas City way. He was picked at the 1944 Democratic Convention in Chicago in a room at the Blackstone Hotel thick with smoke. He was tapped as Roosevelt's running mate and almost certain successor by the party's big-city bosses, the professional pols, who didn't want Henry Wallace, then the Vice President, because Wallace was too left wing, and didn't want Jimmy Byrnes, another Roosevelt favorite, because Byrnes was too conservative, an avowed segregationist and a lapsed Roman Catholic. They wanted Harry Truman, so Truman it was. They knew their man. They knew what stuff he was made of. And remember, this was all in a tradition of long standing. Theodore Roosevelt had been picked by a Republican machine in New York, Woodrow Wilson by the Democratic machine in New Jersey. For Franklin Roosevelt, such "good friends" as Ed Kelly of Chicago, Boss Crump of Memphis, Ed Flynn of the Bronx were indispensable. And because a candidate had the endorsement of a machine, or as in Truman's case owed his rise in politics to a corrupt organization, it didn't necessarily follow that he himself was corrupt. John Hersey, who did one of the best of all pieces ever written about

Harry Truman, for *The New Yorker*, said he found no trace of corruption in Truman's record. Nor did I. Nor did the FBI when it combed through Truman's past at the time Pendergast was convicted for an insurance fraud and sent to prison. Nor did all the Republicans who ran against him in all the elections in his long political career.

I think he was almost honest to a fault. Still he understood, and felt acutely, the bargain he made with loyalty to the likes of Pendergast, and he understood why he was so often taken to task by the Republicans or the press or just ordinary citizens who didn't care for the kind of political company he kept.

Harry Vaughan was for comic relief, Truman's Falstaff. Among the delights of Truman as a biographical subject is that he enjoyed both Vaughan and Mozart. He loved a night of poker with "the boys," and he loved the National Symphony, which he attended as often as possible. If the program included Mozart or Chopin, he would frequently take the score with him.

This same Harry Truman, who adored classical music, who read Shakespeare and Cicero and *Don Quixote*, comes out of a political background about as steamy and raw as they get. And at times, this would get to him and he would escape to the privacy of a downtown Kansas City hotel room. There he would pour himself out on paper, the innermost anguish in long memoranda to himself, and these amazing documents survive in the files of the Truman Library in Independence, Missouri, along with thousands of his letters and private diaries.

Here is a striking example written when Truman was a county judge (a county commissioner really) and one of his fellow commissioners had made off with $10,000 from the county till:

> This sweet associate of mine, my friend, who was supposed to back me, had already made a deal with a former crooked contractor, a friend of the Boss's . . . I had to compromise in order to get the voted road system carried out . . . I had to let a former saloonkeeper and murderer, a friend of the Boss's, steal about $10,000 from the general

revenues of the county to satisfy my ideal associate and keep the crooks from getting a million or more out of the bond issue.

He is not exaggerating with the million-dollar figure. When the Pendergast organization collapsed and its ways of operation were revealed, a million dollars was found to be about standard. But then, importantly, Truman goes on:

Was I right or did I compound a felony? I don't know. ... Anyway I've got the $6,500,000 worth of roads on the ground and at a figure that makes the crooks tear their hair. The hospital is up at less cost than any similar institution in spite of my drunken brother-in-law [Fred Wallace], whom I'd had to employ on the job to keep peace in the family. I've had to run the hospital job myself and pay him for it. ... Am I an administrator or not? Or am I just a crook to compromise in order to get the job done? You judge it, I can't.

This is all very painful for him. He writes of being raised at his mother's knee to believe in honor, ethics, and "right living." Not only is he disgusted by the immorality he sees behind the scenes, he doesn't understand it.

But let me return to 1948, where I think we see Truman, the President, at his best. Consider first the crisis over Berlin. That spring the Russians had suddenly clamped a blockade around the city, which was then under Allied control though within the Russian zone of East Germany. Overnight, without warning, Berlin was cut off. Other than by air, there was no way to supply it. Two and a half million people were going to be without food, fuel, medical supplies. Clearly Stalin was attempting to drive the Allies out. The situation was extremely dangerous.

At an emergency meeting in the Oval Office, it was proposed that the Allies break through with an armored convoy. It looked as though World War III might be about to start. It was suggested that Berlin be abandoned. Nobody knew quite what to do. Truman said, "We stay in Berlin, period." He didn't know how that could be done any more than anyone else, but he said, "We stay in Berlin." Backbone.

An airlift had already begun as a temporary measure. Truman ordered it stepped up to the maximum. It was said by experts, including the mayor of Berlin, that to supply the city by air would be impossible, given the size of the planes and the calculated number of landings possible per day. The whole world was on edge.

"We'll stay in Berlin," Truman said again, "come what may." The supposedly insoluble problem of the limit of plane landings per day was nicely solved: they built another airport. The airlift worked. The Russians gave up the blockade. The crisis passed.

AMONG THE MOST difficult and important concepts to convey in teaching or writing history is the simple fact that things never had to turn out as they did. Events past were never on a track. Nothing was foreordained any more then than now. Nobody knew at the start that the Berlin Airlift would work. It was a model, I think, of presidential decision making, and of presidential character proving decisive.

All this, I should also remind you, was taking place in an election year. Yet at no time did Truman include any of his political advisers in the discussions about Berlin. Nor did he ever play on the tension of the crisis for his own benefit in the speeches he made.

With the question of whether to recognize Israel, Truman faced an equally complex situation but one greatly compounded by emotion. Of particular difficulty for him, personally and politically, was the position of his then Secretary of State, George Marshall, who was gravely concerned about Middle Eastern oil supplies. If Arab anger over American support for a new Jewish state meant a cut-off of Arab oil, it would not only jeopardize the Marshall Plan and the recovery of Europe but could prove disastrous should the Berlin crisis indeed turn to war.

Marshall was thinking as a military man, determined to hold to a policy that was in the best interest of the United States. It was by no means a matter of anti-Semitism, as was sometimes charged, or any lack of sympathy for the idea of a Jewish homeland. But the fact that Marshall was against an immediate recognition put Truman in an extremely difficult position. No American of the time counted higher in Truman's estimate than Marshall. He saw Marshall as the modern-day equivalent of George Washington or Robert E. Lee and valued his judgment more than that of anyone in the cabinet. Further, Marshall was far and away the most widely respected member of the administration, and if Truman were to decide against him and Marshall were then to resign, it would almost certainly mean defeat for Truman in November. He could lose the respect of the man he most respected and lose the presidency.

Truman did recognize Israel—immediately, within minutes—and he never doubted he was doing the right thing. His interest in the history of the Middle East was long standing. He had been a strong supporter of a homeland for Jewish refugees from Europe from the time he had been in the Senate. But he also knew George Marshall and was sure Marshall would stand by him, as of course Marshall did.

I HAVE SPENT a sizable part of my writing life trying to understand Harry Truman and his story. I don't think we can ever know enough about him. If his loyalty was a flaw, it was his great strength also, as shown by his steadfast loyalty to Dean Acheson when Joe McCarthy came after Acheson or the unflinching support he gave David Lilienthal when Lilienthal, Truman's choice to head the Atomic Energy Commission, was accused as a "pink," a Communist. Franklin Roosevelt had not been willing to stand up for Lilienthal. Truman did. And Lilienthal was approved by the Senate.

Perhaps Truman's greatest shortcoming was his unwillingness to let us know, to let the country know then, how much more there was to him than met the eye, how much more he was than just "Give 'em hell, Harry"—that he did have this love of books, this interest in history, his affection for people, his kindness, his thoughtfulness to subordinates, the love of music, the knowledge of music, his deep and abiding love for his wife, his bedrock belief in education and learning. Though he had never gone beyond Independence High School, this was a president who enjoyed Cicero in the original Latin. We should have known that. It's good to know now, too.

A few words about the '48 campaign, which will always be part of our political lore. It's a great American metaphor, a great American story. The fellow who hasn't got a chance comes from behind and wins. Nobody in either party, not a professional politician, not a reporter, not even his own mother-in-law doubted that Tom Dewey would be the next president. The result of a *Newsweek* poll of fifty top political commentators nationwide who were asked to predict the outcome was Dewey 50, Truman 0.

No president had ever campaigned so hard or so far. Truman was sixty-four years old. Younger men who were with him through it all would describe the time on the train as one of the worst ordeals of their lives. The roadbed was rough and Truman would get the train up to 80 miles an hour at night. The food was awful, the work unrelenting. One of them told me, "It's one thing to work that hard and to stay the course when you think you're going to win, but it's quite another thing when you *know* you're going to lose." The only reason they were there, they all said, was Harry Truman.

For Truman, I think, it was an act of faith—a heroic, memorable American act of faith. The poll takers, the political reporters, the pundits, all the sundry prognosticators, and professional politicians—it didn't matter what they said, what they thought. Only the people decide, Truman was reminding the country. "Here I am, here's what I stand for—here's what I'm going to do if you keep me in the job. You decide."

Was he a great president? Yes. One of the best. And a very great American. Can we ever have another Harry Truman? Yes, I would say so. Who knows, maybe somewhere in Texas she's growing up right now.

I live in Massachusetts and this morning, on my way to the Boston airport, I drove by the original home of John Adams. It is very modest. Adams too was a farmer. Listen please to what he said in the year 1765, more than a decade before Philadelphia, 1776: "Liberty cannot be preserved without general knowledge among the people who have the right to that knowledge and the desire to know. But besides this, they have a right, an indisputable, unalienable, indefeasible, divine right to that most dreaded and envied kind of knowledge—I mean of the character and conduct of their rulers."

He put character first.

DWIGHT D. EISENHOWER

1953–1961

by

Stephen E. Ambrose

THE QUESTION IS, Does character make a difference in a president? Speaking as one who writes about the President with the most admired and admirable character, I say yes. How Eisenhower's character affected his presidency is my subject, but before we get into specific issues we need to establish the main characteristics of Eisenhower, as developed from infancy and hardened by his experiences as Supreme Commander, Allied Expeditionary Force.

Dwight David Eisenhower was a great and good man. The two qualities don't always, or even often, go together, but they did with him. Obviously that is an assertion that needs proof. Let me begin with definitions.

In 1954, President Eisenhower wrote his childhood friend Swede Hazlett on the subject of greatness. He thought greatness depended either on achieving preeminence in "some broad field of human thought or endeavor," or on assuming "some position of great responsibility" and then so discharging his duties "as to have left a marked and favorable imprint upon the future."

The qualities of a great man, he said, were "vision, integrity, courage, understanding, the power of articulation, and profundity of character." (To that list, I'd add two others: decisiveness and luck.)

The qualities of goodness in a man, I believe, include a broad sympathy for the human condition, that is, an awareness of human weaknesses and shortcomings and a willingness to be forgiving of them, a sense of responsibility toward others, a genuine modesty combined with a justified self-confidence, a sense of humor, and most of all a love of life and of people.

That last is the key. Eisenhower loved life and he loved people. To me, that is the heart of Eisenhower's character. From it flowed all the rest.

In the fall of 1912, third class Cadet Dwight Eisenhower, twenty-two years old, was walking down a hallway at West Point when a plebe, running full tilt on some fool errand for an upperclassman, ran into him. Reacting with a "bellow of astonishment and mock indignation," Eisenhower scornfully demanded, "Mr. Dumgard [a generic term for plebe], what was your P.C.S. [Previous Condition of Servitude]?"

Eisenhower added sarcastically, "You look like a barber."

The plebe's face went red. He replied softly, "I was a barber, sir."

It was Eisenhower's turn to go red with embarrassment. Without a word, he returned to his room, where he told his roommate, "I'm never going to crawl [haze] another plebe as long as I live. As a matter of fact, they'll have to run over and knock me out of the company street before I'll make any attempt again. I've just done something that was stupid and unforgivable. I managed to make a man ashamed of the work he did to earn a living."

He never hazed again, and as an adult he never shamed a man. Respect for others, honesty in his dealings, love of life, these were some of the basic parts of his character. Where did they come from?

•

NURTURE AND NATURE played their respective roles in shaping Dwight Eisenhower. Physically, he inherited a strong, tough, big, athletic body and extremely good looks, with a quite fabulous grin, along with keen intelligence. He also inherited a strong competitive streak from his parents, plus a bad temper, along with unquestioning love, stern discipline, ambition, and religion. They made him study, read the Bible aloud, do chores. They instilled in him a series of controls over his emotions, his temper most of all. They gave him a solid Victorian outlook on the relations between the sexes and on proper conduct. All his life he would blush if he slipped and said a "hell" or a "damn" in front of a lady.

Thus he grew up in a strong Christian atmosphere. From his parents, and from his experiences in Abilene, he absorbed such values as honesty and fair play in all dealings into the marrow of his bones. He abhorred the idea of cheating or lying, and he never did either. He also absorbed a fervent attachment to democracy; it nearly amounted to a religious faith. This grew naturally in the soil of that little town out there on the Kansas prairie.

At West Point, and in his first twenty-five years in the Army, Eisenhower satisfied few of his ambitions—he didn't get to war and he was still a lieutenant colonel—but he learned his profession and demonstrated another characteristic trait, patience.

After Pearl Harbor his star rose, and soon he was in Washington, making war plans for Chief of Staff George C. Marshall, and then on to London, to take command of the American forces in Britain. This threw him into the middle of the great decision-making process of the Allies, at the highest level, dealing daily with Winston Churchill. He proved to be an outstanding diplomat and politician, not only with Churchill but with Free French leader Charles de Gaulle and other Frenchmen as well. He was successful because he was true to his character.

The situation in French North Africa in the fall of 1942 was exceedingly complicated, with a lot of false promises coming from the British, the Americans, and the various French factions.

But not from Eisenhower. "I know only one method of operation," he wrote in his diary: "To be as honest with others as I am with myself."

When President Franklin Roosevelt pressured him to get tough with the local French, Eisenhower refused, explaining, "My whole strength in dealing with the French has been based upon my refusal to quibble or to stoop to any kind of subterfuge or double dealing."

The French responded. One official told him, "As long as *you* say that, I believe it!" Another said, "I have found that you will not lie or evade in any dealings with us, even when it appears you could easily do so."

Eisenhower was equally successful with his sometimes difficult British subordinates and his sometimes egotistical American subordinates. They might not agree with his decisions, but they gave him their trust.

Indeed, whenever associates described Eisenhower, there was one word that almost all of them, superiors or subordinates, used. It was trust. People trusted him for the most obvious reason—he was trustworthy. British Field Marshal Bernard Montgomery didn't think much of Eisenhower as a soldier, but he appreciated other attributes. "His real strength lies in his human qualities," Montgomery said. "He has the power of drawing the hearts of men towards him as a magnet attracts the bit of metal. He merely has to smile at you, and you trust him at once."

Scrupulous honesty was an integral part of Eisenhower's character, and a learned experience. He saw and experienced the payoff for trust. He knew that telling the truth was the only way to deal effectively with the problems.

He also developed a technique to deliver his message: "I refuse to put anything in diplomatic or suave terminology, and carefully cultivate the manner and reputation of complete bluntness and honesty—just a man too simple-minded to indulge in circumlocution." Thus did the Kansas farm boy approach Charles de Gaulle, and Winston Churchill and Franklin Roosevelt, and so many others, and it always worked.

He was the general who hated war. Some, like General George S. Patton, loved it, but Eisenhower could not. He signed every letter of condolence coming out of Europe for three years, a very sobering experience. He was the one who ordered the bombing and shelling of German cities; he hated doing that, too, hated having to destroy when he wanted to build.

But he did his duty, with all his skill and energy. In 1943, his older brother Arthur sent him a newspaper clipping that stressed Ida Eisenhower's pacifism and the irony in her son being a general. Eisenhower wrote back, saying of the pacifists, "I doubt whether any of them detest war as much as I do. They probably have not seen bodies rotting on the ground and smelled the stench of decaying human flesh. They have not visited a field hospital crowded with the desperately wounded. What separates me from the pacifists is that I hate the Nazis more than I hate war."

"I think that all these trials and tribulations must come upon the world because of some great wickedness," he told Mamie in another letter, "yet one would feel that man's mere intelligence to say nothing of his spiritual perceptions would find some way of eliminating war."

The contrast between Eisenhower and those generals who gloried in war could not have been greater. He had a keen sense of family, of the way in which each casualty meant a grieving family back home.

In 1963, when he was filming with Walter Cronkite a television special entitled *D-Day Plus 20 Years*, Cronkite asked him what he thought about when he returned to Normandy. In reply, Eisenhower spoke not of the tanks, the guns, the planes, the ships, the personalities of the commanders and their opponents, or the victory. Instead, he spoke of the families of the men buried in the American Cemetery in Normandy. He said he could never come to this spot without thinking of how blessed he and Mamie were to have grandchildren, and how much it saddened him to think of all the couples in America who had never had that blessing, because their only son was buried in France.

•

So FAR, he looks like a saint. But he was a healthy, vigorous man in his early fifties during the war, and men at war are notoriously receptive to female charm when they are far from home and close to danger. For many people, the test of character is the marriage vow. In other words, what about Eisenhower and Kay Summersby?

Summersby was Eisenhower's personal secretary in England and sometime driver. She was young enough to be his daughter, very attractive, with a bubbly personality that Churchill and almost everyone else found charming. She had lost her fiancé in North Africa and fallen in love with her boss. For his part, how could he help being responsive? He liked her enormously, may have had a crush on her. They were always together. But almost never alone.

Decades later, in a book published after her death, Summersby claimed that they had fallen in love, and that both had realized it in January 1944, when he returned to England from a visit to Washington. They had an evening together. There was a fireplace. They sat on the floor.

"His kisses absolutely unraveled me," she wrote.

According to her account, it was a passionate but unconsummated experience, because after they took off each other's clothes, Eisenhower was flaccid. This may have been because, as one aide put it in a grand understatement, "Ike has a lot on his mind," or because his stern sense of morality, character, and honesty overrode his passion. He was incapable of cheating on his wife.

Or it may be that the incident never happened. No one will ever know. What is important to note is that not even Summersby ever claimed that they had a genuine love affair. Nor is it true that Eisenhower asked President Harry Truman for permission to divorce his wife, Mamie, in order to marry Kay. What he did ask Truman was permission to have Mamie join him in occupied Germany (Truman refused).

Throughout the war, when Kay was with him always, his love for Mamie remained constant. His sustaining force was the thought that when the war was over, he and Mamie could live together again. He loved Mamie for half a century. Except when he was off at war, they slept in the same bed for fifty years.

EISENHOWER'S CHARACTER traits included a strong sense of responsibility, and a conviction that it was a duty that a man always do his best in whatever his job. These characteristics grew out of his childhood and West Point training, and his experiences as a staff officer. In 1939, when it looked like he might be forcibly retired as a lieutenant colonel, his son John had asked him if he regretted having spent his career in the Army.

Not at all, Eisenhower said. He had found his life in the Army "wonderfully interesting . . . it brought me into contact with men of ability, honor, and a sense of high dedication to their country. The real satisfaction is for a man who did the best he could. My ambition in the Army was to make everybody I worked for regretful when I was ordered to other duty."

Leadership was another part of his character. He was born to lead and trained to lead. He told John that leadership was the one art that could be learned, but of course only the born leader can say that. Eisenhower reinforced his natural talent. He studied the subject of leadership, intensely, and wrote some of his best analytical material on the subject.

An important part of leadership, for Eisenhower, rested on certain matters of character. These included modesty and a genuine eagerness to share the applause. Through the war he never forgot how much he depended on others; he told reporters to go see Omar Bradley or George Patton for their stories.

Sharing the credit for a success and taking the personal blame for what went wrong was Eisenhower's leadership style. In all the announcements of D-Day, the operative words were "the Allies" and "we." In the announcement Eisenhower wrote by hand, to release to the press in the event of failure, the operative word was a personal pronoun, as in It is my fault.

"Always take your job seriously, never yourself," was one of his favorite lines. A corollary to that sentiment was his willingness to sacrifice himself for the good of the whole. In early 1944, Eisenhower wanted to put the Allied bombers to work on transportation targets in France, to isolate Normandy. The bomber commanders said no, they wanted to continue their strategic bombing inside Germany.

Eisenhower felt so strongly about the issue that he told the Combined Chiefs of Staff that either they give him his transportation targets—railroad bridges, turntables, etc.—in France, or he would "simply have to go home." In other words, Eisenhower was not ready to commit his forces to the attack until he was certain that he had utilized every asset he had to the uttermost. If he couldn't use the assets as he saw fit, he would resign his commission.

When he made that threat, he was holding the most coveted command in the history of warfare.

He got his way, and the transportation plan was a big success. He later used the same threat in a knock-down dispute with Montgomery over strategy and command, and again had his way. It was an integral part of him, this ability to know exactly when to use his personal asset, the power of his name and personality. It showed a nice sense of balance about political factors and an accurate measurement of his own strength in a struggle for policy.

He much preferred working with a team to having to act on his own. A stress on teamwork began when he was a child, showed again at West Point, and was reinforced by his experiences as football coach on various Army bases in the 1920s. At the end of his life, he wrote, "I believe that football, perhaps more than any other sport, tends to instill in men the feeling that victory comes through hard—almost slavish—work, team play, self-confidence and an enthusiasm that amounts to dedication."

By 1952, the year Eisenhower entered into politics at age sixty-two, his character, as formed by heredity and experience, was set in concrete. It included the qualities of love, honesty, faithfulness, responsibility, modesty, generosity, duty, and leadership, along with a hatred of war. These were the bedrock.

Or were they? This paragon of virtue had lived in the shelter of the Army nearly all his life. Character-testing opportunities or temptations were almost unknown to him. It is easy to be virtuous when virtue is rewarded, as it was in the Army; not so easy when virtue is ignored and partisanship is rewarded, as in politics. In 1952 it remained to be seen whether Eisenhower's virtues would survive the pounding of politics, the temptations of power.

In the view of many contemporary reporters, some voters, and many historians today, Eisenhower began betraying his principles during the campaign. And they say that this first betrayal made those to come easier, because this was the hardest: he had to betray the man who had made his success possible and whom he admired above any contemporary, General George C. Marshall.

Briefly, this is what happened. Wisconsin senator Joseph R. McCarthy had called General Marshall a traitor. This was outrageous to the Democrats—and to many Republicans. Eisenhower was scheduled to speak in Milwaukee, with McCarthy on the platform.

"Listen," Eisenhower said to his speechwriter, Emmet Hughes, "couldn't we make this an occasion for me to pay a personal tribute to Marshall—right in McCarthy's back yard?"

Hughes was enthusiastic. He drafted a paragraph that praised Marshall and concluded that charges of treason against Marshall "constituted a sobering lesson in the way freedom must *not* defend itself."

Hughes and other younger, more liberal members of the campaign staff began telling reporters on the train running from Chicago into Wisconsin, "Just wait till we get to Milwaukee, and you will find out what the general thinks of Marshall." Everyone on the train was talking about the stinging rebuke McCarthy was going to get.

But in Eisenhower's compartment, Wisconsin's Republican governor, Walter Kohler, was asking the candidate to remove the paragraph about Marshall. Talk about Marshall somewhere else, Kohler said, and he added that Eisenhower had done a good job of defending Marshall in a speech in Denver earlier that week. Mc-

Carthy had won his primary handily and was the Republican nominee; Eisenhower would need his vote in the Senate. Eisenhower's campaign manager, Sherman Adams, nodded his agreement.

Finally, most ominously, Kohler said rebuking McCarthy in Milwaukee would hurt in the election and reminded Eisenhower that Harry Truman had carried the state in 1948. Adams again nodded.

Eisenhower dropped the paragraph from his speech. But advance copies contained it, and the staff had been talking it up. What Eisenhower had not said became a major news item. He appeared ungrateful and unprincipled, unable to stand up to McCarthy or for General Marshall.

He appeared to have put "anything to win" ahead of honor and honesty.

That he was ashamed of himself there can be little doubt. He tried never to refer to the Milwaukee speech. When he came to write his memoirs, ten years later, he wanted to ignore it altogether; when his aides insisted that he could not simply pass it over, he wrote, discarded, wrote again, discarded again, and finally printed a version in which he said that if he had realized what the reaction to the deletion of the paragraph was going to be, "I would never have acceded to the staff's arguments, logical as they sounded at the time." He claimed the critical reaction constituted a "distortion of the facts, a distortion that even led some to question my loyalty to General Marshall."

And, he could have added, caused others to worry about his character.

Some Republicans wondered about how Republican he was. After twenty years of the New Deal, they were eager to tear down the edifice. Lower taxes and abolish Social Security and the regulatory commissions were their battle cries.

But since his boyhood, Eisenhower had feared debt. He had never had a mortgage. He thought FDR's unbalanced budgets eventually would destroy freedom in America. He told the Republicans he would not agree to lowering taxes until the federal budget was balanced. He expanded rather than eliminated Social Security and the regulatory commissions. And to the dismay of many Republicans, he cut rather than expanded defense spending.

Throughout his presidency, he was under great pressure from many Republicans and most Democrats to spend more on defense. He absolutely refused. He explained to Swede Hazlett, "Let us not forget that the armed services are to defend a 'way of life,' not merely land, property, or lives. So what I need to make the Joint Chiefs realize is that they are men of sufficient stature, training and intelligence to think of this balance—the balance between minimum requirements in the costly implements of war and the health of our economy."

ON THE DOMESTIC SIDE, McCarthy continued to plague him. The senator was making wild charges. The U.S. Army had been infiltrated by Communists, he said, and the Eisenhower administration was trying to cover up for the guilty. In 1952 during the campaign, McCarthy had thundered about "20 years of treason" under the Democrats. By the end of 1953, when Eisenhower was President, he was talking "21 years of treason."

Many of Eisenhower's advisers urged him to denounce McCarthy. So did his younger brother Milton, president of Penn State College and the person closest to him. So did the great majority of the press. The reporters made it into a test of Eisenhower's character and political courage.

If it was that, he failed miserably. He never spoke out against McCarthy. In his opinion, however, character and political courage had nothing to do with this case. A one-on-one between a president and a senator could only enhance the influence of the senator. Besides, he told Milton, "I'm not going to get into a pissing contest with that skunk." Anyway he was certain McCarthy would destroy himself, if given enough rope, and he intended to give him the rope by ignoring him.

The President did nothing as the senator ranted and raved, hurling accusations, holding hearings into Communist infiltration of the Army. What finally roused the old warhorse was McCarthy's attempt to use his subpoena power—he was chairman of a Senate subcommittee—to force Eisenhower's White House assistants and other members of the administration to testify.

For Eisenhower, this was a question of executive privilege and thus a matter of principle, not tactics. He spoke bluntly. "Congress has absolutely no right to ask my aides to testify in any way, shape, or form about the advice that they were giving to me at any time on any subject." As he saw it, the modern presidency was at stake. Previous presidents had held that their conversations in cabinet meetings were privileged and confidential, but none had ever dared extend this privilege to *everybody* in the executive branch. Eisenhower did. His predecessors had been exceedingly reluctant to withhold information or witnesses from Congress, and the Justice Department was never able to find any convincing precedent for a doctrine of executive privilege (although Harry Truman had in practice set a precedent in his dealings with Congressman Richard Nixon's House Committee on Un-American Activities in its investigation of Alger Hiss, when Truman refused Nixon's demand for documents).

Eisenhower acted vigorously. He told the Department of Defense that employees had to be completely candid in advising on official matters; therefore, "it is not in the public interest that *any* of their conversations or communications, or *any* documents or reproductions, concerning such advice be disclosed."

This was the most absolute assertion of presidential right to withhold information from Congress ever uttered to that day in American history. In Eisenhower's judgment, it was necessary in the nuclear age. There were so many things Eisenhower felt he had to keep secret that he was willing to vastly expand the powers of the presidency to do it. He told his press secretary, James Hagerty, "If they want to make a test of this principle, I'll fight them tooth and nail and up and down the country. It is a matter of principle with me and I will never permit it."

In his memoirs, Eisenhower complained that the day the

French lost the Battle of Dien Bien Phu, the headlines covered not that event but rather McCarthy's demand for a test of Eisenhower's use of executive privilege. Ten years later, Eisenhower wrote, it was obvious that the fall of Dien Bien Phu was far more important than McCarthy's demand. What Eisenhower could not know was that almost exactly twenty years later, the precedent of executive privilege would be used by President Nixon in defending himself from Watergate charges, which caused the greatest constitutional crisis of the century.

McCARTHYISM was one of the great political issues of the day. The great moral issue was segregation. On racial matters, as on McCarthyism, Eisenhower seemed to come up short. He was a segregationist. He was an infant when *Plessy* v. *Ferguson* established the doctrine of separate but equal, making segregation the law of the land. He grew up in a U.S. Army that was strictly segregated. At southern Army bases, or in Panama or the Philippines or Washington, D.C., he lived under and benefited from a system of apartheid.

He commanded a segregated army in Northwest Europe. That meant keeping 11 percent of the Army's enlisted personnel out of combat. When the Germans launched their counteroffensive in the Ardennes in mid-December 1944, among other problems Eisenhower had to deal with was a clash of his values. He believed in segregation but he wanted to win the war as quickly as possible. Characteristically, he went for the greater goal. He offered black soldiers working as loaders and truck drivers an opportunity to join the combat infantry on an integrated basis. They would be fed into the line individually, thus guaranteeing black volunteers that they would become part of an established team of veterans with good leaders and weapons (the few black combat units that had been formed during the war were notoriously poorly officered and badly armed).

Eisenhower's chief of staff, General Walter B. Smith, vehemently protested integrating the Army. Smith told Eisenhower he didn't want any part of starting a social revolution back home.

Eisenhower did it anyway. In war, he liked to say, everything is expendable for victory, even generals' lives, even racial prejudice.

As President, segregation proved a vastly greater issue and test of character. He appointed Governor Earl Warren of California to the post of Chief Justice, something he later regretted. His Attorney General, Herbert Brownell, and the Justice Department made the case for integration in 1954 in *Brown* v. *Topeka* before the Warren Court, something else Eisenhower regretted but did not prevent. The Court ordered the integration of the public schools with all deliberate speed, which Eisenhower thought was a terrible mistake because the schools were the most sensitive place to proceed, by far. He preferred beginning with public parks, motels, cafes, and the like.

There was uproar over *Brown*. By the summer of 1957, Eisenhower was writing to Swede Hazlett, "I think that no other single event has so disturbed the domestic scene in many years as did the Supreme Court's decision in the school segregation case." Parts of the white South were turning to violence to enforce segregation. Eisenhower could understand their point of view. "Laws are rarely effective unless they represent the will of the majority," he wrote. Further, "when emotions are deeply stirred," progress must be gradual and take into account "human feelings," which always turned out to be the feelings of white southerners. Otherwise, "we will have a disaster." He pointed out that the South had lived for sixty years under *Plessy* as a law-abiding area; it was therefore "impossible to expect complete and instant reversal of conduct by mere decision of the Supreme Court."

There is no doubt of Eisenhower's dislike for *Brown*. But there is also no doubt of his sense of duty and responsibility. Whatever one thought of *Brown*, he told Hazlett, "I hold to the basic purpose. There must be respect for the Constitution—which means the Supreme Court's interpretation of the Constitution—or we shall have chaos. We cannot possibly imagine a successful form of government in which every individual citizen would have the right to interpret the Constitution according to his own convictions, beliefs, and prejudices. Chaos would develop. This I believe with all my heart—and shall always act accordingly."

On the other hand, he abhorred the thought of using force. He said in a press conference in the summer of 1957 that he could imagine no circumstances that would lead him to use the U.S. Army to enforce integration. So he wanted to uphold the Court, but not use force to do so.

Meanwhile his administration was sponsoring a civil rights bill, the first since Reconstruction. The major aim was to grant to black southerners the right to vote. Texas senator Lyndon Johnson led the effort to emasculate the bill, by requiring jury trials for all registrars of voters accused of discriminating against blacks. The jury pool came from the voting roles, so it was all white. Senator Richard Russell of Georgia charged that the Eisenhower administration's civil rights bill was "a cunning device" to use the power of the Justice Department "and the armed forces if necessary, to force a commingling of white and Negro children."

Asked to comment at a news conference, Eisenhower said the purpose of the bill was to protect and extend the right to vote, which he described as the most important of all rights. It was a moderate bill, he said. Now, here come "highly respected men" making statements to the effect that "this is a very extreme law, leading to disorder." The President said that he found such a reaction "rather incomprehensible, but I am always ready to listen to anyone's presentation to me of his views on such a thing."

His willingness to listen, his known sympathy with white southerners, his failure to give his public support to *Brown* v. *Topeka*, and his general lack of leadership on the question of the day, gave one southern governor the notion that he could roll the President. Orval Faubus of Arkansas defied a court order to integrate Central High in Little Rock. He called out the Arkansas National Guard and placed it around the high school, with orders to prevent the entry into the school of about a dozen Negro pupils.

This was the great moral and character test of the Eisenhower presidency. He met it head-on. Despite his own feelings about the mistakes being made in implementing *Brown*, and his horror at the thought of using American troops in American cities, he called out the 101st Airborne and sent it to Little Rock. At Brownell's suggestion, he ordered the Arkansas National Guard into federal service, thus stealing Faubus's army out from under him and putting it to duty helping the 101st ensure an orderly and peaceful integration of Central High.

It was a brilliant stroke and the action of a man of principle. It settled forever the question of whether the federal government would use force to break down segregation.

EISENHOWER WAS almost as blind to the status of women as he was to the status of blacks. He had no women friends, just as he had no black friends. When asked to comment on a proposed constitutional amendment to guarantee equal rights to women, he asked in all innocence what rights American women didn't already have. His view of the role of women in American society was limited to the traditional ones: mother, secretary, teacher, wife. The only women he was ever really close to were his mother, his wife, and his secretaries—Kay Summersby and Ann Whitman.

His secretaries slaved for him, and he took it for granted. They would hand him a perfectly typed, two-page single-spaced letter, and he would change an "a" to an "an," or a "but " to a "however," and have them type the whole thing again. They worked six, often seven days a week, ten and twelve and fourteen hours per day for him, and he never noticed.

WHERE HIS CHARACTER showed most decisively was on questions of war, and more specifically a first strike against the Soviet Union and in Indochina. He was President during the worst decade of the Cold War. He was the only president to have a decisive lead over the Soviets in nuclear weaponry, a lead so decisive that he could have ordered a preventative war which would have destroyed the Soviet Union as a military power, without significant retaliation. Given the amounts of money the United States was spending in the arms race, and the fear it engendered, and the fact that the Soviets would soon be able to retaliate and eventually might pull even in nuclear weaponry, the temptation to use the bomb while we still had the lead was tremendous.

At the time of Dien Bien Phu, during the various crises over the Chinese offshore islands in the mid-fifties, and regularly with regard to the Soviet Union, some of Eisenhower's principal advisers gave in to that temptation. They included his Joint Chiefs of Staff; his Vice President, Richard Nixon; his Secretary of State, John Foster Dulles; members of his National Security Council; and many pundits.

Told on May 1, 1954, that the National Security Council was preparing a paper calling for the use of atomic bombs to save the French at Dien Bien Phu, Eisenhower responded: "I certainly do not think that the atom bomb can be used by the United States unilaterally." He went on: "You boys must be crazy. We can't use those awful things against Asians for the second time in less than ten years. My God."

It was characteristic of him always to ask, What happens next? If we do such and so, what are the likely consequences? Suppose we pull it off, then what do we do? And what do the other players do? It was an attempt to look into the future, and it stood him in good stead as President.

After Dien Bien Phu fell, the Joint Chiefs recommended a preventive attack against the Soviet Union. Eisenhower asked them to think about what they were proposing. "I want you to carry this question home with you. Gain such a victory, and what do you do with it? Here would be a great area from Elbe to Vladivostok ... torn up and destroyed, without government, without its communications, just an area of starvation and disaster. I ask you what would the civilized world do about it? I repeat there is no victory except through our imaginations."

There were war scares throughout his administration. In 1955, the Chinese Communists began shelling Quemoy and Matsu, islands off their coast held by the Nationalist Chinese based on Formosa. This was at a time when the Red Chinese were being insultingly provocative in their acts and words. In November 1955, they had announced life prison terms for thirteen American fliers shot down during the Korean War. The Americans were found guilty of espionage. Voices were raised in the United States to go to war with China, now, and get them back.

At a news conference, Eisenhower was asked to comment. He took ten minutes to reply, in spontaneous remarks that were delivered with visible emotion.

Leaning forward, Eisenhower said he wanted "to talk a little bit personally." He admitted that "a President experiences exactly the same resentments, the same anger, the same kind of sense of frustration when things like this occur to other Americans, and his impulse is to lash out." He said he knew it would be the "easy course" as well. The nation would be "united automatically." It would close ranks behind the leader. The job would become a simple one—win the war.

"There is a real fervor developed throughout the nation that you can feel everywhere you go," he said. "There is practically an exhilaration about the affair." Eisenhower confessed that he was not immune to those feelings: "In the intellectual and spiritual contest of matching wits and getting along to see if you can win, there comes about something . . . an atmosphere is created . . . an attitude is created to which I am not totally unfamiliar."

But tempting though it was to be a war leader, Eisenhower had other memories. He recalled his favorite line from Robert E. Lee: "It is well that war is so terrible; if it were not so, we would grow too fond of it." He told the reporters, "Don't go to war in response to emotions of anger and resentment; do it prayerfully."

ONE OF THE MARKS of Eisenhower's character was his sense of fair play. That showed up often in his presidency. In November 1956, on the eve of the election, the British, French, and Israelis conspired to attack Egypt and seize the Suez Canal. Eisenhower supported Egypt against his NATO partners and Israel, through diplomacy in the United Nations and through direct economic pressure on the conspirators. It was the first and almost only time the United States supported a Third World country in a dispute with its NATO allies.

In explaining why he did it, Eisenhower said, "We cannot subscribe to one law for the weak, another law for the strong, one law for those opposing us, another for those allied with us. There can be only one law—or there shall be no peace."

Fair play included a single standard for all. When Richard Nixon told him in 1957 that Algeria was not ready for independence, so the United States should support the French, Eisenhower replied, "The United States could not possibly maintain that freedom—independence—liberty—were necessary to us, but not to others."

Another of his qualities was patience. "Make no mistakes in a hurry," was a favorite axiom. When his advisers urged him to destroy the Soviet Union while we could still get away with it, he told them to be patient, that in the end the Soviet system would implode because it was rotten at its core, that this would take a long time, maybe fifty years, but they would have to educate their own people to stay up with modern technology and thereby they would sow the seeds of their own undoing.

He was a good steward. "We—you and I, and our government —must avoid plundering, for our own ease and convenience, the precious resources of tomorrow," he said in his farewell address. "We cannot mortgage the material assets of our grandchildren without risking the loss also of their political and spiritual heritage. We want democracy to survive for all generations to come."

A BRIEF ASSESSMENT of Eisenhower's accomplishments as President reveals something of the man and his character. First and foremost, he presided over eight years of prosperity, marred only by two minor recessions.

Under Eisenhower, the nation enjoyed domestic peace and tranquility, at least as measured against the sixties. One of his major goals in 1953 had been to curb the excesses of political rhetoric and partisanship. He managed to achieve that goal by not dismantling the New Deal, as the more conservative Republicans wanted to do. Under Eisenhower, the number of people covered by Social Security doubled as benefits went up. The New Deal's regulatory commissions stayed in place. Expenditures for public works were greater than they had been under FDR or Truman. The Interstate Highway System and the St. Lawrence Seaway were bigger in scope than anything the New or Fair Deal had attempted. Eisenhower, in effect, put a Republican stamp of approval on twenty years of Democratic legislation, by itself a major step toward bringing the two parties closer together.

His special triumphs came in the field of foreign affairs and were directly related to his character. By making peace in Korea five months after taking office, and avoiding war thereafter, and by holding down the cost of the arms race, he achieved greatness. No one knows how much money he saved the United States, no one knows how many lives he saved, by ending the war in Korea and refusing to enter any others, despite a half-dozen and more virtually unanimous recommendations that he order a first strike.

But he made peace and he kept the peace. Whether any other man could have led the country through that decade without going to war cannot be known. What we do know is that Eisenhower did it. Eisenhower seldom boasted, but he did on this one: "The United States never lost a soldier or a foot of ground in my administration," he said. "We kept the peace. People asked how it happened —by God, it didn't just happen, I'll tell you that."

He was an inspiring and effective leader, indeed a model of leadership. The elements of his leadership were varied, deliberate, and learned. He exuded simplicity. He deliberately projected an image of the folksy farm boy from Kansas. But in fact he was capable of a detached, informed, and exhaustive examination of problems and personalities, based on wide and sophisticated knowledge and deep study. He projected a posture of being above politics, but he studied and understood and acted on political problems and considerations more rigorously than most lifelong politicians ever could.

His magnetic appeal to millions of his fellow citizens seemed to come about as a natural and effortless result of his sunny disposition. But he worked at his apparent artlessness. That big grin and bouncy step often masked depression, doubt, or utter weariness, for he believed it was the critical duty of a leader to always exude optimism. He made it a habit to save all his doubts for his pillow.

Anger that is contrived, that is put on for show and a purpose, an actor's anger, can be an effective tool of leadership. It was one Eisenhower used often. But genuine anger, deep, blind anger, is the enemy of leadership. Eisenhower often felt it—with Montgomery, with McCarthy, with others—but he did not act on it. One way he controlled his anger was to do his best to follow his own rule, "Never question another man's motives. His wisdom, yes, but not his motives." He also tried to always assume the best about others, until shown otherwise.

He could do so consistently, even in a world full of high-powered men whose motives were often self-serving or base, because of his most outstanding personal characteristic: he was a man full of love, for life and for people.

No matter how much of his effectiveness as a leader came from conscious study, reflection, and acting, no matter how much of it came from his inner nature, it is clear that Eisenhower's personality was a major contributing factor to his success.

There was, first of all, his intensity and concentration. He would naturally and effortlessly fix those clear blue eyes on a listener or a speaker, and he would draw the person in. He *looked* like an honest man with nothing to hide because he was.

Then there was the depth of his concern, the way he cared about people and events. And his self-confidence, which was based on the knowledge that he was smarter than other men, that he knew more, studied more, understood more, and thought things through more objectively. When he gave an order, he believed in it.

People liked to be around him, to hear that big gutsy laugh, to see that infectious lopsided grin, to note his bouncy step. They responded to his genuine interest in and concern for them. They also responded to his limitless curiosity—about people, places, and things. There was the pure enjoyment he got out of living.

People admired Ike, and worked for him, because he did great and good things for mankind. He was the general who truly hated war, but who hated the Nazis more. He was the President who made a peace and kept the peace and thus provided the conditions that made for the best decade of the century—if you were a white middle-class male. He was old-fashioned, a Victorian who came to power in the mid-twentieth century. His virtues were those of the nineteenth century. Honesty, integrity, and religious devotion and conviction were some of them. To my knowledge, he never lied in his private life. In his public responsibilities, he lied twice—once in 1944 to Hitler about where he was going to invade, and once on May Day 1960 to Khrushchev about what Francis Gary Powers was doing in the U-2 over the Soviet Union.

In my own life, when faced with a moral question or dilemma, or with a personal problem of choice, I am in the habit of asking myself, What would Ike do?

Sad to relate, I often—even usually, perhaps always—come up short of his standards. My only consolation is that so do most of the people I know or whose lives I have studied.

JOHN F. KENNEDY
1961–1963

by

Richard Reeves

THINKING ABOUT the "character" of John F. Kennedy has been a cottage industry for more than three decades—and now it has become a growth industry. Let me start with five questions about the daring young man who made himself our thirty-fifth President. The first of those questions was this:

Were there ever aspects of his character at war with each other?

There certainly were. John Kennedy did not think that the rules applied to him and he did whatever he could get away with, including getting into the U.S. Navy without a physical examination, since there was no way he could have passed any standard medical examination. He sensed, correctly, I think, that if he did not participate in World War II, in the great adventure, the great shared experience of his generation, then he was not going to have much of a public life in this country. So he wanted in. But, of course, to have a man with such frail health as his was as your commander could be dangerous; the John Kennedy who got to be commander of a PT boat numbered 109 never should have been there. However, when PT-109 was run down by a Japanese destroyer, the lieutenant who never should have been there swam six miles holding the belt, in his teeth, of a badly burned man named Pappy McNulty, and saved his life—and then went back into the dark Pacific to try to save others. He lost his boat, but saved most of his crew.

At that time, Kennedy said of the PT-109 incident—"they had to either give me a medal or throw me out." They gave him a medal. And they made a movie about him, after he became President, *PT-109*, an exaggerated World War II morale film—only eighteen years out of date, made in 1963 with Cliff Robertson playing the young Jack Kennedy. But there was a scene to remember in the movie in terms of John Kennedy's character. It's more or less made up. Lieutenant Barney Ross—the names were real in the movie—is half dead after relieving Kennedy in the heroic task of swimming out into a channel in the Solomon Islands, with a flashlight and a pistol, in the hope that other PT boats would come by looking for them. When Ross comes back half dead, Kennedy, who had already done it for two nights, says he'll go again, and gives another pep talk to his men. Then Ross says in the movie—and probably said something like it, or says he did in real life: "Boy, you kill me. We're beat, we're burned, we're given up for dead, we're living on green coconuts and no water. We're surrounded by fifteen thousand Japs and you think the odds are with us." And the movie Kennedy says, "It's a flaw in my character." Well, it was his character. Kennedy had an iron will. And most of the people who rise to this kind of position in any society, begin with that. Their determination knows no bounds and the resources that they are willing to put into it are beyond what other people have.

What attributes of character did he value most?

John Kennedy valued courage above all things. He was a courageous man himself, in pain almost every day of his life. But he did not talk about that or complain about that—in fact, he lied about it, feigning energy and vigor he never had. He, like many junior officers, made fun of "the Old Man," Douglas MacArthur, the Allied commander in the Pacific during World War II. "Dug-out Doug," he was called by some at that time. But after Kennedy failed as commander-in-chief, with the disastrous Bay of Pigs invasion in April 1961, he set up a series of meetings, national unity meetings with leaders, to try to calm a shaken country, uncertain now about its new young leader. One of the old leaders Kennedy called on was MacArthur, whom he had never met. Before he went to see the old general, he asked to read MacArthur's military records—as he often did with people. Many people of his generation would do that as a way of evaluating their peers. In among MacArthur's papers was his nomination for the Congressional Medal of Honor in 1914. Kennedy was enormously impressed by the "old man's" courage as a young man. Their politics were different, but from that moment on, no one could say a bad word about Douglas MacArthur in front of John Kennedy.

What were the pivotal experiences in the shaping of his character?

I think the most important thing in John Kennedy's life, in forming his character and his view of life, was the fact that he was a man who received the last rites of the Roman Catholic Church at least four times. Starting as a young boy, then in the Navy, then as a senator, he always expected to die young and he was a very fatalistic man.

Could a person of Kennedy's character survive the kind of political climate that now exists?

No. There is no way, not so much because of his character but, again, because of his health—rich people have much more latitude in character than other people do. Gary Hart, for one, never understood that. The Kennedys and the Rockefellers have long driveways. You can't sit on their stoop and clock ladies in and out, as the *Miami Herald* did with Hart. Rich people can buy their way out of situations that other people can't, so that perhaps whatever defects there were in JFK's character he could have hidden. What he could not have hidden, though, was his health history. It was all public—but no one really checked. John Kennedy had Addison's disease (a withering of the adrenal glands), which was a terminal disease until maintenance treatment was discovered in 1940. That year, before Kennedy knew he had the illness, a British doctor discovered that it could be treated with cortisone, which would replace adrenaline. When Kennedy collapsed of Addison's in 1947 in a hotel room in London, he was with Pamela Digby Churchill, now Pamela Harriman. She called Churchill's doctor—she was then married to Winston Churchill's son—and the doctor said: "Your young American friend has less than a year to live." Only later did the doctor learn that there was a cure—not a cure, really, but at least a way to sustain Addisonians. The cortisone was extremely expensive at the beginning and the Kennedys kept quantities of the drug in safety deposit boxes around the world. Until artificial cortisone was developed years later, only a rich person could survive on the regimen that JFK did—day by day for the rest of his life.

In addition to that, he had a degenerative back problem that had nothing to do with football or the war—those campaign stories were not true. It was a birth defect, and it was so bad that at a point in 1954, when he was a senator, he gambled on surgery in New York Hospital. He was told he probably would not survive because trauma triggers Addison's episodes. No Addisonian had ever survived traumatic surgery. But the back pain was so great, he said he would rather die than live with it. He did survive the operation, though he was in the hospital for nine months afterward. That bit of medical history was significant enough that the *Journal of the American Medical Association*, in November 1955, ran a report without names on Kennedy's operation. The patient was identified as "the 37-year-old man." But anybody who knew his history, knew that John Kennedy was the thirty-seven-year-old man. This was what they said in the *Journal* in 1955:

A man 37 years of age had Addison's disease for several years. He had been managed fairly successfully for several years on a program of dioxide cortisteroid acetate pellets of 150 milligrams implanted every three months and cortisone in doses of 25 milligrams daily orally. Owing to a back injury, he had a great deal of pain which interfered with his daily routine. Orthopedic consultation suggested that he might be helped by a lumbo sacra fusion together with a sacroiliac fusion. Because of the severe degree of trauma involved in these operations and because of the patient's adrenic cortical insufficiency due to the Addison's disease, it was deemed dangerous to proceed with these operations. However, since this young man would be incapacitated without surgical intervention, it was decided reluctantly to perform the operations by doing two different procedures at different times. Though this patient had marked adrenic cortical insufficiency, and though the magnitude of his surgery was great and though complications ensued post-operatively, this patient had a smooth post-operative course insofar as no Addisonian crisis ever developed.

In the five years after that, and all the years after that, John Kennedy always denied that he had Addison's disease. But in fact, there was a public record that could have revealed his lie. No one in the press ever put two and two together. In the political and journalistic climate today he could not have hidden that information and thus could not have become a candidate, much less President of the United States.

Which of Kennedy's decisions disappointed you?

Vietnam, as I will discuss at length. I believe that John Kennedy, not Lyndon Johnson, was the President who got us into Vietnam.

THOSE ARE my answers, but I suspect those questions will still be around a long time. Robert Louis Stevenson once said that politics is perhaps the only profession for which no preparation is considered necessary. It was true then—it's true now. And John Kennedy had something to do with that. Whatever one thinks of him as a political figure, John Kennedy was a soaring cultural figure. On a level, I think, with the Picassos, the Freuds, the artists and scholars who change the way we look at things. And the most significant thing about John Kennedy, transcending politics, was this: *he did not wait his turn.* And now, no one does. Part of that was because he thought he would die young—and he had to make his move the first chance he got. He went after the presidency out of turn and essentially destroyed the old system of selecting presidents. The only way he could get the job was by creating a new system in which the press was more important than old-fashioned political titans. Political institutions, educational institutions, religious institutions have been broken since then in the same way—using media. The last institution standing, I think, is the courts, and they won't survive without change now that television is in courtrooms. Whatever television touches, it dominates or destroys. Professional football, the presidency, Congress, and now the courts.

Kennedy was the first of the self-selected presidents. He used the primaries, which had basically been showcases before that, to win the press and the nomination before the party itself convened. Since then we have had supply-side politics in the country: the politicians supply themselves. At any given time, there are 15,000 or 20,000 people—I'm making up the number—running for president. Some of them are in college, some are in the eighth grade, some are assemblymen, some are senators from Texas—and they've been running for a long time. They're in a kind of funnel, and out of that group, one will make it—that is the new system. They pick themselves, and it was Kennedy who created the first real model of that.

John Kennedy, I think, whatever could be said of his character, was a pretty good President. The major issue facing his presidency was the danger of nuclear war. He was the first President since the War of 1812 to come to office in a time when the United States could be invaded. We had been almost perfectly protected by the oceans from 1812 on, and by our own military strength—until the advent of guided missiles. In the 1960s, once again, we were vulnerable. But I think that there was less chance of nuclear war when he left office than when he began. I think that was a tremendous achievement.

In addition to that, he was the President who put the government of the United States on the side of the minority in the civil rights years. He didn't want to do that; he did not want to deal with the political ramifications of that question, but he did it. And that was no small thing. He chose the black minority; chose to put the power of the government on the side of the minority, rather than the white majority. Other presidents might have done something different than that. He was, too, though he could never fully understand why, an enormously successful economic president. In the second Eisenhower term, the economy of the United States grew at a little over 2 percent. When Kennedy's presidency ended in November 1963, the gross national product was growing at a rate of 6.5 percent—the greatest growth rate in modern times in the country. I won't talk much about how he did it—but he didn't enjoy talking about it either. Charles Bartlett, his newspaperman friend from the *Chattanooga Times*, and Senator Kennedy used to go out to American University one night a month in the mid-1950s for tutoring on economics. After Kennedy became President, Bartlett asked him: "What ever happened to that guy at American University, do you know?" Kennedy said, "I don't know, but I assume when I got elected he jumped out the window."

His major (and only) agricultural speech during the 1960 campaign was written by a Philadelphia lawyer, Myer Feldman. When he stepped away from the podium, Kennedy nodded to Feldman and said, "Did you understand anything that I said—I sure didn't." Agricultural figures aside, by the end of his presidency, JFK had educated himself very effectively as an economist.

FINALLY, THOUGH, I think Kennedy got us into Vietnam, and Vietnam did terrible things to the country. It kept the Cold War going for another ten or fifteen years. We threw away so much of our moral and political credibility in that period that communism was able to survive beyond its natural time. Accidents of history have hidden and confused what Kennedy did in Vietnam. Beginning in August 1963, Kennedy began to move very directly to try to remove the government of President Ngo Dinh Diem in South Vietnam, basically because they would not take orders from U.S. advisers, and Kennedy thought that was the reason "we" were losing the war. Diem would not take orders from the Americans, who were, after all, paying the bills. We then had 17,000 men in South Vietnam. On November 1, with American involvement, Diem and his brother were assassinated in a coup which Kennedy had personally signed off on.

If you wonder what it is like to be President of the United States, think of this: John Kennedy signed off on the overthrow of the government of South Vietnam on August 28, 1963. That was the day of the great civil rights March on Washington. The Vietnam decision was made while he was waiting for Martin Luther King, Jr., to come down to the White House from the Lincoln Memorial after his "I Have a Dream" speech. King's trip took twenty-five minutes. During that time, Kennedy met with the National Security Council and finally decided to back South Vietnamese generals anxious to overthrow Diem. That done, the President called in King, Roy Wilkins, and other civil rights leaders. From November 1, 1963, on, South Vietnam was an American colony. We paid the money, we gave the orders, we put the generals in charge. They were really little more than sergeants in the old colonial French army and nobody for a moment thought these people could run a country—a large country. Vietnam is a large country, something Americans never got; it is now the twelfth largest country in the world. A country of more than 75 million people. Within three weeks of Diem's murder on November 1, 1963, Kennedy himself was dead. Whether or not he would have expanded the war in the way that President Johnson did—I doubt it—he was not "pulling out," as some of his men still claim thirty years later.

Kennedy's greatest success beyond the specifics of the lessening of nuclear danger was the great test of any democratic politician—that is, whether he brought out the best or the worst in the American people. And I think John Kennedy brought out the best in the American people. I'm not sure, though, that he always knew exactly how or why that was happening. Kennedy saw civil rights, for instance, as a foreign affairs problem. Photographs of black-white trouble made us look bad around the world, it was being exploited by the Communists. Early in the administration, Angier Biddle Duke, his chief of protocol, told Kennedy that African diplomats were having trouble driving to Washington. Thirty-one new countries joined the United Nations in 1961 alone, many of them former African colonies. The ambassadors to the United Nations and the United States from those countries were usually the same person. They would drive from New York down to Washington, through Maryland, a segregated state. "These guys are complaining about driving through there," said Duke. "We've got to do something about it." And Kennedy said, "That's terrible." Duke asked, "Should we do something?" Kennedy said, "Certainly should—tell them to fly."

In May of 1961, Kennedy found out about the Freedom Riders —the group of black and white activists riding Greyhound and Trailways buses through the South to test compliance with federal desegregation laws—by reading the *New York Times*. There was a photograph of a burning bus in Anniston, Alabama, over a report of white attacks on the first Freedom Riders. He called in his civil rights adviser—a young white man named Harris Wofford, later Senator Wofford—and said, What's going on? Who are these people? Wofford told him and then Kennedy said, "OK, get your God damn friends off those buses."

It was too late for that. A second group in Nashville, Tennessee, was getting ready to take up the rides where the first riders had been savagely beaten. The new riders were led by a twenty-one-year-old woman named Diane Nash. One of Robert Kennedy's assistants in the Justice Department, John Siegenthaler, who had been a reporter on the *Tennessean* in Nashville, was sent there by the President himself, to stop her. The next day Siegenthaler called the President and said, "It's like talking to a brick wall. I told her you're going to get killed if you do this, and she said, 'It doesn't matter if we're killed—others will come—others will come.' "

"Did you ask her why she's doing this?" Kennedy demanded. Siegenthaler said she told him she was doing it to show the segregationists and the bigots in the country that they could not defy the President of the United States. So Kennedy was trying to stop them, not understanding that he was a big part of their inspiration. His grand words and the fact that he had not waited—that was what those young Negroes heard and saw. No President ever understands the resonance of his own voice. The rest of us talk: nobody really listens. Presidents talk: the stock market goes up, Haitians build boats. It is very difficult to learn to moderate that. Kennedy, beyond his intentions, was an inspiration for many of the democratizing movements of the 1960s, which, I would say, did bring out the best in the American people. And now, for people who won't accept the change of the sixties, the delayed reaction to those movements brings out the worst in many American people.

How DO THOSE THINGS fit in as "A Question of Character," which is the title of a book written about Kennedy by someone who happens to have the same name I do, Thomas C. Reeves? But this Reeves, me, is not sure I know what character is or how it affects politics and governance.

I did go to the dictionary to find the definitions of character. In Webster's, the first five definitions are things like "a distinctive mark," "a letter, number, or symbol," as in characters on a typewriter. It's not until number six that you get to "essential quality, kind or sort." Then seven, "the pattern of behavior or personality found in an individual or group." And eight, "moral strength, self-discipline, fortitude," and finally, thirteen—"a person in a play or a novel, etc.," and fifteen—"genetics—any attribute as color, shape, etc." So it's a word that seems to define almost all human activity and then some, from genes to presidents.

The *essential* quality of John Kennedy, I think, because of his health, because of the time he lived, was really irony. He was fatalistic; he saw irony. He often would say to people, "Do you think a President of the United States can really do that? . . . Or really has the power to do that?" His favorite saying, which he thought was Irish (actually it is Indian, subcontinent Indian), was that only three things are certain: God, human folly, and laughter. The first two are beyond our comprehension, so we have to do the best we can with the third—with laughter. His favorite line from literature was from *Henry IV, Part I*, when Glendower boasts, "I can call spirits from the vasty deep." And Hotspur says, "Why, so can I, or so can any man; But will they come when you do call for them?" That is the way that John Kennedy saw the world. He loved gossip, but I doubt he would be greatly engaged, frankly, in today's debates about character. He did see the world as larger forces, and men and women as people caught up in them. You do the best you can.

That happens to be close to my own feeling: Power is what you do and character is what you are—I lean to the side of judging people by what they do. But what do other people lump in as character? I assume it is truth and truthfulness, principles and sticking with principles, loyalty, determination—I think all of those are part of it. I want to add, too, that I am a great skeptic about current discussions of character and of the phrase, "character issues," which I see as really, in many cases, a cover for rotten, dirty politics. I think that the current political debate as it revolves around character issues is literally destroying American politics. The problem we face today, in 1995, is that you get to be a public official in this country by screaming louder or more expensively about what a bum your opponent is. And then half the people doing the screaming are elected—and they think that we all forget that this is what they've been saying about each other. Over these years of more and more negative politics and more and more negative advertising, and more and more "character issues," politicians have done a very, very effective job in destroying their own credibility—whatever public character they had to begin with. So I do feel that in the modern context, the word is being overused, greatly to the detriment of public life.

Obviously, John Kennedy would fail most of the current political tests of character, beginning with questions like marital fidelity and infidelity. Even during his presidential campaign, a memo to the director of the Federal Bureau of Investigation from one of his agents—I'm quoting from it—this is July 13, 1960, reads: "As you're aware, allegations of immoral activities on Senator Kennedy's part have been reported to the FBI over the years. These allegations are not being treated in detail in this memorandum. They include, however, gossip that Kennedy carried on an illicit relationship with another man's wife during World War II." (That happened not to be true, by the way.) "That probably in January, 1960, Kennedy was 'compromised' with a woman in Las Vegas and that Kennedy and Frank Sinatra have in the recent past, been involved in parties in Palm Springs, Las Vegas and New York City" —going to a party in New York City being the lowest of the low. However, whatever the specifics of that memo and hundreds of others like it, obviously there is a great deal of truth in the Kennedy "womanizing" stories.

But it is not true that "everyone knew." In fact, most of those stories were told not in 1960 or 1961 or 1963, but in 1975. It was only when "the President's friend," Judith Campbell (later, Campbell-Exner), was mentioned in Senate reports produced by the Church committee investigating the CIA and assassination plots, that the public unraveling of that part of John Kennedy's life began. These things were not, as many people now believe, common knowledge during his presidency or for twelve years after, although you can run into all sorts of people now who say they knew all about it. Perhaps they did, but if they did, they didn't talk much about it until 1975. JFK was a wild man and a terrible man on that level. The first time he met Harold Macmillan, the prime minister of Great Britain, who was in his late sixties then and had been married to the same woman for forty-five years, Kennedy said, "I don't know about you, Harold, but if I don't have a woman every three days, I get these terrible headaches. How about you?" Macmillan, who kept a diary, recorded that. Unfortunately, he didn't record his response.

Kennedy controlled every person who came in contact with him. He was a Brueghel in the sense that he created a world of his own, but instead of squeezing oil paint, he squeezed people to create his own personal world. He was at the center of all he surveyed. He enjoyed using people, and setting them against each other for his own amusement. He lived life as a race against boredom. He used the people around him as pimps and worse. There were a few who were immune, but even Secretary of State Dean Rusk, a very religious man and a very traditional man, had to handle Kennedy's sexual logistics. That was Kennedy's hobby. It was like tennis, and the games were usually easier to arrange. A lot of people, particularly the military attachés, were involved in the coming and going of women. Many of them took pride in it, thinking it showed they were "close" to JFK. But not Dean Rusk. He never forgave Kennedy for all that.

In three separate conversations, Rusk talked to me about the fact that when Kennedy went to Europe in 1963, he made Rusk arrange to get a villa in the lake country of Italy for Kennedy to meet a woman for a night. The villa was owned by the Rockefeller Foundation, of which Rusk had once been president, and Kennedy wanted everybody off the grounds when he spent that night with a rather prominent, very beautiful European woman. It was the night before he met the Pope. Dean Rusk never, never, got over it—even to the point, in 1991 and 1992, of sitting there chatting with me. He talked about how much it hurt him.

Kennedy, like Scott Fitzgerald's Daisy Buchanan, was "careless," taking as a right the control of his own environment, which meant controlling the people around him. It's not an accident that so many presidents have conferences with their people where they're naked and the people are wearing suits. Kennedy held court in the bathtub or the swimming pool, naked, holding meetings with men in suits walking back and forth or sitting on the bathtub or the toilet or the floor—you don't have to be Freud to figure out what's going on there. Lyndon Johnson and Richard Nixon did the same kind of things.

•

JOHN KENNEDY is a very contemporary man in some ways. He may have been the first modern American man, a role model for the generations that followed. Kennedy came to office in a different time, the time of flashbulbs and vacuum tubes and three-button suits, men with short hair wearing hats. But he had long hair, did not wear a hat, wore two-button European suits—and by the end of his presidency, every other American male did too. He was also a master, as many people have become since, of using candor in lieu of truth. He was an extremely candid man, as many people are nowadays—telling most everything about things that used to be considered private. Others walk away thinking they've been told truth. But, in fact, they've really been told nothing of true importance. The small and candid moments set up the big lie.

On larger matters, Kennedy regularly lied and lied to a purpose, like Franklin Roosevelt. Turner Catledge was the White House correspondent of the *New York Times* when Roosevelt was President—years before he became the paper's editor. And Catledge once said, privately, because people didn't write this way in those days, that Franklin Roosevelt's first instinct was always to lie. He always began by lying, and then he'd look out and he'd say, I can get away with the truth with these people. And he would switch from the lie, or the partial truth, to the truth in midsentence. Kennedy's whole life, in many ways, particularly where his health was involved, was a lie. When John Kennedy met with Nikita Khrushchev in June 1961 for the Vienna Summit, he had with him a small platoon of doctors. He had thrown his back out again and was in considerable pain. One of those physicians was Max Jacobson, who later became famous, or infamous, as Dr. Feel Good. Jacobson dispensed amphetamines, and JFK was a regular patient. In Vienna, Jacobson was standing just outside the conference room doors in the U.S. Embassy and in the Soviet Embassy, while Kennedy met with Khrushchev, just in case JFK wanted a shot. When Robert Kennedy confronted his brother and said this stuff is really dangerous, John Kennedy, who took enormous amounts of medication every day of his life, said, "I don't care if it's horse piss—it makes me feel better and I need that."

JFK also lied about his background. Khrushchev ate him alive at that summit, partly because Kennedy had always said he went to the London School of Economics, that he had studied under Harold Laski. Kennedy had, in fact, signed up to study at the school and Laski was to be his tutor—but Kennedy got sick, again, as he often did. He never showed up. But because of that credit on his official biographies, the people he worked with assumed he knew a great deal about communism, or at least about Marxism—because Laski was a great expert in Marxism. But Kennedy knew nothing, and, in 1961, Khrushchev, the old Bolshevik, tied him up within minutes. Kennedy, lost in the dialectic, was defending things he didn't believe in. Colonialism, imperialism, economic-driven foreign policy for the good of the United States. He was confused and bewildered. That was part of the price he paid for juicing his biography over the years.

One result of that lying was that he felt he had to confront the Soviets someplace because he didn't want Khrushchev to think he was weak. After the last meeting with Khrushchev, he walked into a room alone with James Reston of the *New York Times*. The room in the U.S. Embassy in Vienna was dark, because there were two thousand reporters waiting outside, but as is often the case, only the gentleman from the *New York Times* was invited inside. "How was it?" Reston asked, and Kennedy said, "It was awful. Worst thing of my life. He rolled right over me—he thinks I'm a fool—he thinks I'm weak." None of this ever appeared in the papers, of course. Again, in those days, people didn't write things like that. Reston said, "What are you going to do?" The President answered, "I have to confront them someplace to show that we're tough." "Where?" Kennedy said: "We're going to confront them in Vietnam. We'll stop them in Vietnam."

But there was a good result, too, out of that summit disaster. Face to face, JFK recognized the leader of the Soviet Union as just another practicing politician—and he developed a relationship with

Khrushchev that served the world extremely well. Only three months later, Kennedy and Khrushchev communicated well enough not only to avoid military confrontation over the building of the Berlin Wall but to use the Wall to gradually and greatly reduce the chances of nuclear war. JFK knew the Berlin Wall was going up in August 1961; in fact, he was practically a co-contractor with Khrushchev. It was one of the greatest achievements, if not the greatest achievement, of his presidency. But it was secret; if people had known about it at the time, it would have been a political disaster for him and even, conceivably, could have led to impeachment. If there were to be a nuclear war in those years—and that's when the danger was the greatest—it was not going to be in Cuba or Asia, it was going to be in Europe, and it was going to begin in Berlin. It would have happened if the Soviets had made good their threats to take Berlin. The people of East Germany and other Communist countries—at the rate of two thousand a day by the middle of 1961—were using Berlin to escape to the West. And it wasn't just that people were running, it was who they were. They were the best and the brightest—they were the doctors, engineers, the writers, lawyers, the young people. The Soviet Union had to try to stop it. That was their problem in Berlin.

Our problem was that we and our allies, the British and French, had only fifteen thousand soldiers in West Berlin and they were surrounded by dozens of divisions of the Red Army. If the Soviets chose to use military means to solve their problem, our troops could not have lasted a day, maybe only a couple of hours. If we intended to keep Berlin, or keep Germany, or perhaps even keep all of Europe—Western Europe—we had to use nuclear weapons. John Kennedy did not want to use nuclear weapons—and he certainly didn't want to be the first to use nuclear weapons. When he realized that Khrushchev's real (political) problem was only refugees on the run, the two politicians, with intermediaries, some working in public, some in secrecy, were able to work things out.

The Wall was the solution—though Kennedy could never

admit that. Their words in public were essentially in code. Kennedy repeatedly said that as long as our occupation rights were not violated, what the Communists did on their territory was their business. He knew they could build a wall on their territory. And that's what they did—because Khrushchev knew Kennedy was willing to settle for the continuation of access rights for allied occupation patrols. After the Wall went up on Communist territory on August 13, 1961, JFK did not appear in public for more than a day. He was sailing in Cape Cod and did not comment. And, from the day the Berlin Wall went up until the day it went down, the chance of nuclear war in the world declined most every day. It was the great achievement of the leadership of that time, but it could not be talked about at the time. JFK defused the great threat he faced, the greatest threat we all faced on his watch.

The two politicians, of perhaps dubious character, collaborated again the next year in October of 1962, when the Americans discovered Soviet missiles in Cuba. The concept of the book *Is Paris Burning?* has always interested me greatly—that Hitler ordered the German general in charge of occupied Paris to burn the city down as the Allies approached in August of 1944. He was sending messages from Berlin saying, "Is Paris burning?" General Dietrich von Choltitz decided on his own that he did not want to be remembered through history as the man who destroyed Paris. And I think that by October of 1962, Khrushchev and Kennedy knew each other well enough to know that neither of them wanted to be remembered as the man who first fired nuclear missiles. Three years before, Kennedy had become President largely because of a supposed "missile gap" and the perception (false) that the United States was in danger of falling behind the Soviets. In fact, we had overwhelming superiority. It is possible at the time of the 1960 campaign the Soviets had only four intercontinental ballistic missiles (strategic missiles) and there was a real question as to whether their guidance systems were good enough to get them to a target in the United States.

The real trigger of the Cuban Missile Crisis was Kennedy's

decision in early 1962 to make sure that the Soviets and the world knew that *we knew* we were ahead. So in a series of speeches, most particularly one by Deputy Secretary of Defense Roswell Gilpatric, U.S. strength was laid out in detail—and leaked to the press. At that point, the Soviet Union (Khrushchev) was faced with the revelation that the USSR was not the kind of superpower they had been perceived to be for five years or so. Khrushchev then made his move, figuring since after all we have a picket fence of missiles around their border, why shouldn't he try to get some in close to us—turning medium range Soviet tactical missiles into strategic missiles, and putting them south of the U.S., where we had no defenses. All our defenses faced north—assuming attack over Alaska and Canada. Khrushchev took the gamble of taking a goodly part of their stuff and putting it in Cuba. Kennedy understood, as only a national leader could; privately he said that if he were Khrushchev he would have done the same thing. JFK thought Khrushchev did the right thing in his position. By that time, they could deal without sending notes.

ONE OF THE THINGS John Kennedy lied about as President was speed reading. In the Kennedy Library, I read an oral history by Hugh Sidey of *Time* magazine, which first "revealed" that John Kennedy was a speed reader, reporting that he read 1,200 words a minute. People loved it, a real intellectual in the White House. But what actually happened was that the President's sister, Eunice Shriver, was sitting next to Henry Luce, the editor of *Time*, at a party, talking about how much her brother read and how quickly. Luce thought that was a good story, so he sent Sidey to talk to Kennedy. This is from Sidey's oral history:

> We called up the reading institute where he was supposed to have taken the course, but nobody could really remember him being there. They suggested that he probably read about 700 or 800 words a minute, which was twice normal. So I went to Kennedy and told him what the people are saying—Kennedy didn't like that a bit—he

thought he read faster than that and he wasn't a bit modest about it. So we made some rough calculations and it came out that he read 700–800 words a minute, which is pretty good. But most people of relatively high I.Q. do that. And then he brought in John Kenneth Galbraith as a witness, and Galbraith said that JFK had read a 26 page memo and it had taken him just 10 minutes, because he noted it on the clock. That came out to about 1,000 words a minute, but the President thought that was still too slow. So we negotiated and we rounded the figure out and we wrote that he read 1,200 words a minute.

I guess that's a flaw in his character, too. But it's like Lincoln and the paper dolls—at night Lincoln would go upstairs in the White House and play with paper dolls. Did that have anything to do with the conduct of the Civil War? Lincoln's dolls? *I made that up totally. I have no idea what Lincoln did in the privacy of the night.* And would it have made any difference if he played with paper dolls? Kennedy played with human dolls—live ones—but would it, or did it, really make any difference? I don't know because I can't come to conclusions about character myself. Should Kennedy have told the truth about the Berlin Wall? Should Franklin Roosevelt have told the truth about Pearl Harbor? That, for all practical purposes, the U.S. Pacific Fleet had been destroyed. Should he have let the Japanese know that? Should Dwight Eisenhower have stood behind his beliefs on race and civil rights—he thought the Supreme Court was wrong on *Brown* v. *Board of Education.* What would have happened if President Eisenhower had said that out loud? What is character? Should Charles de Gaulle have kept his promises on Algeria rather than forsake his promises and withdraw? It seems to me that all leaders must face some crisis where their own strength of character is the enemy. Should President Nixon have acted out of his real (or at least spoken) beliefs on China and tried to destroy it? Or should he have betrayed his following and made the opening to China? The great moral dilemma of Western history is still this, should Thomas à Beckett be loyal to Henry or to the Church?

People in leadership positions have to make these choices. Was Napoleon a man of great character—I suspect he wasn't. Was Caesar? After John Kennedy was dead and his brother was in a deep depression, Richard Goodwin, trying to cheer up Robert Kennedy about his brother's place in history, said that he had been reading the night before and he realized for the first time that Julius Caesar held power for only three years in Rome. And Robert Kennedy said, "Julius Caesar had Shakespeare."

As far as I can tell from reading, Herbert Hoover was a man of absolutely sterling character. They don't make people any better than Herbert Hoover. But he was a failed President. Perhaps being a journalist rather than an historian has something to do with the way I think, because we tend to put events in the context of their time, while many historians tend to put events and decisions in the context of a complete life or in the context of ideas. When I set out to write about John F. Kennedy, my structure was rigorously chronological. I wanted, to the extent I could, to isolate Kennedy as to where he was, what he knew, when he knew it, who he talked to, what he thought, what he said, what he did at a given point in time, because I knew that history books, which talk in terms of issues—civil rights, foreign policy, the economy—totally distort what being President is like. All of these things happen at the same time to a president.

FINALLY I want to construct "a day in the life" of the presidency of John Kennedy. It's an extended day because of time zones in the world. On June 9, 1963, John Kennedy began the day in Honolulu, where he was at a meeting of the U.S. Conference of Mayors. He had gone out there because sit-ins and other violence had begun in the South and the mayors were the people on the line. He wanted to talk to them about that. Flying back, he picked up Ted Sorenson in San Francisco and they finished editing a speech which Kennedy gave at 10:00 that morning at American University in Washington, June 10, 1963. It was the greatest speech he ever made, one of the greatest speeches ever made by any American. He talked

101

about the assumptions of the Cold War and raised the questions for the first time that perhaps all of these things were not inevitable and perhaps we should reach out to the Soviet Union.

When he came back to the White House he was told that George Wallace, the segregationist governor of Alabama, was standing in the door of the University of Alabama at Tuscaloosa to prevent the entry of the first two Negro students into that school. From South Vietnam on the wires came the story that a monk had burned himself to death in Saigon to protest American policies, and worse than that, UPI had a photo of it that the whole world would see. In Moscow that day, a Chinese delegation led by Deng Xaio-ping arrived and was officially snubbed, an act that eventually led to public proof that U.S. fears of monolithic communism were exaggerated—or just foolish. The situation at the University of Alabama was taking most of Kennedy's attention. He still hoped to avoid making civil rights an issue partly because he needed the southerners in Congress and partly because he thought the American people weren't ready to accept equal rights for Negroes. He was not a bigot; he was a politician. He would do it when it was ready to be done.

But, that day, Vice President Lyndon Johnson convinced him that the time had come. John Kennedy was a man susceptible to argument. He was not a man of great passion, but he was a man of serious intellect in the sense that he changed his mind based on information. Johnson told him that the black-white problem was escalating in the country because as long as the President did not take a position, either with the majority white or the minority black, both sides believed that in his heart, the President was with them. The blacks listened to his rhetoric and it sounded like liberation music to them. And whites, including southern congressional leaders, thought that secretly he was one of them—but was just another Yankee politician who had to talk the way he did because of black votes in the North. But, Johnson said, that was the problem: As long as both sides think that, they're both going to keep going; you have to take sides.

Kennedy accepted that argument. He went on television that night and in another great speech, done largely without notes, he said, This is not a political question, this is a moral question, this is a question of what kind of people we are. And if we do believe in equality, then who among us would choose to be black? The field secretary of the NAACP in the state of Mississippi was in his car when he heard that speech and turned around to go home because he wanted to talk to his children about what the President had just done. The President had taken sides! He pulled into his driveway, stepped out of the car, his children ran out the door, and he was shot. Medgar Evers bled to death in front of his children. That's a day in the life of the President. That's what it's like to be President of the United States.

Whatever character is, John Kennedy had it that day. I suspect that there is such a thing as *presidential character*, which is separate from the way most of us would judge each other or judge our work or responsibility or duty. Edmund Morris, who is Ronald Reagan's designated biographer, wrote a great biography of young Teddy Roosevelt. He concluded that three factors constitute the "essence" of the presidency, then and now, at the beginning and end of the century:

> Articulating what is unspoken in the heart of the American people. The kind of mystical gift to divine what people really want.
>
> To initiate and push policies that are in the people's interest.
>
> To represent the best in us, not only to bring out the best in us, but to represent it in public and with [an] overwhelming positivism of the kind that both the Roosevelts had. They weren't people who told you why things couldn't happen; they told you why things could happen.

Presidents are not paid by the hour. I have spent time with President Bill Clinton and been driven nuts by his explaining to me how hard he's working. I think hard work is the last refuge of scoundrels. We pay our presidents for four, five, one or two big decisions. They represent the 250 million when something happens: when communism falls; when black people riot. At the point of crisis and judgment, what matters is whether they can connect with what is unspoken in the hearts of Americans.

In the end, I come to the conclusion that perhaps what is most important is not the character of the President of the United States, but the character of the American people.

LYNDON B. JOHNSON

1963–1969

by

Robert Dallek

FATE IS CHARACTER, the ancient Greeks said. Lyndon Johnson's political career is a good case in point. He was as outsized and memorable a figure as any to sit in the White House. He has been described as a human dynamo, a whirlwind, a tornado in pants, a cross between a character Mark Twain and William Faulkner could have invented, a Jekyll and Hyde, a magnificent, inspiring leader one minute and an insufferable bastard the next. He was Winston Churchill's puzzle inside a riddle wrapped in an enigma. He was, in the words of one associate, an octagonal figure, and in the judgment of another, a protagonist in Luigi Pirandello's *Six Characters in Search of an Author*. The play "leaves you with the most baffled wonderment as to whether there really were six characters in search of an author or whether the whole thing was a figment of someone's imagination," George Reedy, a longtime aide to LBJ, says. ". . . Johnson would leave you like that."

Johnson was an example of what the Japanese call the contradiction of opposites. Driven, tyrannical, crude, insensitive, humorless, and petty, he was also empathic, shy, sophisticated, self-critical, uproariously funny, and magnanimous. "He was a man of too many paradoxes," Reedy adds. "Almost everything you find out about him you can find out a directly contrary quality immediately, and your problem is always which quality was real and which was assumed. Or maybe neither quality was real. Or maybe both were real, who knows."

New York Times columnist Russell Baker remembers Johnson as "a human puzzle so complicated no one could ever understand it. . . . Johnson was a flesh-and-blood, three-volume biography, and if you ever got it written you'd discover after publication that you missed the key point or got the interpretation completely wrong and needed a fourth volume to set things right." Johnson, Baker concluded, "was a character out of a Russian novel, one of those human complications that filled the imagination of Dostoyevsky, a storm of warring human instincts: sinner and saint, buffoon and statesman, cynic and sentimentalist, a man torn between hungers for immortality and self-destruction."

Johnson was much loved and greatly hated—not just liked and disliked but adored by some and despised by others. Some people remember him as kind, generous, compassionate, considerate, decent, and devoted to advancing the well-being of the least advantaged among us. Others describe him as cruel, dictatorial, grandiose, and even vicious.

Bryce Harlow, a House and Senate staffer and later White House counsel under Eisenhower, remembers LBJ as a sort of fabulous, unique character:

> Wherever he'd sit down there was a cloud of dust. Something was happening all the time, even if he were seated. . . . He was talking to the guys next to him. . . . He was getting up; he was sitting down. . . . His alarm clock watch, which he just loved to harass people with. . . . It was a stunt . . . he always set it off at some propitious time to attract attention to himself. He couldn't stand not

being the cynosure of all eyes. He had to be at the head of the table. . . . And people had to do what he thought they should do. And ordinarily he made them do it. How many people do you know like that? None. You never know anybody like that, because they don't make them. But, yes, they do, once in a millennium. That's Lyndon.

The journalists Rowland Evans and Robert Novak have given us an indelible picture of Johnson applying "The Treatment" to people who needed persuading. It was

supplication, accusation, cajolery, exuberance, scorn, tears, complaint, the hint of threat. It was all these together. It ran the gamut of human emotions. Its velocity was breathtaking, and it was all in one direction. Interjections from the target were rare. Johnson anticipated them before they could be spoken. He moved in close, his face a scant millimeter from his target, his eyes widening and narrowing, his eyebrows rising and falling. From his pockets poured clippings, memos, statistics. Mimicry, humor, and the genius of analogy made The Treatment an almost hypnotic experience and rendered the target stunned and helpless.

Benjamin Bradlee of the *Washington Post* compared Johnson's technique to going to the zoo:

You really felt as if a St. Bernard had licked your face for an hour, had pawed you all over. . . . He never just shook hands with you. One hand was shaking your hand; the other hand was always someplace else, exploring you, examining you. And of course he was a great actor, bar fucking none the greatest. He'd be feeling up Katharine Graham and bumping Meg Greenfield on the boobs. And at the same time he'd be trying to persuade you of something, sometimes something that he knew and I knew was not so, and there was just the trace of a little smile on his face. It was just a miraculous performance.

Hubert Humphrey said: "He'd come on just like a tidal wave. . . . He went through the walls. He'd come through a door, and he'd take the whole room over. Just like that. . . . There was nothing delicate about him." But Johnson's persuasiveness also rested on a capacity to become, in some undefinable way, a physical and psychological extension of someone else. A shared perspective or an affirmation of someone else's thinking complemented the grabbing and holding, the chest-to-chest, nose-to-nose closeness for which he was famous.

Johnson's complexity should not become an excuse for abandoning efforts to understand him. There are patterns to his behavior that help us understand why he acted as he did and how his personality contributed to his successes and failures in the White House.

JOHNSON WAS A MAN possessed by inner demons. From early in his childhood he manifested character traits that shaped his behavior throughout his life. As a boy and a man he suffered from a sense of emptiness: he couldn't stand to be alone; he needed constant companionship, attention, affection, and approval. He had insatiable appetites: for work, women, food, drink, conversation, and material possessions. They were all in the service of filling himself up —of giving himself a sort of validity or sense of self-worth.

"I never think about politics more than 18 hours a day," he once said. He worked at his vocation as if his very life depended on it. He couldn't relax; he needed to be constantly busy. Humphrey described rest for him as "controlled frenzy." Friends and associates remember him as a frenetic character, always in motion, talking politics at ball games, in the swimming pool, at the dinner table. A childhood friend said: "I don't believe he ever got tired in his life. The time that I knowed him . . . he just never did run down."

Johnson's neediness translated into a number of traits that had a large impact on his political actions. He had a compulsion to be the best, to outdo everybody, to eclipse all his predecessors in the White House and become the greatest President in American history. As journalist Nicholas Lemann says, Johnson "wanted to set world records in politics, as a star athlete would in sports. 'Get those coonskins up on the wall,' he would tell people around him." Another childhood friend remembers that "if there was an argument, he *had* to win. He *had* to. . . . If he'd differ with you, he'd hover right up against you, breathing right in your face, arguing your point with all the earnestness. . . . I got disgusted with him. Sometimes, I'd try just to walk away, but . . . he just wouldn't stop until you gave in."

As a senator, he had to be top dog, and drove himself to become Majority Leader. He turned a post with limited influence into the most powerful position in the Senate, from which he directed the passage of significant laws affecting labor, the elderly, housing, civil rights, defense, and space exploration. As Majority Leader, he was thrilled to be the first legislator in Washington with a car phone. When Everett Dirksen, Republican Minority Leader and a friendly rival, also acquired one, he telephoned Johnson's limo to say that he was calling from his new car phone. "Can you hold on a minute, Ev?" Johnson asked. "My other phone is ringing."

In 1951, only three years after LBJ had come to the Senate, the journalist Alfred Steinberg interviewed him in the President's room off the Senate floor, where presidents since Lincoln had come when visiting the chamber. Steinberg wanted to do an article on congressional leaders, but Johnson urged him to do "a whole big article on just me alone." Johnson "sat with his knees pressed against mine, a hand clutching my lapel, and his nose only inches away from my nose. When he leaned forward, I leaned back at an uncomfortable angle. 'What would the pitch of an article on you be?' " Steinberg asked. " 'That you might be a Vice-Presidential candidate for 1952?'. . . 'Vice President hell!' he whispered. 'Who wants that? . . . President! That's the angle you want to write about me. . . . You can build it up by saying how I run both houses of Congress right now.' " Steinberg asked for an explanation of this extraordinary claim: " 'Well, right here in the Senate I have to do all of [Majority Leader] Boob McFarland's work because he can't do any of it. . . . And then every afternoon I go over to Sam Rayburn's place. He tells me all about the problems he's facing in the House, and I tell him how to handle them. So that's how come I'm running everything here in the Capitol,' he finished, gripping me above the knee."

After Johnson won election to the vice presidency in 1960, he "looked as if he'd lost his last friend on earth. . . . I don't think I ever saw a more unhappy man," one of his secretaries recalls. He found it hard to explain how John Kennedy, a more junior and less accomplished senator, could have bested him for the presidential nomination. He expressed his distress and rivalry with JFK during a telephone call on the evening of the election. " 'I see you are losing Ohio,' " he told Kennedy. " 'I am carrying Texas and we are doing pretty well in Pennsylvania.' " "Doesn't that sound like him," his old friend Jim Rowe told Hubert Humphrey.

He was a reluctant Vice President. He had hoped and planned for the presidency, but fate or the limitations of his time, place, and personality had cast him in the second spot. And he despised it.

Initially, one of the hardest assignments for Johnson to accept was that of goodwill ambassador abroad. In the nearly three years he served as Vice President, he spent almost two and a half months making eleven trips to thirty-three foreign lands. Most of it consisted of showing the flag. But Kennedy saw it as a good way to fill Johnson's time and improve his disposition. Kennedy told Florida senator George Smathers, "I cannot stand Johnson's damn long face. He just comes in, sits at the Cabinet meetings with his face all screwed up, never says anything. He looks so sad." Smathers suggested that the President send Johnson "on an around-the-world trip . . . so that he can get all of the fanfare and all of the attention and all of the smoke-blowing will be directed at him, build up his ego again, let him have a great time." Kennedy thought it "a damn good idea," and in the spring of 1961 he sent Johnson to Africa and Asia.

Johnson was reluctant to spend his time on what he saw as

mostly frivolous business. But his craving for center stage, which he could have traveling abroad but not at home, quickly made him an enthusiast of foreign trips. Indeed, they became a kind of theater in which he could act out his zany, irreverent, demanding, impetuous characteristics that amused and pleased some and offended and amazed others. They also gave him an opportunity to bring a message of hope to needy people in distant lands. In Africa and Asia, his trips partly became a crusade for the New Deal reforms that had transformed America. Eager to combat Communist appeals to poor developing nations, Johnson pointed to economic change in his native South as a model for Third World advance.

A four-day trip to Senegal in April 1961 was part comic opera and part serious diplomatic mission. Kennedy's decision to send Johnson there largely rested on a desire to compete with Communist efforts to woo emerging nations. For Johnson, it immediately became a chance to play the great man offering enlightened guidance to an impoverished people. He insisted that a seven-foot bed to accommodate his six-foot, three-and-a-half-inch frame, a special showerhead that emitted a needlepoint spray, cases of Cutty Sark, and boxes of ballpoint pens and cigarette lighters with "L.B.J." inscribed on them travel with him to Dakar.

There, he ignored the diplomatic niceties urged upon him by the U.S. Embassy. One morning at four-thirty he and Lady Bird traveled to a fishing village, where the American ambassador refused to leave his limousine. "It was too smelly a town for him," a Johnson traveling companion recalls. The ambassador counseled Johnson against any contact with these people, whom he described as dirty and diseased. But the Vice President strolled among the villagers, handing out pens and lighters, shaking hands with everyone, including a few fingerless lepers, and advising the bewildered natives that they could be like Texans, who had increased their annual income tenfold in forty years. The trip was a microcosm of Johnson's career: a grandiose, temperamental man doing outlandish things simultaneously to get attention and improve the lot of the poor.

•

JOHNSON'S GRANDIOSITY had a large impact on what he did as President. One can easily take offense at LBJ's impulse to make himself a larger-than-life character. "I understand you were born in a log cabin," German chancellor Ludwig Erhard said during a visit to the President's ranch. "No, no," Johnson replied. "You have me confused with Abe Lincoln, I was born in a manger." When the historian William E. Leuchtenburg interviewed Johnson for an article on the Great Society in September 1965, Johnson's grandiosity amazed and offended him. Throughout the interview, LBJ "had been comparing himself with others, past and present, and finding no peer." Johnson believed "his accomplishments were the most important in all our history. . . . He held a conviction of his own centrality in the universe bordering on egomania."

Johnson's grandiosity both served and undermined him as President. Throughout his career, Johnson held to the proposition that political power was meant to be used for large purposes. "Some men," he told Doris Kearns Goodwin, "want power simply to strut around the world and to hear the tune of 'Hail to the Chief.' Others want it simply to build prestige, to collect antiques, and to buy pretty things. Well I wanted power to give things to people—all sorts of things to all sorts of people, especially the poor and the blacks."

From 1935 on, when he became director of the National Youth Administration in Texas and then, in 1937, a congressman from the Tenth District, which included his impoverished native Hill Country, Johnson used government programs to serve the well-being of his constituents. He believed that Texas and the South could improve living standards and enter the mainstream of the country's economic and political life through federal largesse, New Deal agricultural, conservation, public works, electrification, labor, and housing programs like the Agricultural Adjustment Administration, Works Progress Administration, Civilian Conservation Corps, Tennessee Valley Authority, National Youth Administration, Rural Electrification Administration, Farm Security

Administration, Wages and Hours, and public housing. When World War II erupted and the United States began to rearm, building an Air Force and expanding the Army and the Navy, Johnson pressed the case for defense spending in the South as another way to develop the region's economy. The onset of the Cold War in the late 1940s produced additional subsidies for the southern and western economies that contributed to their emergence as new centers of national economic and political power. It was not by accident that during the 1950s, when Johnson became a powerful U.S. senator, Texas had more air bases than any other state in the Union.

One can see a direct line from Johnson's preoccupation as a congressman and senator with using federal programs to raise living standards to the War on Poverty and Great Society laws of his presidency. Within days of coming to the White House, he learned from Walter Heller, JFK's chairman of the Council of Economic Advisers, that a plan was in motion to bring the 20 to 25 percent of the country who were ill-fed, ill-housed, and ill-clad out of poverty. "That's my kind of program," Johnson told Heller. And less than two months later, in his first State of the Union Address, Johnson announced an "all-out war on human poverty and unemployment in the United States." This "unconditional war on poverty" was not to be "short or easy," but an all-out campaign in which "we shall not rest until that war is won." The aim was "not only to relieve the symptom of poverty, but to cure it and, above all, to prevent it."

In May 1964, in a speech at the University of Michigan, the President announced his plans for a Great Society. The goal was "to move not only toward the rich society and the powerful society, but upward to the Great Society." It was to rest on "abundance and liberty for all." It was "a place where men are more concerned with the quality of their goals than the quantity of their goods. . . . Those who came to this land sought to build more than just a new country. They sought a new world. So I have come here today to your campus to say that you can make their vision our reality. So let us from this moment begin our work so that in the future men will look back and say: It was then, after a long and weary way, that man turned the exploits of his genius to the full enrichment of his life."

Two months before announcing the Great Society program, Johnson had given an interview to representatives of the three TV and radio networks. Eric Sevareid of CBS asked if the President had settled on a catch phrase like "New Deal" or "New Frontier" to describe his administration. Johnson answered that he had been too busy to think of "any slogan, but I suppose all of us want a better deal, don't we?" Although saying he didn't believe in labels, Johnson described himself as a prudent progressive.

"A better deal," "a prudent progressive" were two of the phrases Johnson had come up with in an avid search for a "big theme" to characterize his presidency. Despite his protestations about being too busy and not believing in labels, Johnson had been "badgering" Richard Goodwin, a JFK aide and now LBJ speechwriter, to find a popular slogan that would resonate with voters in the 1964 campaign and give his administration its historical identity. In February, Johnson had summoned Goodwin and his press secretary, Bill Moyers, to join him in the White House swimming pool. "We entered the pool area," Goodwin recalls, "to see the massive presidential flesh, a sun bleached atoll breaching the placid sea, passing gently, sidestroke, the deep-cleft buttocks moving slowly past our unstartled gaze. Moby Dick, I thought. . . . 'It's like going swimming with a polar bear,' Moyers whispered. . . . Without turning his body, Johnson called across the pool: 'Come on in, boys. It'll do you good.' " Stripping on the spot, they joined the President in the pool, where he "began to talk as if he were addressing some larger, imagined audience of the mind." He declared his intention to go beyond Kennedy and create a "Johnson program, different in tone, fighting and aggressive. . . . Suspended almost motionless in the water," Goodwin "felt Johnson's immense vitality," as he presented his plans to move the nation "toward some distant vision—vaguely defined, inchoate, but rooted in an ideal as old as the country."

Johnson's twenty-minute Great Society speech before more than 80,000 people in the University of Michigan's stadium on a warm sunny day was a great hit. The jubilant crowd, grateful for the President's attendance at their children's graduation, sensing that they were hearing a landmark address and stirred by the President's words, interrupted him for applause twenty-nine times. For Johnson, the approval and enthusiasm were intoxicating. On the plane ride back to Washington, he was "manic" or "just . . . absolutely euphoric." Violating a self-imposed rule, he had a scotch highball and joined the pool reporters in the back of the plane. Asking them what they thought, and warming to their positive assessment, he "read, with emphasis, portions of the speech to us. He wanted to make sure we got the story. He'd say, 'Now did you get this?' and 'Back here I said this and that.'"

JOHNSON'S PASSION to leave an unsurpassed mark on the country also translated into a commitment to a civil rights revolution. In 1957, as Majority Leader, he had led the first major civil rights law through Congress since 1875. Though the bill was more symbol than substance, it nevertheless opened the way to the far more telling 1964 and 1965 measures, which ended segregation in public facilities across the South and assured African-Americans of the right to vote. Johnson believed that justice, morality, and the Constitution required the passage of these laws. He also understood that before the South could become part of mainstream American politics, it would have to abandon segregation: he accurately saw that the Jim Crow laws not only segregated the races in the South, they also separated the South from the rest of the nation. His commitment to dismantle the system of legalized racism in the South also partly rested on his determination to become the greatest civil rights president in American history.

The same neediness that made Johnson so eager for personal grandeur contributed to his desire to help the least advantaged. Throughout his life he identified with poor folks who had neither the material possessions nor the social regard held by and accorded to the most affluent members of society. He remembered his first teaching job at Cotulla, Texas, in an elementary school with Mexican-American students as an awakening of his desire to help "those poor little kids. I saw hunger in their eyes and pain in their bodies. Those little brown bodies had so little and needed so much. I was determined to spark something inside them, to fill their souls with ambition and interest and belief in the future." Both in Cotulla and later, there was an almost desperate urgency to Johnson's desire to give sustenance to the poor, as if he were filling himself with the attention and affection he so badly craved.

Johnson's affinity for grand visionary programs produced some extraordinary legislative gains for the nation. Consider, for example, that no twentieth-century president with the exception of FDR comes close to matching Johnson's legislative achievements: the creation of NASA, the 1957 and 1964 civil rights acts, the 1965 voting rights law, Medicare, Medicaid, federal aid to elementary, secondary, and higher education, clean air and clean water laws, the creation of the Departments of Housing and Urban Development and Transportation, highway, automobile, tire, fire, gas pipeline and mine safety measures, the Office of Economic Opportunity, food stamps, Head Start, Aid to Small Businesses, the Fair Immigration law ending the discriminatory National Origins Act, the National Endowments for the Arts and the Humanities, National Public Radio and Television, Truth in Securities, Lending and Packaging, the Product Safety Commission, model cities, Fair Housing, Freedom of Information, and much more.

Johnson's rhetoric about curing poverty, building a Great Society, and ending racial strife undermined his credibility with the public and ability to govern and lead. Johnson celebrated his War on Poverty as cutting in half the number of Americans living below the poverty line, but his claim impressed most people as essentially an act of self-promotion. To be sure, millions of poor Americans found themselves better off as a consequence of the President's war on deprivation. But this was more the consequence of a fourfold increase in the welfare rolls than of social and economic changes ending poverty or of endowing the disadvantaged with more than a fixed dole. With inner-city blight as pronounced as ever, few in America took seriously Johnson's assertion that his administration had found the answer to the centuries'-old problem of economic want for great numbers of people, even in as rich a society as ours. Johnson's excessive claims for what his poverty fight could achieve not only undermined his believability but also made for public cynicism about the value of big social engineering programs under the control of government bureaucrats spending large amounts of money with limited results.

The public had a similar response to Johnson's exaggerated accounts of what the Great Society and civil rights legislation were achieving. After five-plus years of LBJ's presidency, few Americans were convinced that the massive body of laws passed in the service of building a Great Society was doing anything of the kind. Individual measures enjoyed considerable popularity, like Medicare and Head Start, but crime, social and racial tensions, and bouts of inflation coupled with periodic economic downturns left most Americans cynical about the capacity of the government to manage national affairs very effectively, let alone create a Great Society.

THE INNER-CITY RIOTS during the "long hot summers" of the late 1960s and subsequent racial strife in America, including fights over busing, quotas, and affirmative action, have given the lie to Johnson's promises of race harmony once de jure segregation disappeared and everyone in the country had the right to exercise the ballot. The current surge of conservatism embodied in Newt Gingrich's Contract with America is as direct a repudiation of LBJ's Great Society programs as anything we have seen since their passage in the mid-sixties.

This turnabout is reflected in recent surveys of public attitudes toward LBJ and other presidents. During Johnson's five-plus years in the White House, he enjoyed an average approval rating of 56 percent, higher than that of Harry Truman, Richard Nixon, Gerald Ford, Jimmy Carter, and even Ronald Reagan, who averaged 52 percent. Well into 1966, Johnson received positive assessments for his presidential performance of between 50 and 60 percent. In 1966 and 1967, a majority of Americans described Johnson as the most admired man in the world. In January 1968, he placed second on the list behind Dwight Eisenhower.

Since then, however, Johnson has become one of the least admired men ever to sit in the White House. At the close of his presidential term in 1969, frustration over the Vietnam War, his abrasive personality, his "credibility gap," and costly domestic programs producing less than he promised drove Johnson's approval rating down to 49 percent. A Harris Poll in 1988 on presidential performance from FDR to Reagan consistently ranked LBJ at or near the bottom of eleven categories. Who was the best among these presidents in domestic affairs? Harris asked. Only 6 percent chose LBJ. Who was the greatest moral leader? John Kennedy topped the list. Johnson came in dead last, with only 1 percent of the vote. Even Nixon beat him out with 2 percent. In 1990, Johnson's approval rating had fallen to 40 percent. Only Nixon stood lower among recent presidents, with 32 percent. And the outpouring of regard for Nixon at his death may now have boosted him past Johnson. Given the current assault on the Great Society programs, it is not hard to imagine this as the case.

Much of Johnson's drop in public standing had to do with the losses and defeat in Vietnam. Americans across the political spectrum see the war as a disaster for which Johnson must take considerable blame. Critics on the right complain that Johnson failed to use sufficient power to win the struggle against communism in Vietnam. On the left, opponents of the war, then and now, see the conflict as a struggle for American empire in which approximately 3 million Vietnamese and 58,000 Americans died. Most Americans in the middle now see the war as a poor idea in which we squandered much blood and treasure to no good end. Johnson's failure to understand that this was a civil war which had nothing to do with consequential U.S. interests resulted in divisions at home and distrust of presidential authority that won't go away.

The war brought out the worst in Johnson. His failure to deal effectively with the conflict partly rested on his character flaws: his grandiosity that could overcome every obstacle and his impulse to view criticism of his policies as personal attacks which he would overcome by increasing his efforts to make his policies succeed. Johnson fought in Vietnam for many reasons. He genuinely believed it essential to hold the line in Vietnam against Communist advance. Otherwise, the United States would face the loss of all of Southeast Asia to a hostile ideology. He also believed that a failure to stop the Viet Cong and North Vietnamese in South Vietnam would embolden Moscow and Peking and raise the likelihood of another larger, possibly nuclear, war. If all this weren't enough to keep Johnson fighting in Vietnam, there was his concern that losing the country to communism would touch off another round of McCarthyism in the United States and defeat him and the Democrats in the next election. The victory of conservative Republicans would then lead to the dismantling of the War on Poverty and the Great Society and the eclipse of the Democrats for a long time to come.

Johnson clung to these assumptions to the end of his life in 1973. Arguments by thoughtful opponents that a Communist Vietnam would not necessarily lead to like-minded regimes in Laos, Thailand, Cambodia, Malaysia, Singapore, and the Philippines did not convince him. Assertions that the war in Vietnam was essentially a civil conflict between national rivals more intent on controlling their country than promoting the advance of international communism also left him cold. A product of his experience with appeasement leading to World War II and of the commonly held belief in the forties and fifties of a "worldwide Communist threat," Johnson could not walk away from the war in Vietnam.

"We are in bad shape in Vietnam," Johnson told Turner Catledge of the *New York Times* in December 1964. "Uncertainties in that area are far more than the certainties. Yet we can't afford to, and we will not, pull out. We must find some way to bring the job off even if we have to set it up so that a withdrawal would have a better face. . . . Whether we spread military operations across

North Vietnam is yet to be decided. We certainly haven't decided against it. We've got to do whatever it takes, either to get a good settlement there, or to furnish a good face behind which we can withdraw. Again, withdrawal is not in the picture, certainly not now."

The escalation of U.S. involvement in the fighting in 1965, first through the sustained bombing campaign, "Rolling Thunder," and then by the introduction of 500,000 American troops beginning in the summer, confronted Johnson with a new dilemma. How much U.S. power would it take to force Hanoi into negotiations that would preserve South Vietnamese independence? Neither Johnson nor any of his advisers could ever come up with the answer to that question. As Johnson and others in his administration came to see, U.S. bombing and troop escalations produced not negotiations but additional military action by the other side.

Johnson and most Americans until at least the beginning of 1968 held to the belief that at some point the Communists would crack; it was accepted wisdom that they could not hold out forever against American power. But how long that would be, no one could say. In these circumstances, the greatest danger Johnson saw to the U.S. war effort came not from the North Vietnamese but from war opponents in the United States. He believed that their constant expressions of dissent—warnings that this would be a ten- or possibly twenty-year war that would take tens of thousands of American lives and expenditures that would weaken our economy—was encouraging Hanoi and sapping the American will to fight.

The opposition attacks brought out the worst in Johnson. Criticism wounded and enraged him, making it difficult for him to respond in sensible ways to manageable political problems. He should have taken a page from Franklin Roosevelt's book. From 1939 to 1941, when confronting a nation divided by the European war, FDR encouraged a debate about how to respond. A believer in the proposition that you could not have an effective policy abroad without a stable consensus at home, Roosevelt assured that debate and general agreement preceded any major foreign policy action. Johnson would have been well advised to do the same: A debate about Vietnam in 1965 probably would have led to a consensus for escalation. A continuing dialogue in the country about how to proceed also probably would have convinced the Congress to abandon the conflict by 1968, understanding then that Saigon could not sustain itself without American arms, and that the price of a continuing war was not worth the questionable gains of keeping South Vietnam free of Communist control.

But Johnson couldn't bring himself to do this. His escalation of the war was done without directly consulting the Congress or the country. There was nothing resembling the debates that preceded involvement in World Wars I and II. Truman's experience with Korea made Johnson mindful of the political dangers to a president committing fighting men to a conflict lacking a declaration of war. Johnson saw the Gulf of Tonkin Resolution in the summer of 1964 as an antidote to this problem. But war opponents, including a number of prominent senators who voted for the resolution, never took it seriously as a blanket endorsement of an American commitment to fight in Vietnam.

JOHNSON'S EFFORTS not to stir dissent by clearly acknowledging steps escalating American involvement produced what journalists described as the "credibility gap." How do you know when Lyndon Johnson's telling the truth? a joke made the rounds of Washington. When he pulls his earlobe, scratches his chin, you know he's being straight with you. But when he begins to move his lips, you know he's lying. It was a terrible burden to bear for any president as intent on aggressive leadership as Johnson.

In dealing with dissenters, Johnson's overbearing and controlling temperament served him poorly. He took criticism of anything he did as intensely personal. Though he understood that differences played a large part in politics, he could never take his distance from objections to his most intensely felt public actions, especially by people he counted among his allies and friends.

Hubert Humphrey tried to persuade Johnson that what he was

doing in Vietnam might be "the most fateful decisions of your Administration." Humphrey believed it essential that Johnson make the war "politically understandable" to the American public. "There has to be a cogent, convincing case if we are to enjoy sustained public support," he told LBJ in February 1965. "In World Wars I and II we had this." Even in Korea, where "we could not sustain American political support for fighting Chinese," the public had a better understanding of what we were doing than in Vietnam. Humphrey predicted that if "we find ourselves leading from frustration to escalation and end up short of a war with China but embroiled deeper in fighting in Vietnam over the next few months, political opposition will steadily mount." And he warned that this opposition would come from "Democratic liberals, independents, [and] labor" and would gain a hold "at the grassroots across the country."

Johnson was not happy with Humphrey's criticism and warnings. Senator J. William Fulbright, chairman of the influential Senate Foreign Relations Committee, told the President that Humphrey had introduced him to men who believed that the problem in Vietnam "could get started toward solution if we would replace our military provincial proconsuls and advisers with civilians who knew the peasants and village people." Johnson responded: "In a choice between Humphrey and General [Maxwell] Taylor as our major strategist I am disposed toward Taylor in this matter." Humphrey's warnings made him persona non grata with LBJ. As Humphrey described it, he contributed little to discussions on Vietnam in the next several months. Johnson sent him into "limbo," with his access to the President "limited," and his "counsel less welcome."

In April 1965, after Canada's Liberal prime minister Lester B. Pearson had given a critical speech in Philadelphia about the President's Vietnam policy, Johnson invited him to Camp David, where he vented his frustration. Johnson did all the talking. "If there had not been a kind of 'et tu, Brute' feeling about the assault, without any personal unpleasantness of any kind," Pearson writes in his memoirs, "I would have felt almost like Schuschnigg before Hitler at Berchtesgaden!" Pearson was reluctant to reveal how overbearing the President had been, even, one eyewitness said, grabbing the prime minister by the lapels. When asked at a cabinet meeting what had really happened, Pearson recounted "the story of a British policeman giving evidence at a murder trial. 'My Lord,' the policeman told the judge, 'acting on information received, I proceeded to a certain address and there found the body of a woman. She had been strangled, stabbed and shot, decapitated and dismembered. But, My Lord, she had not been interfered with.' " At Camp David, Pearson explained in conclusion, he had at least not been "interfered with."

The burden of Johnson's complaint was that Pearson "had joined the ranks of the domestic opponents of his Vietnam Policy: [Senator Wayne] Morse, [Walter] Lippmann, the *New York Times*, ADA [Americans for Democratic Action], the ignorant liberals, the 'know nothing,' 'do gooders,' etc." Johnson seemed "forlorn at not being understood better by friends." He impressed Pearson as being

> tired, under great and continuous pressure, and . . . more worried about US policy in Vietnam than he was willing to show. His irritation at any indication of lack of full support for his policy; his impatience of criticism and his insistence that everything is working out in accord with a well-conceived plan; all these really indicate a feeling of insecurity about the situation, rather than the reverse. As the President said: "It's hard to sleep these days." "I'm beginning to feel like a martyr; misunderstood, misjudged by friends at home and abroad."

Johnson saw liberal opponents of his Vietnam policies as disloyal to him and the country. Vietnam was a war he believed in; it was nothing he wanted to do, but he felt he had no choice, it was vital to the country's well-being. He kept asking: Why couldn't dissenters see that the war was a blight on his greatest hopes of altering the face of domestic America? Didn't they understand that he was acting out of necessity?

The only satisfactory explanation he saw for the dissent was

Communist influence. He believed that the driving force behind the marches, rallies, teach-ins, sit-ins, draft-card burnings, and written and oral expressions of opposition by intellectuals and prominent public officials like Senators George Aiken, J. William Fulbright, Eugene McCarthy, George McGovern, and Wayne Morse was the Communists.

In January 1966, when Fulbright's Senate Foreign Relations Committee began Vietnam hearings that it believed would serve the national interest, Johnson was furious. He thought the open debate would encourage the Communists to see the United States as divided and likely to quit the war. He feared that Fulbright, Morse, and other members of Congress were under the unwitting influence of Communist diplomats. He asked the director of the FBI to study comments made at the hearings to see if they reflected Communist views. Though J. Edgar Hoover was unable to show that Communists or other subversives had influenced Johnson's Senate critics, the President asked the FBI to keep a close watch on Communist envoys in the United States to see if they were "making contacts with Senators and Congressmen and any citizens of a prominent nature." The President believed that "much of this protest concerning his foreign policy, particularly the hearings in the Senate, had been generated by [Communist officials]."

Johnson now took the position that there was no neutral ground in the debate over Vietnam. People were either with him and the war or against him. After retired General James Gavin testified against the war, Johnson—or so Gavin believed—arranged an Internal Revenue Service audit of his tax returns. When retired Ambassador George Kennan, who was also critical of American involvement in Vietnam, appeared before the committee, CBS president Frank Stanton, a friend of LBJ's, decided to show reruns of *I Love Lucy* and *The Real McCoys* instead of continuing to televise the hearings. News Division head Fred Friendly, who opposed Stanton's decision, resigned in protest.

Soon after, in a meeting with state governors at the White House, Johnson declared that "our country is constantly under threat every day—Comm[unists] working every day to divide us, to destroy us. Make no mistake about the Comm[unists]," he said. "Don't kid yourself a moment. It is in the highest counsels of gov[ernment]—in our society. McCarthy's methods were wrong— but the threat is greater now than in his day."

Who was Johnson thinking of? Were his remarks just hyperbolic rhetoric meant to scare war critics into "getting on the team"? Or did he actually believe that congressmen, senators, and journalists were intent on overturning the country's traditional institutions? It is difficult to take his comments at face value. Whatever his propensity for suspicion—even paranoia—it is hard to imagine that he genuinely saw high government officials and prominent reporters as secretly promoting communism at home or abroad. But at the same time, he could not accept the view that his opponents were expressing independent judgments. From his perspective, anyone in America who thought carefully about the war would see the need and wisdom of the administration's policy. Johnson believed that some academic critics were "gullible" men, mesmerized by romantic assumptions about the virtues of communism in Vietnam. Their naivete made them vulnerable to the Communists, who skillfully encouraged and orchestrated their opposition to the war.

In 1965–66 the war became a personal crusade for Johnson. It was his war, being fought by his "boys," with his helicopters and his planes and guns. Withdrawal and defeat became unthinkable. In 1967, when Leonard Marks, LBJ's director of the United States Information Agency and a close friend whom Johnson had always treated with consideration and respect, privately suggested that the President follow Senator Aiken's advice in Vietnam—declare victory and leave—Johnson glared at him until Marks asked: "What do you think?" Johnson shouted at him: "Get out." As increasing numbers of Americans died in the fighting and Johnson couldn't appear in public without risk of protests, he became emotionally distraught. By 1967, Georgia senator Richard Russell, a Johnson mentor, couldn't bear to see Johnson alone at the White House, because the President would cry uncontrollably. The journalist William S. White has similar memories of LBJ weeping when presented with casualty reports.

JOHNSON'S PRESIDENCY was one of the most tumultuous in American history. Great numbers of groundbreaking laws, a landmark electoral victory in 1964, the longest and most controversial war in the country's experience, repeated explosions of civil strife, assassinations of major public figures, a presidential withdrawal from an election campaign, and the most violent national Democratic Party Convention ever punctuated Johnson's sixty-two months in office.

It would be too simple, too easy to say that the times reflected the controversial, overdrawn, and imperfect character of the man. However much of a mark LBJ left on the sixties, this was not the age of Johnson; the sum of the times was larger than any of its parts, even one as huge as Lyndon Johnson. Nevertheless, we risk diminished understanding of the period without close consideration of what this man contributed—positive and negative—through the weight of his powerful personality. His presidency, for good and ill, was greatly shaped by his character. And surely one of Johnson's lasting contributions to American history will be a continuing struggle to understand and assess what he tells us about the country's life during his day and ours.

RICHARD M. NIXON

1969–1974

by

Tom Wicker

YEARS AGO, in what seems now like another world, I went to Stockholm as a columnist for the *New York Times* and interviewed the late Olof Palme, the Swedish prime minister. Before I could ask a question, he said to me:

"I was in Paris yesterday for the funeral of President Pompidou, and I met your President Nixon."

"What did you think of him?" I asked.

Palme's eyes widened and he leaned toward me to whisper conspiratorially:

"He was wearing pancake makeup!"

That's not an unfitting description of a man who sometimes thrived on, sometimes suffered from, and was a genuine pioneer of television. The morning after Nixon delivered his famous "Checkers" speech in 1952, defending himself from charges of accepting improper contributions, to what was then the biggest TV audience ever assembled in the United States, the waitresses in a Missoula,

Montana, coffee shop "damn near fainted" when they saw Nixon enter—but not, his friend and later Secretary of State William P. Rogers recalls, because he was running for Vice President. They might not even have known that. They were excited because, the night before, they had seen him on television, then a new and mysterious medium.

In the 1950s, when he was Vice President carrying much of the political burden for President Eisenhower, Nixon's beard-shadowed face and upturned nose became familiar to the increasing number of Americans who owned TV sets. By 1960, he was running for President against John F. Kennedy; and when the two engaged in the first of the televised debates that have since become common campaign events, the watching audience was the first to surpass in numbers the one that had watched the Checkers speech eight years earlier.

Thus, Nixon was a star attraction for the first two big national television audiences, as TV was beginning to transform American politics and American life. It transformed Nixon, too; he learned at least two hard lessons from that first debate.

One was: Never give your opponent an even break. In early 1960, Nixon was inaccurately regarded as the natural as well as the chosen heir to President Eisenhower, and as one whose vice-presidential experience made him far more ready to be President than the lesser known Kennedy. Those who watch tapes of that first debate today won't find much difference in the capacity the two men showed. What did matter was that Kennedy proved to be as knowledgeable as Nixon; and after that, Nixon's advantage as the supposedly more experienced man was gone forever. Giving a lesser known opponent the opportunity to show his wares before that record-setting audience probably cost Nixon his first chance at the presidency.

The second lesson was that Kennedy *looked* better than Nixon, who had recently been ill, had a tendency to perspire, and suffered a lifelong case of five o'clock shadow. And as candidates well know today, but did not necessarily realize thirty-five years ago, appearance and manner count more on TV than substance. Nixon's gaunt and sweating face was not attractive, nor did his staff's inept use of makeup hide his beard shadow. So when Nixon met Olof Palme in Paris more than a decade later, he was wearing plenty of pancake makeup and was ready for any camera that might turn up.

Television thus had a large part in "making" Nixon in the fifties and then helped to "break" him in 1960. As the world came to know, however, the man was nothing if not indomitable. When he again ran for President in 1968, he used TV as skillfully as any candidate had, up to then; he may have been the first president elected *primarily* because of television. His commercials were candid shots of Nixon in action and at his best before carefully screened audiences; his so-called telethons were an early version of the now familiar "town meeting" campaign style; and both were expertly tailored to make him look like your friendly neighbor, rather than the unshaven menace pictured in Herblock cartoons.

Television's huge role in Nixon's career continued into his presidency. In 1969, with a single nationally televised speech he reversed a tide of opposition to the war in Vietnam, if only temporarily. But in the seventies, in the throes of Watergate, and especially in some bear-pit news conference, the TV cameras showed him to the nation at his defiant and unconvincing worst.

IT'S FITTING, for another reason, to think of Richard Milhous Nixon in the context of the television era, which began at about the same time as his political career, in the early postwar years. Television is a medium that can cruelly expose, as it did Nixon's unattractive appearance in the first debate with JFK; but it's also a medium through which contrived and artfully presented images can be convincing to a host of viewers, as were his commercials in 1968. And with rare exceptions like the 1960 debate, what the public usually saw of Nixon, on TV or in person, *was* contrived and artfully presented.

That's not quite as damning as the blunt statement may make it seem. For in my judgment, Richard Nixon was an introvert in the extroverted calling of the politician. And as if that were not problem enough for him, he was an intellectual appealing to a public that puts low value on eggheads. I don't mean an intellectual in the stereotypical sense of a cloistered scholar; I mean that Nixon was a highly intelligent man who relied greatly on his own intelligence and that of others, who had a considerable capacity to read and understand technical papers, who retreated to a room alone and wrote in longhand on a yellow legal pad the gist of his major speeches, who impressed associates with his ability to evaluate disinterestedly the pros and cons of a problem, who in the opinion of Arthur Burns, whom he appointed to head the Federal Reserve, could have "held down a chair in political science or law in any of our major universities."

Any number of Richard Nixon's associates will tell you that glad-handing and pressing the flesh did not come naturally or congenially to him. When closely observed, he always seemed somehow ill at ease. His gestures when he spoke—the counting of points on the fingers, the arms upstretched in the victory sign or sweeping around his body like a matador flicking a cape before a bull—the body language always seemed a little out of sync with what he was saying, as if a sound track were running a little ahead of or behind its film.

Lyndon Johnson once called him a "chronic campaigner" but Nixon actually shrank from the accustomed rituals of politics. In an interview early in his career, he told the columnist Stewart Alsop: "I'm fundamentally relatively shy. It doesn't come naturally to me to be a buddy-buddy boy . . . I can't really let my hair down with anyone." Yet he forced himself to engage, sometimes even to excel, in the exhibitionary skills of campaigning over a political career that lasted nearly thirty years—a remarkably successful career during which he served in both houses of Congress and as Vice President, was twice elected President of the United States, and became the only American other than Franklin Roosevelt to be nominated by a major party on five national tickets.

Ray Price, Nixon's highly respected aide before, during, and after the White House years, told me that throughout that career Nixon presented to the general public a false image of himself. Not, Price insisted, the common politician's deception of claiming to be smarter, more courageous, better qualified than he or she actually is. Rather, Nixon's pretense was to be *less* than he was—less thoughtful, less introverted, less skeptical and analytical, less cerebral—to present himself deliberately as an Average American: patriotic, conventionally religious and responsible, gregarious, sports-loving, hardworking and hard-nosed.

One can only imagine what maintaining that appearance must have cost, psychically and personally, a studious introvert like Richard Nixon. I recall hearing him speak, many years after he had resigned the presidency, to the Los Angeles Council on Foreign Relations. He gave a typically knowledgeable *tour d'horizon* of world affairs, apparently speaking extemporaneously. But he actually had memorized his remarks so accurately that they coincided almost totally with a printed text handed to reporters in advance. And all during this remarkable performance, his hands were clasped in front of him, twisting together, writhing white-knuckled, in what I took to be effort and anxiety.

One *political* consequence of Nixon's constant effort to appear to be in tune with ordinary Americans, of course, was his remarkable appeal to American voters. He became a discounted, sometimes derided figure during and after Watergate. But the career he achieved before his disgrace was extraordinary by any standard.

He was elected President in 1972, for instance, by one of the largest margins in American history. That was no more remarkable than the virtual dead heat he ran in 1960 against one of the most attractive candidates ever to seek the presidency. That election was so close and so disputed that Thruston Morton, the Republican Party chairman, did not concede defeat until two months after John Kennedy's inauguration. I was the reporter to whom Morton finally gave a concession statement—and I had to wring it out of him.

Nixon's appeal was attested by the long lines of Americans who paid their respects at his funeral in 1994. That was evidence of what the November 1994 elections confirmed—that the "silent majority" he counted on is alive and well today, and perhaps growing. Many of those funeral goers, of course, never had the chance to vote for or against him since he last sought public office in 1972. To many of these, the fiercely partisan, harshly hawkish Nixon so strongly supported or furiously denounced by their elders may not have been visible in the "wise old man" that in his last years he appeared to be—and may even have become.

During his active political life, Nixon was an undeniably popular figure, if not to the millions who voted for John F. Kennedy in 1960, then to the approximately equal number of millions who did not. His efforts, even if sometimes transparent, to identify himself with the ordinary American surely flattered that not-quite-mythical figure, of whom there are many. His hard-hat patriotism and his Americanism echoed theirs, as did his piety and his sentimentality about mothers and sports. He was by no means Dwight Eisenhower's chosen heir, but his close identification with and his defense of the Eisenhower years of peace and prosperity struck a responsive chord with millions of Americans who had never had it so good.

Nixon's victories in 1968 and 1972 surely reflected, moreover, the fact that in the rebellious sixties and during the years of Vietnam and civil rights protests, he stood squarely in the mainstream, with the common man against the "longhairs" and the "hippies," the draft-card burners and those he was not slow to call "America-haters." That he was elected President in 1968 partially as a result of his so-called Southern strategy and of the national "backlash" against racial integration suggests again the extent to which ordinary Americans—ordinary *white* Americans—saw themselves reflected in him.

Nixon's cutting of ethical or political corners, both real and imagined, was viewed with shock and horror by his opponents. But even those actions may well have been seen more sympathetically by millions of American voters. Most were strongly anti-Communist themselves. And which of them, after all—which of us —never sought an edge, never lied or cheated a little, never got out front any way he or she could? Most Americans have reason to know that the ideal often must yield to the necessary or the expedient, that right seldom conquers might.

Another consequence, however, of Nixon's public persona was that even those who supported him sensed something contrived and artificial. A "new Nixon" was proclaimed so often in the fifties and sixties, as he ran again and again for office, or in support of other Republicans, that the phrase became a standing joke. My colleague Russell Baker wrote a classic column sometime back in the sixties about a row of suits he said were hanging in Nixon's closet. Each suit represented a "new Nixon": all the man had to do was to put on a different one to make himself into another "new Nixon."

Reporters frequently tried to get behind the man's mask of patriotism and propriety but were seldom successful; one of them said there must be a "cardboard man" underneath. Even Dwight Eisenhower, whose patronage cemented Nixon's position as a national figure, worried whether he had the character and strength to be President. In 1956, Eisenhower sought to "dump" Nixon as Vice President; in 1960, he tried hard to find an alternative Republican candidate for President. In both cases, Eisenhower badly underestimated Nixon's standing within the Republican Party and with the general public.

Still another consequence of Nixon's calculated presentation of himself was that, when he finally made it to the White House, he was one of two presidents in my personal experience who were mistrusted by a large segment of the American people. All presidents are opposed, of course, and many are disliked; but few suffer widespread attacks on their personal integrity or veracity. Nixon did; so did Lyndon Johnson.

Distrust of both Johnson and Nixon as presidents arose not least from public opposition to the war in Vietnam and the belief of many Americans that neither was telling the whole truth about it. In Nixon's case, however, distrust had been evident earlier, before his presidency, even before he ran in 1960—on the part of liberals because of his Communist-hunting and rough campaign tactics, but on a wider scale because of that vague feeling that he was not what he seemed. Even people who followed him could not know exactly what lay beneath the facade he constantly presented. But one could sense that from behind his appearance of pious responsibility and somewhat strained good fellowship, someone else was looking out, with a gaze shrewd, sharp, measuring, menacing to some, enigmatic even to those who stood with him—and baffling today, to those who try to understand the man.

EARLY IN LIFE Nixon seems to have thrown in his lot with those he called the "have-nots" rather than on the side of those he once described to his former aide Ken Clawson as having everything and therefore "sitting on their fat butts." As a freshman at Whittier College he helped organize the Orthogonians, a men's club in sharp contrast to the existing Franklins. "Orthogonians" meant "Square Shooters," Nixon explained in his memoirs; and in the college yearbook, Franklins were pictured in tuxedos while Orthogonians wore open-necked shirts, as befitted what Nixon termed "athletes and men who were working their way through school."

The Franklin-Orthogonian distinction is a constant in Nixon's life. His first two major opponents, Jerry Voorhis, a millionaire banker's son, and Helen Gahagan Douglas, a famous actress and friend of Eleanor Roosevelt, could be seen as Franklins. So could his most prominent victim, the elegant diplomat Alger Hiss. Two of his most frequent Democratic targets, Adlai Stevenson and Dean Acheson, surely were Franklins. John F. Kennedy, rich and cool as Nixon would never be, obviously was another. Whether or not Nixon actually saw these adversaries as Franklins, their presence and manner are bound to have whetted his class instinct; and Kennedy's disputed victory in 1960 must have been the more crushing because of it.

What were the origins of that instinct? Here we enter psychological turf to be trodden only at peril. But we know Nixon came from a near-poor background just this side of poverty. As a worker in his father's grocery store, his lowly status was quite visible—and we have the testimony of a childhood acquaintance, Lucille Parsons, that "he didn't like to wait on people in the store" and "didn't want anybody to see him go get vegetables" from the Los Angeles market.

He couldn't make the Whittier College football team, despite near-suicidal attempts, thus flunking one of the established tests of orthodox American males. Another youthful contemporary recalls that Nixon "didn't have the glamour about him that interests the opposite sex"—a second grievous failure in youth, or at any age. Bill Rogers, who befriended Nixon when the latter was a young member of Congress, recalls that Nixon always believed people didn't like him.

His father, volatile, cantankerous, loud, and not much of a provider, may have embarrassed the young Richard. And Frank Nixon repeatedly told his sons how fortunate they were to go to school and get an education, as he had not been able to do. That must have sharpened Nixon's sense of being a "have-not" who would need to work for everything he got. At Duke Law School, he lived on next to nothing, and though he did well academically was known primarily for having "an iron butt"—the ability to study for hours and hours in the library. Upon graduation, he was rejected by the big New York law firms to which he had applied, and only reluctantly accepted a position in a small firm back home in Whittier—symbolically returning from the East with his tail between his legs.

Is it too much to suppose, then, that Richard Nixon suffered from feelings of inadequacy and was lacking in a sense of self-worth? That he felt bitterness toward those gifted Franklins in their tuxedos to whom good things came easily and who thus deserved them less? A decade after he resigned the presidency, he told Ken Clawson:

> . . . what starts the process really are laughs and slights and snubs when you are a kid. . . . But if you are reasonably intelligent and *if your anger is deep enough and strong enough*, you learn that you can change those attitudes by excellence, personal gut performance, while those who have everything are sitting on their fat butts [emphasis added].

I believe it is possible to see the life of Richard Nixon as a long, relentless effort to "change those attitudes by excellence, personal gut performance." If he was not liked, if he was not attractive to women, if he was a poor athlete, if he had to do menial labor for an embarrassing father, if he was not one of "those who have everything," if the eastern establishment scorned him, still Richard Nixon with his "iron butt" could show them all by "excellence, personal gut performance." And he would.

It would be a battle, of course, but Nixon throughout his career seems to have regarded life as battle, even to have welcomed struggle. He may have inherited his father's aggressive temperament; he certainly gloried in the appellation his political tactics soon earned him—that of a "gut fighter." The "battle" metaphor appears constantly in his writing and he liked to tell the public that he was at his best when under challenge or attack. Typically, his first book of memoirs was titled *Six Crises* and concerned those moments when he regarded himself as battling for his political life.

But where was he to find the field for the "personal gut performance" he was determined to display? His early experience in the law was not encouraging. His World War II naval experience had taught him primarily how to win at poker. But his officer's uniform was not the least reason a group of his home-town elders chose him, more or less out of the blue, to run for Congress in 1946. His hard-hitting campaign and smashing victory over Jerry Voorhis disclosed to him his calling, his metier, his life. But if he were to succeed in politics, on a broader stage than the Twelfth Congressional District of California, if "personal gut performance" were to give him through politics the status and standing he craved, it could hardly be as introvert or as an intellectual, much less both.

So the Nixon who had believed or feared he would not be accepted by the Franklins, and who helped form the Orthogonians in defiance, who had been turned away by the eastern establishment, carried over into his political career the conviction that his future lay with the Average American. He would become one, or at least appear to be one. His natural self would be concealed; an unnatural self would be devised. But that, too, was only a matter of "personal gut performance."

A MAN OR WOMAN of real gifts might conclude that a successful politician has to appear to be an ordinary middle-class American, with all the attitudes and prejudices attributed to that vast cohort, for exalted or even noble reasons—in Nixon's case, he certainly did hope to build "a structure of peace." But I believe such a profound personal transformation could be contemplated only if one held ordinary Americans in a certain basic contempt. Rather than saying, "I will try to make them better," one is saying, "I will lower myself to their level in order to win their votes."

Nixon himself once conceded to Hugh Sidey of *Time* magazine, "You've got to be a little evil to understand those people out there. You have to have known the dark side of life to understand those people." Even if that's true, the idea nevertheless seems to me to represent a condescending and contemptuous attitude toward the commonality of the American people. If Nixon really did understand them, I believe he also held them in less than high regard, except for their votes.

Nor did he trust them. A close associate, a man who knew him well, the late Bryce Harlow, speculated to me that "as a young person, [Nixon] was hurt deeply by somebody he trusted. . . . He never got over it and never trusted anybody again. But in life we get back what we plow into it." Such a personal betrayal may have happened, but in any case we seldom trust those we hold in contempt.

It's clear, for instance, that as President, Nixon did not trust the American people to understand his conduct of foreign policy. A devotee of *realpolitik*, aided by Henry Kissinger as his national security adviser, he proceeded usually in secrecy, often by threat and manipulation, sometimes by duplicity, and rarely believed enough in his own associates or the American people to take them into his confidence, share with them his goals and ideas.

The "opening to China" was carried out by Nixon and Kissinger in all but total secrecy, even from the Secretary of State, at the cost of allies' anger, and was delivered to the public as a successful fait accompli. The first Strategic Arms Limitation Agreement was reached partially in a "back channel" unknown even to the State and Defense departments or to the administration's official arms control negotiators, much less to the public. The final SALT agreement was hyped as the beginning of a "detente" between the superpowers. When, inevitably, the supposed detente was shown to be hollow and the agreement itself flawed and limited, arms control as a concept was nearly discredited. Worse, Nixon's lack of trust prevented him from using the "bully pulpit" to build solid public support for his strategic vision.

Nixon's penchant for secrecy did not arise solely from his mistrust of the public. It was also a natural outgrowth of his preference for solitude. Richard Nixon was a true loner—another anomaly in a successful politician, another aspect of personality to be painfully concealed beneath the broad smile and the glad hand. One of his Whittier acquaintances recalls that, even in his youth, "he had a room up over the garage that was his room where he could be alone to study. . . . He liked to be alone to study."

In all his years as a major public figure, he still liked to be alone to study. While Vice President, he told Stewart Alsop that "a major public figure is a lonely man . . . you can't enjoy the luxury of intimate personal friendships." Reporters who covered his 1956 campaign remember that he once emerged from a hotel wearing a bathing suit, dived in the pool, swam a lap, got out, and walked away without having greeted or spoken to anyone around the pool, even those in his entourage.

On election night in 1968, he closeted himself alone in a hotel room, with his wife and daughters in another. The next day, after a victory luncheon, he again secluded himself in his library, listening to Richard Rodgers's music for *Victory at Sea*. Once in the White House itself, he spent hours by himself in a hideaway office in the old State, War and Navy Building next door.

Describing in his memoirs the traumas and triumphs of his

public life—the Hiss case, the 1952 fund crisis, Eisenhower's efforts to dump him, his loss to Kennedy, his victories in 1968 and 1972, the major events of his presidency, even his Watergate ordeal—in all these Nixon cites important periods of seclusion, of silent contemplation, of deliberate retreat from the consolations or plaudits of family, staff, advisers. He never seems to have indulged himself in intimate personal friendships. Solitude was Richard Nixon's chosen environment, his reward in victory, his solace in defeat. No wonder, then, that he chose to operate in secrecy, taking counsel of few but himself, confiding in even fewer, as he made decisions and devised policies that affected millions of people throughout the world.

Arthur Burns once asked me if I thought Nixon ever had had a good, close personal friend, in whom he could confide his deepest thoughts, from whom he might have been willing to heed straight talk? Neither of us could recall any such person.

Thinking of Watergate, Burns concluded: "A friend like that could have saved him."

NIXON WORKED HARD during his presidency and even harder after his forced resignation to foster his reputation as a master of foreign policy. That reputation and his real achievements, such as the opening to China, have obscured the fact that he actually was a strong domestic president. And Watergate, understandably, has caused many of his achievements to be forgotten.

The nation's major environmental laws were signed and the Environmental Protection Agency was established by President Richard Nixon. So was the volunteer army. The first wage and price controls ever imposed in peacetime by any president were decreed by the supposedly conservative Nixon. Calling himself a "Keynesian," he also tried out the first "full-employment budget" and doubled funds for food stamps. Nixon set affirmative action as an official government policy, with the so-called Philadelphia Plan, and he supported both the Equal Rights Amendment and legislation against sex discrimination.

139

Nixon began and sustained a program of sharing federal revenues with the states and cities—a program ultimately killed by President Ronald Reagan that actually did what so many Republicans like to talk about: turn power away from Washington. Perhaps most remarkably, he formulated, but Congress and the Democrats defeated, what is still the most far-reaching welfare reform ever proposed: the Family Assistance Plan, which would have provided a federal floor under the incomes of the poor, "a guaranteed annual income," in fact. And in 1971, nearly a quarter century ago, Nixon proposed a comprehensive health insurance plan (CHIP) requiring employers to provide health insurance for their employees. Not unlike 1994's more complex proposals, CHIP went nowhere.

In 1970, despite the "Southern strategy," the Nixon administration also forced more school integration than had been achieved in the sixteen years since the Supreme Court ruled segregated schools unconstitutional. It's true that the courts had left Nixon little choice; but he carried out legal requirements he disapproved of more effectively than any president up to that time.

None of that is as surprising as it may seem because Nixon's domestic political outlook had been shaped at a time when New Deal liberalism, and later the civil rights movement, dominated American politics. That was true even during the eight years of the Eisenhower administration and Nixon's vice presidency. When he became President himself, following Lyndon B. Johnson, he did turn back some of what Republicans considered the excesses of the Great Society program; but in domestic affairs, the Nixon administration was far more nearly in line with New Deal ideas than with those on which Ronald Reagan and Newt Gingrich later triumphed.

THAT WAS NOT the case in foreign policy. Nixon, it must be remembered, made his early reputation, both good and bad, as a scourge of domestic communism. And just as his domestic views were heavily influenced by the New Deal years, his foreign outlook was largely shaped by the Cold War. It began about the time he entered politics and was still the prime fact of international life when he left the White House in 1974.

Richard Nixon was a child of the Cold War, the prevailing ethic of which, on both sides, was that power had to meet power. Only power could thwart or even "contain" power. Only fire could fight fire. A missile system had to be met with another missile system, and topped with an anti-missile system. Nixon was not alone in saying, and undoubtedly he believed, "The Communists only respect force."

From the day he entered politics, Nixon took the hard line of power for himself, his party, his country. He was not only a political beneficiary of Cold War views, he was an instigator. His early California campaigns, the Hiss case, his national campaigns in the fifties—all emphasized the anti-Communist orthodoxy that prevailed for so many years. He was selected for Vice President on the Eisenhower ticket primarily because of his record against communism. During the first Indochina crisis in 1954, he urged the use of nuclear weapons; fortunately, Eisenhower knew better. Even when, as President, Nixon sought the opening to China and arms control agreements with the Soviet Union, he was not trying to end the Cold War but to strengthen the United States for the contest. And as crises of whatever magnitude arose, he invariably viewed them geopolitically, as Cold War confrontations between Moscow and Washington.

Just as the nation, in its determined pursuit of the Cold War, to some extent sacrificed its ideals and its moral position in the world, so Richard Nixon followed a course that in a crucial sense belied his upbringing. He had been raised a Quaker, and his mother, Hannah Nixon, by the testimony of all who knew her and by Richard's own frequent tributes, not only lived and preached Quaker ideals but was considered virtually "a saint."

The same testimony and tributes disclose no suggestion, however, that she also was a warm and loving mother, likely to caress or comfort a lonely little boy rather than give him moral instruction. Nixon himself has recalled that she "never said 'I love you' because she considered that to be very private and very sacred." Some of his early recollections, though carefully worded, suggest clearly that he craved more manifestations of love and affection, perhaps just hugs and kisses, than he apparently received. Persons more qualified in psychology than I may see in that deprivation the seeds of his later austerity and reserve.

What he did get in plenty from Hannah Nixon, who dominated his early life and remained a prominent force in his later years, was a powerful example of rectitude, idealism, and restraint. As a public man after 1946, however, Nixon quite clearly turned away from her calm and "saintly" preachings, the Quaker idealism she had sought to instill in him, and followed instead the more combative, rancorous, confrontational ways of his father, Frank Nixon. I don't suggest that Richard made a deliberate choice to do so; I'm not even certain that one parental strain, like blue eyes or left-handedness, overcame another. I do think that the public man who chose and pursued the course of power must occasionally have reflected that he was following more nearly in his father's footsteps than his mother's; and that to a man who revered her as a saint, that knowledge could hardly have been comfortable or comforting.

In fact, Richard Nixon's repeated emphasis on building a "structure of peace" may well have been the justification he offered to himself, and therefore to his mother's memory, for his abandonment of her ideals and his politician's reliance upon power in trying to build that structure. And among all those, including himself, to whom he sought so tenaciously to prove his worth, Hannah Nixon may well have been foremost. The most powerful of the forces that drove him, it seems plausible to suggest, may have been the wish to go in spirit to Hannah Nixon—despite all the un-Quakerish grapplings and betrayals of his political life—and say: "Mother, I have made peace. Now I am worthy of you."

BEING ELECTED President is something that only forty-two Americans—all white males, so far—have achieved. Reaching that pinnacle of power, one might assume, would make ordinary apprehensions seem less fearful. Surrounded by the Secret Service, transported on Air Force One, truckled to by yes-men, his every personal want satisfied, "Hail to the Chief" ringing in his ears, even nuclear weapons at his beck and call—what kind of insecurities could possibly afflict a president?

The answer obviously is that what's in a person's heart and soul will not likely be changed by the ability to command a helicopter to land on the South Lawn. Lyndon Johnson could have a drink dispenser installed in his armchair but he couldn't shake the feeling that his education was inadequate. Bill Clinton can get an expensive haircut and entertain Hollywood stars but he can't rid himself of the problems of growing up with an alcoholic stepfather. And Richard Nixon brought anxieties to the presidency that not even a hot line to Moscow could assuage.

In a limited way, however, Nixon apparently did find the White House liberating from the contrived personality he had assumed to get there. He had still to campaign, of course—the words "Nixon" and "campaign" go as naturally together as bacon and eggs. But shielded by the White House grounds and his assiduous gatekeeper, Chief of Staff H. R. Haldeman, he could sometimes be the shy and introverted loner he naturally was.

"We've got the reputation of . . . building a wall around the President," John Ehrlichman, another White House aide, remembered, speaking of himself and Haldeman. "The fact is that [Nixon] was down under the desk saying 'I don't want to see those fellows' and we were trying to pull him out."

When Ehrlichman and Pat Moynihan, then also a White House aide, tried to get the President to visit a Washington supermarket to check the prices housewives had to pay—a harmless photo op—he flatly refused. "Too hokey," he said. Old adversaries like Harry Truman and Adlai Stevenson, who believed Nixon capable of any deception or duplicity, must have been rolling in their graves.

With a few such exceptions, however, Nixon seems to have found his personal fears and insecurities rising almost to the level of paranoia when he reached the White House. Perhaps once there, he realized that he had more to lose, if the enemies he imagined all around him were to succeed in their plots. Or perhaps all those years of shaking hands, slapping backs, kissing babies, eating rubber chicken, making orotund speeches, signaling the ephemeral victories and defeats of politics—perhaps all those years of denying one's true self, playing to the despised crowd, took their ultimate toll. After all, if one were both contemptuous of the people and fearful of their power, might not one's deepest fear be that they would someday turn upon one and take it all away?

And, of course, in Richard Nixon's case, they did; and it seems to me that his personal demons were to some extent responsible. It's easy to say, and it often is said, that had Nixon come clean about Watergate in the beginning, when he had no direct responsibility, the affair would quickly have blown over and he would have survived. That may be true, but it ignores the fact that the man Richard Nixon was by 1972 *couldn't come clean.*

What actual excesses or even crimes he might have believed he had to cover up are still a matter of speculation; but with his view of life as battle and crisis as challenge, his determination to prove his worth, particularly to himself, his consequent inability to "give up" and his reluctance to show weakness, as well as his conviction that through "personal gut performance" any height could be scaled—for all those reasons, it would have been impossible for Nixon to do anything but fight back, stand fast, "stonewall" his enemies.

So he did—and the indelible marks Richard Nixon left on American history are Watergate and his resignation from the presidency before he could be impeached. Those events cause many to believe him an evil man who schemed to subvert the Constitution; they cause others to consider him a victim of the press, the liberals, the Democrats, even the CIA or the Pentagon. And looking back at Watergate, many Americans can't see beyond it the achievements of a president who often responded to the pressures of his time with knowledge and skill and sometimes even with courage—qualities the American people apparently don't find in most of their leaders today.

As a reporter, I interviewed, traveled with, reported on, and deplored Richard Nixon's actions for much of his career. As a columnist, I frequently criticized his presidency. Later, after his political career was ended, I studied Nixon and his record, talked to his friends and enemies, reviewed my own words and memories, and concluded that he was neither evil nor a victim, except of himself—and we're all that kind of victim. So I wrote in *One of Us: Richard Nixon and the American Dream* and repeat here:

> If John F. Kennedy embodied, as Norman Mailer once wrote, something like the nation's "romantic dream of itself," perhaps . . . Americans could have seen in [Nixon] themselves as they knew they were, not as they frequently dreamed of being. They could have recognized in Nixon their own sentimental patriotism and confidence in national virtue, their professed love of God and family, their . . . preference for action over reflection . . . and their vocal if not always practiced devotion to freedom and democracy.
>
> They also might have seen reflected in the ambiguous figure of Richard Nixon—even in his reputation for sharp practice and his transparent presentations of himself —their own melancholy knowledge, hard-earned in a demanding world, that ideals sometimes had to yield to necessity. . . .
>
> Rarely, if ever, in my judgment, has the extent to which dreams and reality live side by side within a people been so dramatized as it was in the great Kennedy-Nixon confrontation of 1960.

Richard Nixon came within a hair of winning that election. Many people still believe that, in reality, he did—that victory was stolen from him by ballot-box chicanery.

Nixon neither challenged the results in court nor in any way clouded the legitimacy of John F. Kennedy's presidency. In devastating defeat, his better instincts prevailed.

GERALD R. FORD

1974–1977

---

by

James Cannon

GERALD R. FORD became President not because he was popular with the American public, not because he campaigned for the job, but because of his character.

More than any other president of this century, Ford was chosen for his integrity and trustworthiness; his peers in Congress put him in the White House because he told the truth and kept his word. He was nominated for Vice President after Spiro Agnew was forced to resign to avoid indictment for accepting bribes. Ford was confirmed by a House and Senate that expected him to replace a President who was also facing indictment for crimes. Eight months later Ford succeeded to the presidency when Richard Nixon, facing impeachment in the House and conviction by the Senate, resigned.

From our beginning we in this nation have had the good fortune to find the right leader, often from an unexpected quarter, whose character, ability, and experience fit the tide of history. In the most dangerous constitutional crisis since the Civil War, a crisis that President Nixon created by defying Congress and a federal court, this obscure workhorse of a congressman assumed the presidency.

Gerald Ford was the right man in the right place at the right time to replace the President who had dishonored himself and the office.

Ford personified what Nixon was not. Ford was honest. He could be trusted. Throughout twenty-five years in the House of Representatives, Ford had proved himself to be a man of integrity. It was for that integrity that the highest powers of Congress, Democratic and Republican, chose Ford to be Vice President, knowing that Nixon's presidency was doomed.

CHARACTER: THE BEGINNINGS

The qualities of character that placed Ford in the White House and guided his decisions as President run like golden threads to his childhood, leading back to a time and place and family that instilled in the boy the integrity, loyalty, courage, stamina, ambition, patriotism, idealism, and the habit of hard work that became part of his being.

Character: the word comes from the Greek *charakter*, for the mark or impress on a coin or seal. Euripides defined it as "a stamp of good repute on a person." The Greeks believed that character was formed in part by fate and in part by parental training, and that character was exemplified not only in acts of bravery in battle but in the habits of daily conduct.

Webster's Third International Dictionary defines character as "A composite of good moral qualities typically of moral excellence and firmness blended with resolution, self-discipline, high ethics, force, and judgment." This definition is an accurate description of Ford, and an appropriate standard for every president.

Surely character begins at home, and in Ford's case we know for certain that it began with his mother.

Dorothy Gardner Ford was a strong and resourceful woman

whose own character was tested at the age of twenty. She grew up in a warm, loving family in a small town in northern Illinois where her father prospered as a businessman and served as town mayor.

In college Dorothy met the brother of her roommate, and fell in love with him. Leslie King was the blond, blue-eyed, charming son of a wealthy Omaha banker who also owned a stage-coach line and a wool business.

On their honeymoon she discovered that she had made a tragic mistake. Her new husband struck her, not once but repeatedly. When they reached Omaha, where they were to live with his family, she found out that King was not only brutal, but a liar and a drunk. His outward charm concealed a vicious temper. He was unstable emotionally, a scoundrel who took money from the till in the wool warehouse where his father had given him a job.

She decided to leave King, but discovered she was pregnant. With the encouragement of King's mother and father, she decided to have the baby in Omaha, and did.

On July 14, 1913, the thirty-eighth President of the United States was born in the mansion of his paternal grandfather, and named Leslie King, Jr. Unaccountably, a few days later, King came into his wife's room with a butcher knife and threatened to kill mother, child, and nurse. Police were called to restrain him.

As soon as she was well enough, Dorothy wrapped her sixteen-day-old baby in a blanket, left the King mansion, and hired a carriage to take her across the Missouri River bridge to Council Bluffs, Iowa, where her parents were anxiously waiting to take her and her son away.

Divorce was rare in 1913, but an Omaha court found King guilty of extreme cruelty, granted custody of the child to the mother, and ordered King to pay alimony and child support. King refused to pay anything.

For a proper young woman who had led a sheltered girlhood, Dorothy Gardner King's brief marriage was a brutal end to innocence. Yet she came out of the experience with a resolute self-confidence and sunny optimism that remained with her all her life. She imparted these and other good qualities to her son.

Too embarrassed to go back to their home town, Dorothy's father moved his wife, daughter, and grandson to Grand Rapids, Michigan, to begin a new life.

They had come to the right place. In the first quarter of this century, Grand Rapids was America at its best—a diverse community of enterprise, self-reliance, and opportunity. Dutch settlers dominated the area and had imposed the habits of civic responsibility, thrift, hard work, and cleanliness. Good public schools, thriving businesses, strong churches, home ownership that ranked second in the nation—all made Grand Rapids a model community for a boy growing up.

By good fortune, in her son's first year, Dorothy Gardner King met a man whose character matched and complemented her own. He was a tall, dark-haired, and amiable bachelor named Gerald R. Ford. By trade, Ford was a paint salesman; in the community he was respected as honest and hardworking, kind and considerate, a man of integrity and character—everything Dorothy's first husband was not.

The next year she married Jerry Ford, and her two-year-old son grew up as Jerry Ford, Jr., believing his stepfather was his true father.

By Jerry Ford, Sr., Dorothy had three more sons, and the Fords provided a strong combination of love and discipline. Ford house rule number one was: "Tell the truth, work hard, and come to dinner on time."

Mother was a strict disciplinarian. She resolved that her oldest son must learn to control the hot temper he had inherited from King. When the boy raged in anger, she would try to reason with him, or send him to his room to cool off. During one episode, she had young Jerry memorize Kipling's poem "If." After that, she would have him recite it every time he lost his temper.

The home-cooked dinner was the focus of the Fords' family life. Her sons remember dinner as the daily center for family discussion: personal matters, civic affairs, school happenings, sports. Everyone was encouraged to comment, ask questions, or express an opinion. After dinner everyone helped clear the table, wash and dry the dishes. Then the boys trooped back to the dining room for homework—supervised by Mother and Dad.

The father was determined that all his sons would have the education that he had missed. Homework every night; and every mark in school, every report card was reviewed by Dad, Mother, and child. In addition, the Fords encouraged their boys to read. By the time he was ten, young Jerry had read every Horatio Alger book in the Grand Rapids Public Library. He never forgot these idealized accounts of the poor boy who made his way by pluck and hard work to success.

On his twelfth birthday Jerry Ford, Jr., took the oath to become a Boy Scout, an oath of duty to God and country that would guide his life. As a Scout he got his first lessons in leadership as a camp counselor and swimming coach, and at fifteen Ford was chosen by the governor of Michigan as one of eight outstanding Eagle Scouts to be a guide at Fort Mackinac one summer. It was his first opportunity to meet the public, and he found he liked it.

For high school, the Fords chose to enroll Jerry in South High, which was the most socially diverse of Grand Rapids' three high schools. The Fords had also learned that South High had the best teachers.

Jerry was not only a good student at South High, but at fifteen he was the star center on the football team. To Coach Clifford Gettings, "Ford was a leader—first in the huddle, first out of the huddle, knew everyone's assignment—it was like having a coach on the field. On defense, he was all over the field making tackles. I never saw him make a bad pass from center, and I never saw him play dirty. Yes, he could make a mistake in an easy game, but in the hardest games, Jerry Ford was at his best."

In his senior year Ford was elected captain of the South High team that won the state championship, and he was chosen all-state center and captain of the all-state team.

For Ford, the football field at South High was preparation

for life. There he learned to listen to coaching and carry out his assignment, that a team is greater than the individual players. He learned that a good attitude is infectious and can generate in teammates the extra effort that brings victory. He met defeat, but saw a loss on the field not as an end but as the first step in trying harder the next time.

As a teenager, Ford had neither the time nor the money for girls or social life. He earned his pocket money mowing lawns and at other odd jobs, and for a while he worked in a diner across the street from South High.

One afternoon a stranger came in and stood silently near the door as he watched Ford at work.

"Can I help you?" Ford asked.

The stranger walked over and said, "Are you Leslie King?"

"No," Ford said.

The man paused, looked at Ford intently, and said: "I'm your father. You're Leslie King. I'm in town with my wife, and I would like to take you out for lunch."

Startled, and hesitant, Ford said, "I'm working."

"Ask your boss if you can get off."

Ford went to see the owner and said: "This man wants to talk to me. He says he's my real father. Can you let me go have lunch with this person?"

The owner looked over at the stranger, and said, "Sure."

Ford took off his apron and walked outside, where a woman waited in a new Lincoln and a small girl played nearby. King introduced his wife of ten years and their daughter.

At a small restaurant, King explained to his son that he found him by going to all the high schools in Grand Rapids and asking for Leslie King. At South High, when he was told there was no Leslie King enrolled, King—who knew the last name of the man his first wife had married—asked: "Do you have a boy named Ford here?"

"Oh yes," the principal at South High said. "You mean Jerry Ford. He's at work at Skougis's diner across the street."

King boasted to his son that he owned vast acres of ranchland in Riverton, Wyoming, and had taken the train to Detroit to pick up a new Lincoln.

"Wouldn't you like to come out and live with us in Wyoming?" King asked.

"No," his son said. "I like it here."

As King talked, Ford studied his face, looking for some resemblance. In his mind were questions he wanted to ask: Why have you never tried to find me before? Did you come because I'm a football star and you can brag about it? Here I am, working for $2 a week to make it through high school, and you can afford a new Lincoln —why have you never helped pay for my education?

But Ford asked none of these questions. "I bit my tongue to stop myself from being impolite," he said later.

As King took his son back to the diner, he said: "Can I help you financially?"

"Well, that would be nice," Ford said.

King gave his son $20. It was the only financial assistance Ford ever received from his father.

Back home, after dinner, he told his mother and stepfather what had happened and they did their best to console him.

In his room that night, he lay in the darkness trying to find good in the person who claimed to be his father.

He could not. His real father left the lasting impression of, as Ford put it, "a carefree, well-to-do man who really didn't give a damn about the hopes and dreams of his son."

Unable to hold back the tears of anger that night, he remembered a prayer from Proverbs that his mother had taught him:

> Trust in the Lord with all thine heart; and lean not unto
> thine own understanding.
> In all thy ways acknowledge him, and he shall direct thy
> paths.

Ford turned to look ahead. Early in high school he had made up his mind that he would somehow go to college. In 1931, with the Great Depression getting worse, the Fords could not afford college. The outlook was bleak.

But Ford was not only a promising athlete, he was also a National Honor Society student. Arthur Krause, principal of South High, talked to Michigan's football coach. No football scholarship was available, but Coach Harry Kipke got Ford a job waiting on tables for his meals. Krause arranged an award of $100 for Ford's first-year tuition.

With his own savings to pay the $2 a week for room rent, Jerry Ford had found a way to go to college. And at eighteen, Ford was ready for this new challenge.

His character, resting firmly on the moral and religious foundation established by his parents, had developed through Scouting, good teachers, homework at the dining-room table, earning his own pocket money, the teamwork and challenge of football—with each activity of his boyhood and youth successively reinforcing the values set earlier.

Success in athletics, academics, and personal relationships had instilled in the young Ford a quiet confidence, a readiness for any challenge.

From his mother Ford drew energy, self-discipline, and a sure and abiding sense of morality. From her and from his stepfather he learned to trust, and to be worthy of trust; both taught, practiced, and enforced honesty, fairness, and self-reliance, a respect for learning, and the obligation of every citizen to take part in public affairs. In times of setback and misfortune, both demonstrated cheerful hope and resolution in putting things right again. Their good habits, their strong values, became those of the son in whom they took such great pride and to whom they were both so devoted.

From his first days in college at Ann Arbor, Ford did well. He made first-string center on the freshman team, and was voted the most promising of all the freshman players. Then came a great disappointment.

In his sophomore year, Ford ended up on the sidelines, benched in favor of Michigan's all-American varsity center, Chuck Bernard. For two years Ford was substitute center on a Michigan team that was undefeated national champion. The experience taught Ford a lesson he never forgot. He said later: "Not playing was tough, but I learned that there could always be some-body better at the job than you. And I learned to be patient."

In 1934, his senior year, Ford finally made center on the first team, and was all-Big Ten center. The Detroit Lions and the Green Bay Packers offered him contracts to play pro football.

Ford turned down the offers. He was graduating with a B average and a B.S. in Economics, and he was determined to go to law school, even though he had no money. Worse than that, he was $1,000 in debt for college expenses.

Again, a mentor helped. Michigan's football coach recom-mended Ford to Yale's football coach, who offered Ford a job as an assistant line coach at the then princely salary of $2,400 a year. Ford took the job, believing that somehow he would manage to go to law school at Yale.

In his first year in New Haven, Ford paid off the $1,000 he owed and resolved never to go into debt again. By sheer persever-ance, Ford persuaded the Yale Law School to admit him on a part-time trial basis. Once in, he proved he could do well in his law classes and coach football at the same time.

Ford graduated in the top third of his class at Yale. There he learned, as he put it, "the process of thinking and analysis, the application of logic to issues." As he planned, Ford went home to Grand Rapids to practice law and begin a political career.

On his first try he passed the Michigan Bar examination. He and a college friend opened a new law partnership, and they were just getting started late in 1941 when the Japanese attacked Pearl Harbor. Ford volunteered for the Navy and served forty-seven months, including two years in battle on an aircraft carrier in the Pacific.

On the USS _Monterey_ he and his ship earned eleven battle stars in thirteen months, and survived repeated attacks by Japanese bombers and torpedo planes. Then, in the worst Pacific typhoon the Navy had ever recorded, the _Monterey_ was saved by the execu-tive officer, an experienced merchant seaman who took over from a Navy captain who was a good pilot but green at handling a ship.

Ford would always remember what the executive officer had done: by calm and deliberate steps in a crisis, a subordinate had stepped in to save ship and crew from defeat and disaster.

Like four other future presidents, Ford was motivated by what he had seen and experienced in World War II to commit to the profession of politics, imperfect as it was, as the way to make a difference.

MAN OF THE HOUSE

Ford first ran for public office in 1948, as a reformer, determined to defeat the isolationist congressman representing the Fifth District of Michigan and that congressman's corrupt political boss. On that first try, he won—one of the few new Republicans elected in the year that President Truman defeated Governor Thomas Dewey.

In Washington, immediately after Ford was sworn in for the first time, a slender young man came up to Ford on the floor of the House of Representatives and stuck out his hand. "I'm Dick Nixon from California," he said. "I heard about your big win in Michigan. Congratulations." Ford was surprised that anyone outside Michigan had ever heard of him.

As a new member of the House, Ford was earnest, likable, and hardworking. He earned respect for his diligence, and quickly came to be known as a man of his word—he had learned that in childhood. By making the right friends Ford won a seat on the Appropriations Committee, a small group of members who decide how many federal dollars to spend, and for what. In that key spot Ford mastered national defense, intelligence, foreign policy, and the varied mix of politics and purpose that makes democracy work.

Duty on the powerful Appropriations Committee also gave Ford a close-up opportunity to watch five presidents govern: Truman, Eisenhower, Kennedy, Johnson, and Nixon. But Ford never aspired to *be* President. He loved the House of Representatives. His ambition was to be Speaker of the House.

In doing his job as a congressman, Ford won the respect of Democrats as well as Republicans. He was conservative in fiscal affairs, moderate on social programs, and committed to a strong national defense. On the floor in debate he knew his subject and was forceful in the argument; but when the debate ended, Ford always made a point of going over to shake hands with his opponent.

His popularity, and the professional respect he commanded among his peers, made him a natural choice to be the Republican leader in the House. After the Goldwater debacle in 1964, when the Republicans lost thirty-eight House seats, a group of Ford's friends persuaded him to challenge the incumbent leader, Charles Halleck. Ford won, narrowly, 73–67.

His friendship with Nixon had grown, and Ford supported Nixon for President in 1960 and 1968. During President Nixon's first term, Ford successfully carried the Nixon legislative program in the House.

And Ford hoped that in 1972 Nixon would be reelected by such a landslide that the Republicans would win the House and Ford himself would become the Speaker.

WATERGATE

Ford was delivering a number of speeches in Michigan on the weekend of June 17, 1972, and heard on his car radio about the burglary of Democratic headquarters in the Watergate office building in Washington.

His first thought was: How could anyone be so dumb as to break into any party headquarters?

Two days later Ford confronted John Mitchell, Nixon's campaign manager: "John, did you or the Nixon Campaign Committee have anything to do with the break-in at the Democratic National Headquarters?"

"Absolutely not!" Mitchell replied. Later, Nixon also assured Ford that neither he nor the White House staff was involved. Ford believed Mitchell and Nixon.

In fact, most of the American people believed Nixon was too smart a politician to let himself be involved in anything so ridiculous as Watergate. On November 7, 1972, Nixon won reelection by a landslide, but Congress stayed Democratic.

Ford was so disappointed that the Republicans would remain a minority that on that election night he and his wife, Betty, decided he should retire from politics.

Two months later, in January 1973, two separate events began to change history.

First, the public heard the initial evidence that President Nixon's White House was directly involved in Watergate. One of the Watergate burglars in jail told Federal Judge John Sirica that Nixon's senior staff was not only involved in the Watergate break-in but was paying off the other burglars, also in jail, to keep quiet about it. Simultaneously, the Senate Watergate Committee began the investigation that would reveal Nixon had taped his own criminal actions in the White House.

Second, the U.S. Attorney in Baltimore learned that Vice President Spiro T. Agnew had accepted bribes, including at least one in the White House itself.

By October 1973, Agnew was forced to resign. Under the new Twenty-fifth Amendment, Nixon would nominate a new vice president—subject to confirmation by the House and Senate.

THE ONLY CHOICE

With Agnew's resignation, Nixon saw the opportunity to hand the vice presidency to John Connally, a former Democratic governor of Texas who had become Nixon's choice to be the next Republican president. At Nixon's urging, Connally had just turned Republican. Connally's action offended the leaders of both parties: Democrats considered him a turncoat, and Republicans saw him as an opportunist. Consequently, Democratic and Republican leaders told Nixon that Connally could not be confirmed.

On the afternoon of Agnew's resignation, Nixon invited the two Democratic leaders, Speaker Carl Albert and Senate Majority

Leader Mike Mansfield, to the White House to get their advice about the best nominee to replace Agnew.

Albert suggested Jerry Ford. He would be easily and quickly confirmed, Albert said. Nixon turned to Mansfield. He agreed that Ford would be a good choice.

Nixon had asked the two powerful Democrats for suggestions. The political reality was that their response identified the one man who could be confirmed in both the House and Senate. With impeachment already an issue in Congress, Nixon could not afford a battle on another political front.

Speaker Albert said later: "We gave Nixon no choice but Ford. Congress made Jerry Ford President."

In choosing Ford, both Albert and Mansfield believed they were selecting the next president, and that Ford had the experience, the qualities of leadership, and the character to serve as President.

To a lesser degree, Nixon also believed that Ford might succeed him. "By the time I selected Ford," Nixon wrote later, "I felt that as a political realist there was at least a fifty percent chance that Ford might become President."

For this first-time use of the Twenty-fifth Amendment, Congress ordered the most extensive investigation of a presidential nominee in history: 350 FBI agents probed into his life, going back to his childhood, his bank accounts, his campaign expenses, his associates. The Library of Congress compiled a record and summary of every vote and speech in his twenty-five years in the House. For days the Senate Rules Committee and then the House Judiciary Committee questioned Ford under oath.

In these hearings, Congress, and the American public, learned more about Jerry Ford—his beliefs, character, experience, philosophy of government, political record—than has ever been disclosed about any other presidential candidate, before or since. And with that knowledge the Senate and House confirmed Ford to be Vice President with a combined vote that was an extraordinary endorsement: 479 to 38.

When Ford was sworn in, in his beloved House of Representatives on December 6, 1973, he fully expected to serve out the balance of Agnew's term and retire from public life.

But over the spring of 1974 Ford began to change his mind. His belief in Nixon turned to wonder, from wonder to doubt, from doubt to suspicion, and finally, to use Ford's word, "denial" of the reality that his friend, the President, was guilty.

Nixon's mind and energies were focused on survival. He was President in name only. His chief of staff, General Alexander Haig, was Acting President for ten months.

On July 24, 1974, the Supreme Court ruled 8–0 that Nixon must give up the White House tapes. Nixon knew he was trapped. His lawyers told him that refusing the Court order would bring impeachment. Only Nixon knew, at that point, that disclosing the tapes of his crime would also be cause for impeachment, and probably prosecution.

In desperation, Nixon telephoned John Mitchell, his senior lawyer and trusted friend, for advice, in the hope of avoiding prison.

Mitchell's reply was characteristically brief and blunt: Dick, he said, make the best deal you can and resign.

Nixon made his decision: he would send General Haig, his chief of staff, to see Vice President Ford and suggest that he would resign as President if Ford would agree in advance to pardon him.

Nixon's attempt at a deal turned out to be an extraordinary test of Ford's character.

On the afternoon of Thursday, August 1, 1974, Haig went to Ford's office in the Executive Office Building, next door to the West Wing of the White House. At Haig's insistence, they met alone.

Haig told Ford there was new evidence, taped evidence that would force Nixon to resign or be impeached.

The President had six options, Haig said. He could step aside temporarily; negotiate for a congressional censure; pardon himself and resign; pardon the Watergate defendants and himself and then resign; or simply postpone any decision.

Or the final Haig option, as Ford described it: "Nixon would agree to leave in return for an agreement that the new President—Gerald Ford—would pardon him."

To make it easy for Ford, Haig handed him two sheets of paper written in longhand by Nixon's lawyer, Fred Buzhardt: one describing a president's power to pardon, and the other a ready-made pardon for Nixon.

Sitting there alone with Haig, Ford faced a decision that no Vice President and no other man in American history had ever confronted. There, in Ford's grasp if he would accept the terms of the deal, was the presidency. One word, one "yes" would make Ford President of the United States.

Instinct, caution, and political experience made Ford pause. He needed time to think, time to talk to his wife and his counselors. So he told Haig neither yes nor no. He said he would have to think over the promise of a pardon for Nixon's resignation.

When Haig left the Vice President's office, the full impact of Haig's message struck Ford. He had never expected to be President. But now Ford knew that Nixon would either resign or be impeached—and he would become President.

He was confident that he could handle the job; he had no doubt about that. But he also knew that forcing an elected president out of office would be a calamity. At the same time, although he had never said so to another soul, Ford knew that Nixon had lost the capability to govern. Would it be in the best interests of the country to provide an incentive for Nixon to resign and avoid putting the country through a national ordeal—months of House impeachment proceedings and a trial in the Senate?

For twenty-four hours Ford pondered Haig's proposal. He listened to his wife and three other advisers. All pleaded with him to reject the deal. Still he debated: What was best for the country?

On the afternoon after Haig had proposed the deal, Ford brought in Bryce Harlow, a close friend who had counseled every president since Eisenhower. Harlow listened to Ford's account of what Haig had proposed, and with quiet eloquence brought Ford to see that any deal was tainted, and that the national interest would not be served by replacing one flawed presidency with another. So Ford called Haig and told him no deal.

When Nixon learned that there was to be no deal, he told Haig he would fight on and force Congress to impeach and convict him. Four days later, after the evidence became public that Nixon had been part of the Watergate cover-up since the beginning, Nixon saw his last friends in Congress turn on him in dismay and anger.

Nixon counted his last supporters—seven votes in the Senate at most. With impeachment and conviction certain, the President finally resigned.

INTO THE WHITE HOUSE

Ford took the oath of office at noon on Friday, August 9, 1974.

He took command of the ship of state in a sea of troubles. Unemployment was bad and getting worse. Inflation and interest rates were going up. The energy crisis mounted; long lines stretched for blocks at gas pumps. The Vietnam War dragged on. The USSR still presented a threat to the United States and to the rest of the world.

Ford fixed his first priority: to calm and stabilize the country. In his inaugural speech, he told the nation: "Our long national nightmare is over."

At first, Ford's inexperience in managing anything larger than a congressional district office showed. He made mistakes: To deal with inflation, an aide suggested to Ford a voluntary citizens campaign to be called Whip Inflation Now. Ford liked the idea: The purpose was high, the cost minimal. He believed the innate goodness of the American people could be mobilized to control inflation. To advance the program Ford, wearing an oversized WIN button, appeared before Congress to call on "every American to join in this massive mobilization." But WIN failed; economic forces overpowered the best of intentions. Consequently, Ford's first economic decision made him look inept, almost comical. But he learned a

161

lesson: never again would President Ford endorse a proposal until it had been analyzed, scrutinized, and debated by his ablest advisers.

Although WIN embarrassed Ford, he was roundly commended for his choice of former Governor Nelson Rockefeller of New York to be Vice President.

Some of his advisers were concerned that Rockefeller, twice a candidate for President, might upstage him. Ford was unconcerned. He had never hesitated to surround himself with people who knew more than he did about a subject.

THE NIXON PARDON

Two weeks into his presidency, at his first press conference, Ford bungled his answers to questions about whether he would pardon Nixon.

Seething with anger at his own contradictory responses, Ford spent two days deliberating privately about what he might do to clear the national agenda of Nixon and Watergate so that he could focus attention on more compelling issues: the worsening recession, the Vietnam War, foreign policy.

After forty-eight hours of deliberating, Ford called in his four senior advisers and told them he had decided to pardon Nixon. He would, he said, listen to contrary views, but in his mind, in his judgment, and in his conscience, he believed the pardon of Nixon would be in the best interests of the country.

At Ford's direction, White House counsel Phil Buchen asked Watergate special prosecutor Leon Jaworski how long the indictment and trial of Nixon might take. When Jaworski replied that a Nixon trial could take two years or longer, it was the deciding factor for Ford. He would grant the pardon, and thereby—he thought—dismiss the issue from the national agenda.

Ford hoped that Nixon would make a statement of contrition in accepting the pardon, and sent a young lawyer to negotiate that. But Haig, without Ford's knowledge, got word to Nixon through Ron Ziegler, who had been Nixon's press secretary in the White

House and became Nixon's chief of staff in exile in San Clemente, that Ford had already made up his mind to grant the pardon. In addition, Haig told Ziegler, no apology or statement of contrition from Nixon would be necessary.

On Sunday, September 8—just one month after he became President—President Ford granted a pardon to Richard Nixon for all the crimes he committed while he was President. The reaction across America was outrage. Instead of ending the Watergate tragedy, the pardon seemed to reopen the wound.

Ford was shocked. He expected his pardon of Nixon to be unpopular, but he was stunned by the vehemence of the public reaction. Forgiveness was so great a part of Ford's nature that he thought the American people would be forgiving, that they would accept Nixon's resignation as punishment enough. Ford's naivete about the public mind led him also to expect that the country, like him, was ready to turn to more urgent business—the recession, Vietnam. It was a momentous miscalculation. Not only that, but the pardon, coming only one month after Nixon's resignation and Ford's inaugural, also provoked a new suspicion to imperil Ford's fledgling presidency: Was there a deal between Nixon and Ford?

Responsible voices in Congress raised the question. To get the answer, the House of Representatives sent an official Resolution of Inquiry to the President, demanding a written explanation. To make a truthful response, Ford knew that he would have to disclose that Al Haig, Nixon's chief of staff, had proposed a pardon as a condition for Nixon to resign. With his usual directness, Ford decided the best way to handle the problem was for him to go up to the House, testify, and spell it all out.

"That's the only way to clear the air," he said.

Buchen tried to talk Ford out of testifying, but Ford said: "Look, I've got nothing to hide. I'm going up there."

Ford did testify before Congress, as no president had ever done before. Before the House Judiciary Committee, Ford gave his account of what happened in his meeting with Haig. Was there a deal? one representative asked.

Ford's reply was blunt: "There was no deal. Period. Under no circumstances."

Ford recognized that not everyone would believe him, or understand his own rationale: to Ford, a deal in August would have benefited Nixon, but his decision in September to grant the pardon was a necessary act to begin to heal the nation.

With his public defense of the pardon of Nixon, Ford hoped that the American people would see him for what he believed himself to be, a president with the courage to do what he thought was right, whatever the political consequences.

By pardoning Nixon, Ford hoped to close Watergate. In that he failed. But it was his judgment then, and it remained his judgment, that a two-year public trial of former President Nixon in the courts and by the press would be far more damaging to the progress and well-being of the country than a pardon. Ford blamed himself for not doing a better job of justifying his decision, but he never doubted that he acted in the national interest. Two decades later, Ford reflected on his decision to pardon Nixon and said: "My feelings are even stronger today than they were at the time. It was the right thing to do. I know there are people who want to believe that a deal was made. I have a clear conscience. I am absolutely certain that there was never a deal arranged between Haig and me, or between Nixon and me, or by anybody else."

Watergate, the crime that impelled Congress to make Ford President, remains a mystery. There is no folly in the American political experience that compares with Watergate. Why did Republicans break into Democratic headquarters? Why did President Nixon, with his campaign experience and highly sensitive political antennae, get himself involved in the cover-up of a senseless burglary? The answer, if there was one, was lost with Nixon's death.

THE THIRTY-EIGHTH PRESIDENT

Character, and the courage to do what was right despite the political consequences—these were Ford's greatest assets as President, as they had been throughout his public life. He also had the three additional qualities that every modern president needs most: an understanding of how the federal government works, common sense, and the guts to say yes or no.

Ford came quickly to like his new job. Up early every morning, he couldn't wait to get to the Oval Office, hear the latest intelligence reports, get his morning briefing from Capitol Hill, and deal with the problems of the day. Governing was what he liked; he had spent the best years of his life in training for it.

In the Oval Office, Ford was personable, intelligent, engaging, and on top of the job. He worked away at his daily tasks with quiet resolution and good-humored intensity. His genial nature was matched by unshakable self-confidence. He searched out and listened to those who knew more about a subject than he did. There was not a trace of envy in his being. He knew exactly who he was, and he liked being the man he was. Duty was the impelling force of his presidency, every day.

Ford was a practical man; political theory did not interest him much. Nor did grand government schemes. Over a quarter century he had dealt with federal programs left over from the New Deal, World War II, and the New Frontier; and he had heard a thousand new solutions to public problems.

As President, Ford said: No more new federal programs; let's see if we can fix the programs we already have. Let's make them work, or drop them.

Ford was best at what every president spends most of his time doing—reacting to events and circumstances over which he has no control. Every unmanageable problem that humanity confronts anywhere in the world ends up on the White House doorstep.

With every crisis, domestic or international, great or small, Ford's first instinct was to listen, to ask questions, to reach out for diverse opinions, to hear the facts from those who knew most about a situation or problem. He enjoyed constructive debate. He welcomed a dissenting view so long as it was delivered succinctly and factually.

At the end of a discussion he would pause, ask if anyone had anything further to say, and then go to the Oval Office. There he would make his decision, without delay. He knew that cabinet members and congressmen, by habit, hear what they want to hear. To prevent any misunderstanding about his decision or intentions, he put them in writing. Thoroughness—it had been a habit since early schooldays. Once he decided, he did not worry over his decision, or second-guess himself. He moved on to the next task at hand.

As an executive, Ford was disciplined. He had developed good habits of managing his time, beginning at South High. He was invariably prompt. His mother and stepfather had instructed him about the precious nature of time. He didn't waste your time; and you didn't waste his.

By nature he was gregarious, but he liked to work alone. He often reserved an hour or so just to sit back and think about things.

Presidents are remembered more often for their words than their actions. Ford's thoughts and words were plain, everyday; he spoke with the Midwest directness that was his heritage. Any suggestion that he orate, or articulate soaring goals, or declare his vision for America, left him embarrassed. Except for "Our long national nightmare is over," few remember much about what Ford said.

THE RECORD

Always an eclectic, Ford knew a good idea when he saw one. In 1975, he proposed the variable rate mortgage to ease the interest burden on new home buyers, and the press scoffed that it would never happen. During his congressional years, he had become something of an expert on monetary affairs and the American banking system. He immediately saw the possibilities in the transfer of money electronically, and put in place the regulations for automatic teller machines that would become commonplace.

Ford advanced a plan that would have created a vast American nuclear fuel industry, a partnership between the federal government's nuclear resources and private entrepreneurs. Ford foresaw that the United States could become to nuclear energy what the Middle East was to oil, that we could create an industry to fulfill world demand for cheap power and simultaneously assure greater control over nuclear material for peaceful purposes or weapons.

But Congress blocked him and thereby opened the world market for nuclear material produced and sold by less responsible nations, such as France and the USSR.

Ford was a strong conservationist and initiated a plan to double the size of the National Park system. His successors let the project languish.

Ford did not know how to make himself a popular president. He was so incapable of pretense that he was bereft of showmanship. He lacked the sunny grin that made America like Ike. He did not have, nor could he affect, the aw-shucks bonhomie that would later endear Ronald Reagan to the country.

Since he had never run for national office, Ford had not developed the knack for television, or the art of symbolism that was essential to effective governing in the media age.

From his first to last day in the White House, Ford held to the conviction that the first responsibility of every president is to protect America's national security.

To Ford, that meant he should take the lead in strengthening alliances, maintain a strong and ready military force, and diligently negotiate with potential adversaries. At his first summit, with Leonid Brezhnev in Vladivostok, Ford not only negotiated new limits on nuclear weapons but also created a structure of arms control followed by his successor presidents.

AN END AT LAST

Next to the stain that Nixon left in Washington, Ford's worst legacy was the war in Vietnam. Intent on healing America's wounds over Vietnam, Ford offered young Americans who had dodged the war a chance to earn amnesty. It was not popular with veterans who had served in Vietnam and earlier wars, but Ford believed it was the right thing to do.

To resolve Vietnam, Ford sent a trusted Army general to Vietnam to bring back a fresh estimate on what could be done and what it would cost. With that information in hand, Ford went up to Capitol Hill and asked for $1 billion for military, economic, and humanitarian aid.

In reply, the Senate Foreign Relations Committee offered money to evacuate Americans, "but not one nickel for military aid." In what Ford said was "the saddest hour of my life," he watched the television pictures of the last Americans leaving the embassy roof under fire.

Two weeks later, when an American merchant ship, the *Mayaguez*, was seized off Cambodia, Ford acted swiftly, determined that the United States would not suffer another international humiliation. Combining military might and diplomacy, Ford simultaneously ordered a Navy carrier and helicopter assault force to move into position to rescue the crew and retake the ship, and sent messages to Cambodia through the United Nations and China to release the *Mayaguez* and its crew. Cambodia rejected the message, and Ford responded. Marines landed on the Cambodian island where the crew was held, and other Marines boarded and secured the *Mayaguez*. In darkness the Cambodians moved the crew off the island and into a small boat. Before it reached the mainland, a U.S. destroyer intercepted the boat and rescued the crew. With crew and ship again in U.S. hands, Ford ended the operation. But the cost was high: fifteen Marines killed, three missing in action, and fifty wounded. In addition, twenty-three U.S. Air Force security troops died in a helicopter crash in Thailand in support of the operation.

BREAKING UP THE EMPIRE

As a congressman and as President, Ford was always ready to use military force to defend American interests, but by upbringing and conviction he was a man of peace. He negotiated and signed the Helsinki Treaty, over the protests of conservative Republicans such as Ronald Reagan, and over the protests of hawkish Democrats such as Senator Henry Jackson. At Helsinki, Ford persuaded Brezhnev to agree to renounce the use of force against Russian satellite nations, and to accept new standards for human rights, self-determination, and the free movement of people and ideas across all borders in Europe.

Years later, when other presidents were enjoying credit for the dissolution of the USSR, historians looked back and said that the breakup of the Soviet empire began at Helsinki.

A central tenet of Ford's beliefs was that a man or a family or the federal government ought to live within its means. Ford was not in office long enough to stop the nation's headlong plunge into national debt, but he did show that a president could slow it down. In the budget he sent to Congress in 1976, he made a specific and realistic combination of spending reductions and tax increases that would have balanced the budget in three years. There was no magic to it. Ford was the only president since Eisenhower who had the stomach to stop Congress from spending money and the professional expertise to do it.

In 1976, President Ford ran for a full term as President, but he lost to Jimmy Carter, for several reasons.

Initially, he was naive about how to run for President. He believed that if he did a good job as President, the Republican Party would nominate him and the American people would elect him. That was how he won reelection in the Fifth Congressional District of Michigan, and he saw no reason to believe that strategy would not work for him in the White House.

As had been the case before, his persistent optimism and trust in people put him in political jeopardy. He delayed and delayed in getting started, and his slow beginning encouraged Reagan's followers and, in time, Reagan himself.

When Ford did get started, he adopted the campaign strategy of winning southern Republican conservatives, but most were already committed to Reagan either openly or in their hearts. To appease party conservatives, Ford dumped Rockefeller. With uncommon political loyalty, Rockefeller still delivered New York and other moderate Republican delegates—enough to get Ford the nomination.

Later Ford realized he had made, in his words, "the biggest political mistake of my life." Dumping Rockefeller, Ford said, was "one of the few cowardly things I ever did."

Ford won the nomination, barely, chose Kansas senator Bob Dole to be his nominee for Vice President, and left the convention thirty-four points behind Jimmy Carter. Ford gained steadily until the second debate with Carter, when President Ford said, "There is no Soviet domination of Eastern Europe." Ford meant that the United States did not *accept* Soviet control of Eastern Europe, and thought he had said that.

His temper and stubbornness about what he thought he said got the better of his normal good judgment. By the time Ford admitted his mistake three days later, the damage was done.

In October, in the final days before the election, Ford was hit by bad economic news: unemployment up, farm prices down. But the biggest single cause of Ford's defeat was the pardoning of Nixon. He knew when he granted the pardon that it could cost him the election. It did. But he never changed his mind about the correctness of his decision.

When the election was over, he conceded to Carter and assigned his most experienced counselor, John O. Marsh, to bring about the best possible transition to the new President. To Ford, that was his duty.

FORD WAS PRESIDENT for 895 days, and his record in the White House is like the man himself: solid. He took the country through and out of the worst recession since the Great Depression of the 1930s. He brought the Vietnam War to an end. It was not a glorious end, but Ford did accomplish in Vietnam what five presidents before him did not. With foresight and determination, and against intense political opposition, Ford negotiated and signed the Helsinki Treaty that opened the way to end Communist Russia's domination of Eastern Europe. To the historian Edmund Morris, "Gerald Ford was our most underrated modern President."

Gerald Ford did not aspire to be President. He accepted the nomination to be Vice President not because he wanted the job but out of his sense of duty, and because he was honored to be asked. He took over as President after the most dangerous constitutional crisis since the Civil War, and by his honesty and openness he led a frightened and angry nation back to a measure of accord and confidence in constitutional government. In doing so, moreover, Ford demonstrated that one honest, hardworking politician can make a difference.

JIMMY CARTER
1977–1981

by

Hendrik Hertzberg

THE RELATIONSHIP between a politician and his speechwriter is fraught with awkward emotions. They say that no great man is a hero to his valet; and while there are differences between a valet and a speechwriter, from the speechwriter's point of view those differences are not always as striking as the similarities. The relationship is problematical from the politician's point of view as well. The speechwriter's very existence is an affront to the politician, because it intimates that the politician is too lazy or too stupid to decide for himself what it is he is going to say. A retinue of secretaries and bodyguards and advance men and special assistants adds to a politician's glory, because these people are an outward sign of the politician's power and importance. The speechwriter is different from the other members of the court. The politician does not seem bigger or grander because he has a speechwriter. Having a speechwriter is apt to diminish the politician in the eyes of the public, because the one thing a leader cannot delegate is his inner essence, and if what the leader says is not a reflection and product of his inner essence, then what *is*, and who *is* he, and where *is* his inner essence? If someone else is writing the words he speaks, then what *do* those words express? By giving the politician *something* to say, the speechwriter suggests by implication that the politician has *nothing* to say. So a politician is generally a little resentful toward and ashamed of his speechwriter—not ashamed of the particular person who holds the job, simply of the fact that the job exists. By the same token, a speechwriter is always, on some level, just a little bit contemptuous of his politician, even if that contempt is a grain of sand compared to the mountain of respect and even awe in which the squire holds the knight.

There is a peculiar and not always comfortable intimacy about the relationship between politician and speechwriter. This intimacy exists even if the two are not close, even if they seldom or never speak to each other, and it derives from the fact that because the speechwriter, sitting alone in a room by himself, has written certain words and not others, therefore the politician says certain words and not others—says them in a very physical and definite and sensory way, using his tongue and teeth and throat and voice. Speechwriting is what doctors call an invasive procedure. It is not necessarily conducive to a serene, untroubled relationship, free of the emotional complications and hidden agendas historians endeavor to avoid. What a speechwriter says about his President may or may not be insightful, but it should always be viewed with suspicion.

DISCLAIMERS out of the way, then, here is the thesis of my character assessment of Jimmy Carter:

Jimmy Carter is a saint.

Now, by saying that, I don't mean to assert that Jimmy Carter is perfect, or that he is a total stranger to base motives, or that he is one of the elite of God's elect—though for all I know that third item, at least, may well be true.

Nor am I referring strictly to Mr. Carter's post-presidential career. It is now the conventional wisdom to say that Mr. Carter is a far better ex-President than he was a President. And in this instance the conventional wisdom has got it right. No historian would place Carter among the three or four greatest presidents of our history, and not even his most fervent admirers would place him in the top ten. But as an ex-President, he has only a tiny handful of rivals. Most of them, like him, served only a single term in the White House. One thinks of William Howard Taft, who served as Chief Justice of the United States after being defeated for reelection, and who performed adequately if not with much distinction in that office. One thinks of Herbert Hoover, that other White House engineer, whose pre-presidential good works in international humanitarian relief anticipated Carter's post-presidential efforts, and who, after his disastrous term of office, did honorable work as founder of the Hoover Institution on War and Peace and as head of the Hoover Commission, the ancestor of today's efforts to tame the federal bureaucracy. One thinks above all of John Quincy Adams, who returned to the capital as a humble member of the House of Representatives, and who in his final term in Congress stood side by side with a newly elected fellow Whig from Illinois named Abraham Lincoln to denounce the evil of slavery—thus linking together in his person America's two wars of liberation, the Revolution and the Civil War.

Jimmy Carter has taken a different route as ex-President. Whether by necessity or inclination, it has not been the route of public office. Carter put his post-presidential ambitions this way in the opening sentence of his farewell address from the Oval Office. He said (and I should note that while I may have typed this line, Mr. Carter, by virtue of his character, was its true author), "In a few days I will lay down my official responsibilities in this office, to take up once more the only title in our democracy superior to that of President, the title of citizen." In the fourteen years he has held that title, he has brought honor to it. He hasn't just talked about housing the homeless, he has built houses for them with his own hands and has inspired and organized others to do likewise. He hasn't just talked about comforting the afflicted, he has mounted a little known program through the Carter Center that is well on its way to eradicating Guinea worm disease, a painful, crippling parasite that has inflicted suffering on millions of Africans. He hasn't just talked about extending democracy, he has put his reputation and sometimes his very life on the line in country after country, often with little or no publicity, to promote free elections and expose rigged ones. And, of course, most controversially, he hasn't just talked about peace, he has made peace, or made peace possible, by using his moral prestige and his willingness to take risks and his persistence and his patience and his stubbornness to bring hostile parties that extra little distance that sometimes makes the difference between war and not-war.

A former President's activities as former President should neither redeem nor tarnish our estimation of his performance in office. James Buchanan was a weak and mediocre President, and the fact that he later became a firm supporter of Lincoln and the Union cannot alter that judgment. Millard Fillmore was a bad President and a worse ex-President—he ended up trying to get back into the White House as the candidate of the anti-Catholic, anti-Jewish, anti-immigrant, anti-everything Know-Nothing Party—but his badness as President is not made worse by his worseness as ex-President. As a former President, Theodore Roosevelt was on balance a less than constructive force—his third-party attempt in 1912 to unseat his handpicked successor had the ironic consequence of grievously damaging his former party's progressive wing—but that takes nothing away from his glittering accomplishments as President.

Nevertheless, it's useful to look at post-presidential careers, because if they can't change our judgment of a presidency they can certainly deepen our understanding of it. Away from the constrictions and exaggerations of office, undistorted by the powers he wielded and was buffeted by, a President's character and personal qualities may emerge in stronger relief once he is back in private life. We can see which of the qualities he projected as President were authentic and which were fake, which of his strengths and weaknesses were inherent in his character and which were products of chance and circumstance.

In Carter's case, the post-presidential career shows that his inner resources—his inner strengths—are extraordinary, far deeper than they appeared to be when he was President. Many other aspects of the character people saw in him then have turned out to be obviously genuine, and some of them are perfectly suited to the work he has created for himself. His tendency to go it alone sometimes damaged him as President, but in his role as a diplomatic privateer it has served him and the world well. His unshakable sense of his own rectitude did not make him popular on Capitol Hill or in the White House press room, but now it seems to focus him single-mindedly on his good works—and not just when he is within camera range.

His trip to Haiti in September 1994 is the best known example of Carter the ex-President at work. Carter's interference—combined, of course, with President Clinton's determination to use force if necessary—turned what would have been a bloody invasion with casualties and bitterness on all sides into a peaceful and apparently quite successful occupation. Carter was roundly attacked for his efforts, and some of the attacks seemed valid on the surface. A lot of people were outraged that Carter treated Haiti's military strongman, Lieutenant General Raoul Cédras, with respect and called him a man of honor. A lot of people were outraged that Cédras and his henchmen initially were permitted to remain in Haiti and allowed to keep some of their ill-gotten financial gains. A lot of people were outraged that at one point Carter said he was ashamed of his country for the way it had treated Haiti over the years. A lot of people were outraged that Carter, in defiance of official State Department policy, allowed the puppet president of Haiti to sign the agreement, thus seeming to give legitimacy to an essentially criminal regime. And, of course, a lot of people were outraged, or maybe just baffled, that Carter kept talking about how slender and attractive Mrs. Cédras was. For those of us who still wince at the memory of Carter's notorious "lust in my heart" *Playboy* interview from the 1976 campaign, that detail was what made the episode true vintage Jimmy.

But the bottom line was: There was no bloodshed. The elected, legitimate president of Haiti, Jean-Bertrand Aristide, was restored, the killings and human rights violations were stopped, Cédras and his pals ended up leaving the country, and Haiti now has a better chance than anyone thought possible to become a relatively normal country instead of a nightmare of death and cruelty.

Many people, including some of Carter's customary critics, understood this in the immediate aftermath of Carter's trip and were willing to give him credit. And if Carter had just come home and issued a statement saying he was glad to have been of service to President Clinton and the country and had then gone back to Georgia and kept quiet for a while, he now would be a universally recognized and celebrated hero. Clearly, this was one of those times when modesty and reticence would have been the most effective form of boasting. But he didn't do that. He went on television and talked and talked, and ended up saying some rather graceless and foolish things. The result was that he ended up reminding a lot of people of what they had never liked about him—the self-righteousness, the assumption of moral superiority—and quite thoroughly taking the shine off his triumph.

For many of us who love and admire Jimmy Carter, it was an exasperating and all too familiar moment of frustration. But the truth is, a person's character is all of a piece. It would be nice if we could separate out the bits we like from the bits we don't and just have the bits we like. But that's not how life works. A person's character is what it is. It's a little like a marriage—only without the option of divorce. You can work on it and try to make it better, but basically you have to take the bitter with the sweet. The same bullheadedness and perhaps overweening arrogance that misled Jimmy Carter into going on TV after he got back from Haiti and raining all over his own parade were just the flip side of the qualities of perseverance and self-confidence that enabled him to come up with an agreement in the first place. If Carter weren't the kind of guy who can go on *Larry King Live* and offend everybody who wants to give him a break, then he probably wouldn't be the kind of guy who can keep the Pentagon, the State Department, and the White House on hold while he goes ahead and changes their policies for them—all for their own good, of course.

We admire ruthlessness in the makers of war, but we're not quite sure how to respond to it when we encounter it in a maker of peace. We respect George S. Patton because he did what was necessary and didn't give a damn what anyone thought about it. We esteem Ulysses S. Grant because he refused to flinch from taking enormous casualties if he was convinced it would yield victory. Jimmy Carter is a kind of Patton for peace. He is a General Grant of the negotiating table. He may have to flatter a dictator or flirt with a dictator's wife or publicly praise a war criminal in order to avert a bloodbath, but if that's what it takes that's what he does. And if he thereby opens himself to ridicule or scorn, he doesn't give a damn.

One of the most curious charges lodged against Carter after his trip to Haiti—and, even more vociferously, after his trip to the former Yugoslavia, where he tried, with little short-term success and no long-term results, to persuade the Serbs to halt the shelling of Sarajevo—was that he has some sort of compulsion to be nice to dictators. His critics recalled that as President, he toasted the Shah of Iran and the authoritarian rulers of the Philippines and South Korea, described Marshal Tito of Yugoslavia, improbably, as one of his "best friends," and, at the Salt II signing ceremony in Vienna, embraced Leonid Brezhnev and kissed the startled apparatchik on both cheeks. But these gestures spoke not to any admiration for tyrants but to a Christian eagerness to redeem sinners—and, as in the later case of Cédras and the Serbs, to a not-so-Christian willingness to manipulate the emotions of his negotiating partners. In practice, Carter has always showed himself as ready to anger authoritarians as to flatter them, in pursuit of peace and human rights.

He kissed Brezhnev, yes; but he also defied him by receiving Alexander Solzhenitsyn, corresponding with Andrei Sakharov, boycotting the Moscow Olympics, and sending arms to the Afghan resistance. And in his post-presidential travels, with the power of the U.S. government no longer at his command, he has sometimes filled the gap with a display of physical courage. When he denounced the rigging of a Panamanian election by the Manuel Noriega regime, he did so not from the safety of Washington or Atlanta, but from a sidewalk in Panama City, under the eyes—and the guns—of Noriega's armed secret police.

The Haiti episode illustrates some of the qualities in Jimmy Carter I've chosen to call, only half-unseriously, saintly. Being a saint isn't all kindness and sweetness and compassion. Being a saint, especially a saint in politics, is a very mixed proposition and not always a completely attractive one. Saints can be intensely annoying. They can be hard on the people around them. They can be blind to ordinary human feelings and ordinary human failings, including their own.

GEORGE ORWELL begins his famous essay on Mahatma Gandhi with these words: "Saints should always be judged guilty until proved innocent." Later in the essay, referring to Gandhi's self-denying way of life and uncompromising moral standards, he writes, "The essence of being human is that one does not seek perfection, that one is sometimes willing to commit sins for the sake of loyalty, that one does not push asceticism to the point where it makes friendly intercourse impossible, and that one is prepared in the end to be defeated and broken up by life, which is the inevitable price of fastening one's love upon other human individuals." And Orwell continues, making a point that today would be judged medically if not politically incorrect, "No doubt alcohol, tobacco, and so forth are things that a saint must avoid, but sainthood is a thing that human beings should avoid."

I should add, before anybody gets the wrong idea, that Orwell's overall assessment of Gandhi is a very positive one. Carter is no Gandhi (and I'm no Orwell). But the fact that it is not completely unnatural to mention the two of them, Gandhi and Carter, in the same breath is suggestive of something worth exploring. This is not something one would be tempted to say about many presidents or many politicians.

Carter's style of leadership was and is more religious than political in nature. He was and is a moral leader more than a political leader. And I think this helps explain not only some of his successes as President but also some of his failures.

Look at how he was elected in the first place. In the early and decisive days of his campaign, he spoke the language of religion and morality far more, and far more effectively, than he spoke the language of politics. He spoke openly and convincingly about his Christian faith—and he managed to do this in a way that was inclusive and tolerant. Nowadays every politician seems to feel obligated to talk about being born again, just as in decades past politicians seemed to feel obligated to have themselves photographed wearing an Indian chief's war bonnet. But Carter was Christian before Christian was cool. Carter was the first and is still the only candidate for President who ever used the word "love"—in its specifically religious and Christian sense—in virtually every campaign speech he delivered.

Carter was nominated because of a number of circumstances. The liberal wing of the Democratic Party formed its usual circular firing squad, splitting its vote among several candidates and leaving Carter with a narrow plurality within the party. Carter alone understood the peculiar timing and dynamics of the nominating season. He used the previously ignored Iowa caucuses to leverage himself a victory in New Hampshire and some other early primaries; by the time he started losing one primary after another, as he did toward the end, it didn't matter because he was able to win enough delegates here and there to put himself over the top. Carter won the general election partly because the incumbent, Gerald Ford, had been damaged by the Nixon pardon and then by a bruising primary campaign against Ronald Reagan's challenge. But in a deeper sense,

Carter was nominated and elected on account of a pair of profound and painful moral dramas in American life: the centuries-long drama of race and the decade-long drama of disillusion over Vietnam and Watergate.

Carter's nomination and election marked the end of the Civil War as a determining factor in American party politics. Carter's political career was a product of the civil rights movement as surely as were those of his fellow Georgians Andrew Young and John Lewis. In his inaugural address as governor of Georgia in 1971, Carter said, "The time for racial discrimination is over." Because he was so clear about that, because he made that simple and electrifying declaration, he was able to become the first President of the United States from the heart of the Old Confederacy. Carter's historic role in the Democratic Party was that he was the agent of the destruction of George Wallace and the southern racist wing of the party. Carter was not the only "centrist" or "moderate" Democrat who sought his party's nomination in 1976; the professionals regarded Senator Henry Jackson of Washington State as a far more formidable figure. But Jackson had been a diehard supporter of the Vietnam War, and Jackson utterly lacked the moral prestige Carter gained by humbling Wallace and ridding the party of what Wallace represented.

Carter was certainly not the first New South politician. Atlanta had long prided itself on the slogan, "The city too busy to hate." But that very slogan implied that if the good people of Atlanta weren't so darn busy, well, maybe they *would* find time to hate. Carter's rejection of racist and racial politics was not based on the idea that racism was bad for business. It wasn't based on technocratic or pragmatic considerations. It wasn't based on notions of legal equity. It was based on Christian love. Carter appealed to blacks—and also to a stratum of southern whites—not on the basis of interest group politics, but on the basis of a fervent shared vision of Christian love, forgiveness, and reconciliation.

There was a remarkable scene at New York's Madison Square Garden after Carter's acceptance speech. On the stage, Carter and his running mate, Senator Walter Mondale, stood arm in arm and side by side with an extraordinary array of friends and former adversaries: Coretta King, the widow of Martin Luther King, Jr., and King's civil rights comrades Ralph D. Abernathy, Jesse Jackson, and Andrew Young; the wheelchair-ridden onetime racist firebrand George C. Wallace; Mayor Richard J. Daley with former Senator Eugene McCarthy, whose youthful followers had been clubbed by Daley's police in the streets of Chicago eight years before; Senators Hubert Humphrey, George McGovern, and Henry M. Jackson, who had struggled with each other over policy and power for a decade; and many more. It was a political Peaceable Kingdom. The anthem of the evening was "We Shall Overcome." I had not yet joined the Carter team; I was there as a reporter. But I wept. Everyone in the room wept. Everyone in the room—even in the press section—linked arms and swayed back and forth and sang. It was a moment of healing that carried tremendous emotional power. It was as if the agonies of slavery and war and racial hatred and the fratricidal bitterness of Vietnam and the lies of Watergate—it was as if all this were being washed away, washed in the blood of the lamb, and at the center of it was this small, slight, soft-spoken man from a tiny hamlet in the depths of the Deep South.

The rest of the campaign was something of an anticlimax. The simple verities that had propelled Carter to the nomination—the simple promise not to lie, the simple assurance that we could govern ourselves through goodness and love—were not quite enough to power a general election campaign in the national arena. Carter left his convention with a huge lead in the polls. His lead melted steadily in the brutal furnace of national politics. If the election had taken place a few days later, he might well have lost. But he won, if only by a hair.

IN THE WHITE HOUSE, Carter established a style of leadership that was pointedly humble. The candidate who had carried his own suit bag became the President who walked down Pennsylvania Avenue in his inaugural parade. President Carter got rid of door-to-door limousine service for top White House staff. He dispensed with fancy tablecloths and seating by rank in the White House mess. He even put a stop to the constant serenades of "Hail to the Chief."

It was typical of him that one of the first things he did was to sell off the presidential yacht, the *Sequoia*. Now the truth is that this was a mistake. It was a mistake because the *Sequoia* was one of the most cost-effective items in the federal budget. A President could take some important senator out on that yacht and give him a few drinks and flatter him and they could sit together on the deck and watch the sun go down in the cool of the evening, and when they got back to the dock the President would have that senator's vote on some important bill. Without the yacht, the President might have to offer something more concrete and expensive to get that senator's vote—like agreeing not to close a big military base in the senator's state. That yacht paid for itself many times over every year.

Carter didn't look at it that way. He probably should have, but he didn't. He simply thought it was wrong for the people's President to put on airs by sailing around on a yacht. He thought it was unseemly for a man in his position to live like a millionaire at the taxpayers' expense.

In a way there was a religious aspect even to this little detail, in my opinion. Unlike President Carter, I don't come from a long line of Baptists. But my mother was a Congregationalist, and she taught me the difference between low church and high church. Jimmy Carter was and is emphatically low church. His discomfort with pomp and circumstance isn't just a matter of personal taste. It goes straight back to the Protestant Reformation.

Fortunately for Carter, his distaste for show worked very well for him as a candidate—almost as if it had been a calculated ploy dreamed up by image consultants. The public was sick and tired of artifice, insincerity, and slick packaging—sick of lies and anything that smacked of lies. Candidate Carter's simplicity, his lack of bombast, even his Sunday School–teacher awkwardness—all this the public found very appealing. They were part of his outsiderness.

His communications director, Gerald Rafshoon, took advantage of these qualities by making ads that were calculatedly amateurish and un-slick looking.

This religious style of leadership continued in the Carter White House. In our speechwriting office, which was populated mostly by diehard secular humanists, we used to joke that it was no accident that the man's initials were J.C. It seemed like one of those odd coincidences that make you think maybe there is a God after all and that He has a pretty good sense of humor—like the fact that in 1995 the anti-welfare leader of the Senate Republicans is named Dole and the reptilian Speaker of the House is named Newt, or that the tax-cuts-for-the-wealthy Republican national chairman in 1992 was named Rich Bond, or that Ross Perot's campaign that year was managed by a man named Swindle.

As President, Carter's disdain for artifice served him well as long as things were going his way, but when things weren't going his way it created problems for him, because it essentially deprived him of the full use of one of the basic tools of statecraft. He didn't like to perform—in the sense of giving a performance. He hated to pretend to be feeling emotions he wasn't actually feeling at that moment. And of course that kind of pretending is essential to making an effective political speech, which is a kind of theatrical performance. You have to act as if you're feeling pride or sorrow or the swell of patriotic feeling or whatever, even if at that particular moment, the moment the speech is scheduled for, what you really want is to be home in bed—or, in Carter's case, back in the little study next to the Oval Office, reading memos and making decisions.

Carter considered making decisions to be by far the most important aspect of his job. Communicating those decisions—communication in general—took a very distant second place. Naturally this was frustrating for those of us who were writing his speeches. He didn't much like to prepare or rehearse. He often removed emotive or inspirational language from his speech drafts.

Sometimes his dislike of artifice reached comic lengths. One day he was scheduled to announce the elimination of several thousand pages of federal regulations. We got a big stack of paper for him, and the idea was that he would sweep it off the table or dump it in the wastepaper basket to illustrate how many regulations he was getting rid of. We thought that this would be very dramatic—excellent footage for the evening news. The only problem was, the President didn't follow the script. Instead, he pointed to the stack and said something like, "This is a prop prepared by my staff. It's supposed to represent the thousands of pages of regulations. Actually, it's just a pile of blank sheets of paper." He then ignored it for the remainder of his statement. The evening news found something else to lead with that night.

On this point, of course, the contrast between Jimmy Carter and the man who beat him in 1980 could hardly be stronger. We Carter speechwriters, after we left office, sometimes felt a twinge of envy for our successors in the Reagan administration. Ronald Reagan *did* know how to follow a script—and I say that meaning no disrespect. If Reagan understood nothing else, he understood the importance of speechmaking and communications.

But Reagan and his speechwriters had an advantage over us that was a good deal more important than his superior talents as a thespian: Reagan and his team always knew far ahead of time what they wanted to say. Carter and his team did not.

This was *not* because Reagan had stronger convictions. It was because Reagan had a fixed *political ideology*, and Carter did not—at least, he had much less of one.

A political ideology is a very handy thing to have. It's a real time-saver, because it tells you what you think about things you know nothing about. Reagan never had to agonize over the merits of this tax versus that tax—if it was a tax, he was against it. He never lost sleep over the proper design of some environmental regulation—if it was an environmental regulation, he was against it. He never worried about whether to build up the Navy at the expense of the Army, or the Army at the expense of the Navy. His view was, if it was military, build it all—and damn the expense.

Another way to put this same point is that Ronald Reagan did all of his thinking and made most of his decisions long before he became President. He had a complete ideological framework that answered virtually every policy question in advance. So, as President, he was able to devote all his time and energy to selling and implementing the ideas he had adopted during his years as spokesman of the conservative wing of his party.

This observation applies as much to ideologues of the left as to ideologues of the right. If, say, a Hubert Humphrey or an Edward Kennedy had ever become President, then he, like Reagan, would not have had to spend a lot of time developing a program. A fully developed, fully worked out political ideology provides a model of how the whole organism works. It may not provide you with the details, but it does provide you with a clear general direction.

Jimmy Carter did not have the advantage of a dogma. In this respect he was like all other presidents of recent times—all except Reagan, who was the only leader of the militant wing of one of the two parties to come to power since World War II. All the other postwar presidents—Eisenhower, Kennedy, Johnson, Nixon, Ford, Carter, Bush, and Clinton—have been drawn from the pragmatic center. (No leader of the left or liberal wing of the Democratic Party has ever become President, which is one reason that the conventional assumption that liberalism has been tried and found wanting is a little unfair. Unlike unalloyed conservatism, unalloyed liberalism has not been tried.) And Carter, even more than Kennedy, Johnson, and Clinton, was a centrist. His only strong tie to the party's liberal wing was through the southern civil rights movement, which was limited both regionally and ideologically.

In Carter's case, the matter was complicated by three other factors. First, he came from a one-party state, Georgia, where politics was traditionally a matter of maneuvering within a single party, usually without much ideological content. Second, Carter—unlike Johnson, the veteran Senate leader, and Clinton, the cosmopolitan Rhodes scholar, former antiwar protestor, and onetime Senate staffer—had had no exposure to national issues and national politics before he started running for President. And, third, Carter was brand new. He had played no role in national political life and was almost entirely unknown outside his region. When I first heard about Carter, in 1975, my initial thought was that it would be interesting to have a country singer in the White House. It wasn't until some weeks later that I realized that Jimmy Carter was not the same person as Jimmie Davis, the singing governor of Louisiana.

Because he was so new, Carter had no ties or commitments to the traditional constituency groups of the Democratic Party, such as labor and the cities. This was a strength for him, because he could argue, correctly, that he would not be a prisoner of pressure groups. But it was also a weakness once he became President, because he did not have the loyalty of those groups. Again, the contrast with Reagan is instructive. Reagan could say to a Republican constituency group like the Christian right, "I'll get to your concerns about abortion and school prayer eventually, but right now I have to concentrate on my economic program. Be patient." Because of his long years in the wilderness with these people, he had the authority to ask them to wait. Carter didn't have the standing to make that kind of request. He was in no position to tell the unions or the cities or the women's rights advocates to be patient. As a result, he was too weak politically to resist pressures from the various Democratic constituency groups to propose legislation on behalf of each and every one of them, and to assure each in turn that its particular concern—youth employment, the Equal Rights Amendment, labor law reform, consumer protection, health care, whatever—was his "top priority." Is it any wonder he quickly earned a reputation for scattering his energies, for failing to set clear priorities, and for getting swamped in details?

The truth is, he was damned either way. If he had set firm priorities, choosing to emphasize one or two issues to the exclusion of others, the disappointed interest groups would have turned on him immediately, making it impossible for him to accomplish even limited goals. So he chose to try to appease the interest groups for a while, and hope for the best. As it was, once they realized he would be unable to deliver on most of his promises, they turned on him anyway.

The interest groups had very high expectations, which were

based on their experience with President Johnson. But Johnson, who had won a huge mandate at the polls after President Kennedy's assassination, had governed at a time when liberal reform was sweeping all before it. (The tide of reform was so strong, in fact, that it continued well into the Nixon administration, bringing about the creation of such agencies as the Environmental Protection Agency and the Occupational Safety and Health Administration.) Carter, elected by a hair, had no such mandate. And he came to office at an essentially conservative moment: his election had more to do with moral revulsion at Watergate than with political enthusiasm for large-scale programmatic innovation. (The interest groups never quite admitted this, but they seem to have learned enough from the experience that they have been willing to give Clinton a little—though only a little—more leeway.)

CARTER APPROACHED domestic issues one by one, as a problem solver. He studied each issue separately and tackled each issue on its own terms. He didn't have the kind of big-picture framework that might have enabled him to explain how the issues all fit together. And he didn't have the kind of political strength that might have enabled him to bring the unruly constituencies into line. So it was difficult both conceptually and politically for him to set priorities. He had little choice but to spread himself too thin.

Though Carter didn't have a political ideology, he did have what I would call a *moral* ideology—and on this he was faultless. *He knew the difference between right and wrong.* This may sound like faint praise—after all, doesn't everybody know the difference between right and wrong?—but it isn't. It is very *high* praise.

Let me explain. I came to the Carter White House from the liberal wing of the Democratic Party. I voted for Carter in the 1976 election, of course, but in the primaries I had first been for Harold Hughes and then for Fred Harris and then for Mo Udall. My liberal friends would sometimes say to me, "How can you work for that guy?" Their questions became more insistent as 1980 approached and Ted Kennedy began making moves to get into the race.

Well, I never had any problems of conscience about working for Jimmy Carter in 1980—for two reasons. The less important reason was that I was absolutely certain that Ted Kennedy could never be elected President of the United States—not because he was too liberal, but because of Chappaquiddick. Even if the public had been willing to forgive Kennedy for the drowning of Mary Jo Kopechne, they would not have been willing to forgive him for the more politically damaging but less widely known aspect of the scandal: Kennedy's abortive attempt in the hours after the accident to establish an alibi and shift the blame to a family retainer. By the time the Republicans were through, I feared, every American would be familiar with the details. For the Democrats to nominate Ted Kennedy, I believed, would be tantamount to turning the country over to the Republicans without a fight.

The second and more important reason had to do with this matter of Carter's moral ideology. I used to say to my liberal friends, "Jimmy Carter is the first President of my adult life who is not criminally insane." I had in mind the legal definition of criminal insanity: the inability to tell right from wrong. It is wrong to kill people for no reason other than political gain or political fear. Lyndon Johnson and Richard Nixon did that. They escalated and continued the Vietnam War, thus causing the deaths of tens of thousands of Americans and hundreds of thousands of Vietnamese, long after it became clear that the war could not be won—and they did this not because they seriously believed that their actions would help America to be secure or Vietnam to be free, but because they were afraid of looking weak. Gerald Ford was not in the same category by any means. Indeed, his simplicity and forthrightness contrasted markedly with the tortured Machiavellianism of his two predecessors. But in what became known as the *Mayaguez* incident, even the gentle Ford sent a number of men to their deaths needlessly. Jimmy Carter never did anything like that.

Carter's moral ideology—his ability to tell right from wrong—would have made him a great President for a time of moral crisis. If the overriding problem facing America in the late seventies had been racial segregation, for instance, or the Vietnam War, Carter would have known how to rise to the occasion because he knew how to do what was right—even when the political cost was high.

Carter was elected in the backwash of a moral crisis, but the biggest problems he faced as President, especially in the domestic arena, were not primarily moral problems. They were primarily managerial, technical problems, involving tremendous vested interests and offering few political rewards. There was no right or wrong way to solve these problems; just effective ways and ineffective ways.

Energy is a good example. Carter devoted enormous amounts of time and political capital to the energy problem. One might argue that he achieved a certain success—you don't hear much about the energy crisis these days, I notice. But he suffered many legislative defeats along the way and alienated many groups of people.

On one occasion, Carter, seeking to go beyond technocratic approaches, tried to cast the energy problem in sweeping moral terms. This was the so-called "malaise" episode, widely recognized as one of the most memorable moments of the Carter administration and almost as widely scorned as one of the most contemptible. The received version of what happened is simple. It goes like this: In the summer of 1979, President Carter was overwhelmed by energy and economic crises. In desperation, he made a disastrous speech blaming the American people and a national "malaise" for his own manifest failures of policy and leadership. The American people, horrified, turned him out of office at the first opportunity.

Variations on this version were used effectively by both Edward Kennedy and Ronald Reagan in the 1980 election campaign. The "malaise" has proved to have a long shelf life. At the 1988 Republican Convention and again in 1992, speaker after speaker trooped to the podium to denounce "Jimmy Carter and the days of malaise." Attacks on Carter and "malaise" have served the Republicans in the eighties and nineties almost as sturdily as attacks on Hoover and "prosperity is just around the corner" served the Democrats in the forties and fifties.

It goes without saying that the historical reality and the political caricature do not comport with one another. For example, here are four details of the episode that are at variance with how most people seem to remember it: (1) Carter himself never mentioned the word "malaise." (2) The speech itself was an enormous popular success. It generated a record amount of positive mail to the White House, and Carter's approval rating in the polls zoomed up by eleven points literally overnight. (3) The sudden political damage came not from the speech but from the cabinet firings a few days later. (4) Although Carter has been flayed for blaming others, the first third of the speech is devoted to the most excoriating self-criticism ever heard from any American president. As these random details suggest, the "malaise" episode has become encrusted in myth.

The episode came at a moment of great political and human vulnerability for Carter. He and his staff had been preoccupied with two difficult overseas trips—one to Vienna to complete and sign the SALT II Treaty with the Soviet Union, the other to Japan and Korea. Everyone was completely exhausted. Meanwhile, back at home, the country was in an uproar because of gasoline lines triggered by the fall of the Shah in Iran. Carter had hoped to stop over in Honolulu for a couple of days and get some rest, but that was politically impossible given the gas lines at home. Almost as soon as we got back to Washington, it was announced that Carter would address the nation on July 5. Actually, Carter had not agreed to deliver a speech, only to look at a draft and then decide. But the premature announcement put him in a corner.

Even so, when Carter got his speech draft, he decided that he didn't want to do it. He said he had made the same points about energy policy over and over again, and the people weren't responding, and, as he pungently put it in the conference call in which he told his senior staff he was canceling the speech, he didn't want to "bullshit the American people." He remained at Camp David and began an extraordinary series of meetings with leaders from all walks of American life. For a long time, Patrick Caddell, Carter's brilliant young pollster, had been saying with increasing urgency that Americans were losing faith in their institutions. (It was Caddell, by the way, who in background briefings for the press would later describe this loss of faith as a "malaise.") At Camp David, the things Carter heard from his visitors seemed to confirm Caddell's analysis.

I was the designated writer for the speech that emerged from this curious process. In truth I was more stenographer-typist than author, smoothing and coordinating bits of draft from various people, including Caddell, Stuart Eizenstat, and Carter himself. The speech had three parts. In the first part of it, wholly conceived and written by Carter, the President criticized himself through the words of those he had spoken to over the previous ten days: "Mr. President, you're not leading this nation—you're just managing the government," and so on. The second part described the erosion of public faith in institutions, in the future, and in the economy—an erosion begun by the shocks of Vietnam, the Kennedy and King assassinations, and Watergate, worsened by inflation and energy shortages, and manifested in declining rates of savings and voter participation. The third and final part outlined a series of proposals for tackling the energy problem and, in the process, beginning to pull ourselves out of the crisis of confidence.

The speech engendered a mixed reaction among the elites, although it did get mostly favorable editorial comment in its immediate aftermath. But three days later, Carter asked for the resignations of the whole of his cabinet and senior staff, telling them he would decide which ones to accept. He hoped that this would be the beginning of a regeneration of his administration—an infusion of new blood and new ideas, and a signal that even those whom he would decide to keep on would be starting anew. Instead, the mass resignations created an unanticipated and unwelcome global sensation; many foreign newspapers and governments, whose grasp of the intricacies of the American political system was imperfect, actually believed that the U.S. government had "fallen." It was at this point, I think, that the elites decided that Carter was finished. Within a few weeks this view had trickled down to the public, and

Carter's popularity ratings dropped back to the abysmal level where they had been at the outset.

The episode was consistent with the religious cast of Carter's leadership. It had elements of sin, confession, and redemption, via a process of "witnessing," prayer, and rededication. It was part of a pattern of symbolic death and resurrection that had marked Carter's personal and political life. He had been politically reborn before—after his first, unsuccessful runs for state senator and then governor, and then, as an obscure southern ex-governor, to the presidency itself. And of course he had been "born again" as a Christian. The "malaise" episode was his most spectacular effort to be "born again"—and, this time, to bring the country with him.

The episode was an exercise in national pastorship or, to use secular terms, in national psychotherapy. Acknowledging the trauma (the "crisis of confidence" brought on by Vietnam, Watergate, and the sense of national vulnerability triggered by energy shortages) was to be the key to healing it. The therapy's failure, of course, opened the way to a period of hedonism and boastfulness.

The episode may also be seen as mythmaking, in the sense popularized by Joseph Campbell. It was an attempt to create one myth (the notion of a crisis of confidence that could be overcome by tackling the energy problem) that inadvertently created another (the notion of Carter as the personification and cause of national weakness and vulnerability). A side effect was the discrediting of candor about unpleasant truths and the enshrinement of "optimism." Carter's diagnosis of the country's spiritual ills was accurate, and was recognized as such by millions of people, but when he proved unequal to the task of curing those ills (or even palliating them, as Reagan did), he was reviled with special bitterness.

In the cabinet and staff shakeup that followed the speech, Carter got rid of a number of officials who might have been described as disloyal but competent. If he had first gotten rid of a few who were loyal but incompetent, the episode might have turned out quite differently. But that, apparently, he could not bring himself to do. The rebirth was stillborn. The speech was a truthful and prescient diagnosis of what was wrong with the country and what in many ways continues to be wrong with the country. But a President who sets out to diagnose a problem had better be able to offer a plausible solution to it. The Carter of the "malaise" episode was a prophet. But he was not a saviour.

IN FOREIGN POLICY, Carter's moral ideology was a clearer guide to action. He could pursue his vision relatively unhampered by the built-in frustrations and roadblocks that hobble our political system in the domestic arena. Carter was very much in charge of his own foreign policy. His two top foreign policy advisers, the hawkish Zbigniew Brzezinski and the dovish Cyrus Vance, were often in disagreement with each other. I don't know whether he intended it to work this way, but the result was that he himself made all the important decisions.

Carter believed in peace—in preventing war—and in human rights. These two values were the lodestars by which he guided his conduct of foreign affairs. And again, these values were expressions of his sense of religious and moral duty.

Four areas of Carter's foreign policy show his character and style of leadership quite clearly: his human rights policy; his fight for the Panama Canal treaties; his Middle East diplomacy; and his handling of the Iran hostage crisis.

Carter's advocacy of human rights as a central goal of American foreign policy was an innovation, but it was one that connected directly with the values of the American civic religion. He said a number of times that while America had not invented human rights, human rights had invented America. The United States was unique among nations in that its very sense of nationhood was based not on ties of blood or kin or ethnicity or even language, but on the shared political and moral values of the American political compact —especially the value of universal human rights.

Carter insisted on applying the human rights test not only to our adversaries—to the Soviet Union—but also to countries allied with us. This angered a number of dictatorial governments that had traditionally done our bidding in the Cold War and now found themselves criticized by their patron. It also angered a good many foreign policy experts in this country. They saw it as naive and moralistic and even dangerous. Some of them saw in it a squeamish failure to understand that the global struggle against Soviet Communist totalitarianism carried an overriding moral imperative of its own, one that sometimes required the use of dirty methods and unsavory allies.

Carter's human rights policy invited charges of hypocrisy and inconsistency. It was inevitable that there would be times when larger strategic concerns had to take precedence over human rights concerns. And there were times when the policy did indeed weaken leaders of governments that had been American clients—Somoza of Nicaragua, for example, and the Shah of Iran. But on balance the policy was a success. It saved thousands of lives and won freedom for thousands of prisoners of conscience. It was crucial in launching the process that has seen country after country in Latin America replace military dictatorships or oligarchies with constitutional democratic governments.

The implication of the human rights policy was that America's enemy was not communism per se but tyranny in general, regardless of ideology. Many assumed that the policy would succeed only in weakening America's friends while having no effect on the countries of the Soviet bloc, which understood only force and strength and could not be swayed by lectures about human rights. This view prided itself on being hardheaded and tough-minded, but it turned out to be less hardheaded and tough-minded than it claimed to be. We have it on no less an authority than Vaclav Havel that Carter's human rights policy undermined the legitimacy and self-confidence of the Communist bosses and gave hope and encouragement to the dissidents. Communism collapsed from within, non-violently. America's embrace of human rights played a role in that magnificent triumph.

The human rights policy is one reason that Jimmy Carter remains a hero today in much of Latin America. Another reason is his fight for the Panama Canal treaties, which was an epic struggle, though it is now almost completely forgotten in this country. But the truth is that if Carter had ducked that fight, or if he had lost it, Central America would have been plunged into instability and probably into war.

The Panama struggle was fairly typical of the kind of fights Carter took on. Though failure would have been disastrous, success offered no political rewards—Carter could hardly run for reelection on the boast that he had successfully given away the Panama Canal. The opposition to the treaties was led by Ronald Reagan, who used the issue to galvanize his political movement and build up its mailing lists and fund-raising apparatus. Perhaps Reagan was sincere in saying that the loss of the Canal would be a blow to America's vital national security interests. Yet the fact is that once Reagan became President, he did absolutely nothing to abrogate—or even to modify—the treaties he had so passionately denounced.

President Carter's most important single foreign policy achievement was making peace between Israel and Egypt—an extraordinary breakthrough, one that permanently changed the dynamics of events in the Middle East and laid the groundwork for all the progress that has been made since. Carter's role at the Camp David summit with Anwar Sadat and Menachem Begin is well known. His perseverance, his determination, his ability to listen, his refusal to quit when others lost hope—these qualities of his came into focus like a laser beam at Camp David. But six months later, negotiations on the peace treaty itself had stalled, and it looked as if the entire agreement might collapse.

So in March 1979 Carter decided to go to the Middle East. I went along on that trip. It was very different from any other presidential trip that I have ever read about, let alone experienced. Presidential trips abroad are carefully scripted. Advance teams go to the site weeks or months beforehand to make preparations down to the tiniest detail. If there are agreements to be signed, they are worked out well ahead of time. Nothing is left to chance.

This trip wasn't like that. The decision to go was made only five days before Air Force One took off. There was very little time for preparation. As we flew across the Atlantic, everybody tried to get some sleep—everybody except me. I was up working on the address Carter would make to the Egyptian parliament after we landed. I remember tiptoeing through the darkened plane and seeing Cyrus Vance, the Secretary of State, and Zbigniew Brzezinski, the President's national security adviser, sleeping head to toe next to each other on a banquette that ran the length of a hallway opposite the President's cabin. When these men were awake there was a certain rivalry between them. But now, as the plane sped east through the night, they had their little Air Force One pillows under their heads and their socks peeking out from under their little Air Force One blankets over them, and they looked as peaceful as a couple of kids at a slumber party.

Not just for me but for many of us, that journey was the zenith of our White House service. The point that the episode illustrates about Carter's character and leadership is that he was willing to risk everything for peace. There was absolutely no guarantee of success. In fact, right up to the last day of the mission we were convinced that it was going to fail. And it would have been a very public, very costly, very humiliating failure. It would have cemented the notion that Carter was a well-meaning incompetent.

But it didn't fail. And I think the reason was that Begin and, especially, Sadat were deeply impressed by Carter's courage. He had put his presidency on the line. He had made it personal. He had taken the leap into the abyss and dared them to follow. They could not refuse.

Coming home from that trip, being greeted at Andrews Air Force Base by our friends and co-workers and loved ones, we all got a taste of what it must be like to return in triumph from a victory in war. The fact that it was a victory in peace made it all the sweeter.

Again, the political rewards were minimal. We had an easier time of it on Capitol Hill for a few weeks, but then the bump in the polls faded and we were back to the normal backbiting and bickering. But the satisfaction remains to this day; and every time ex-President Carter goes on one of his quixotic journeys, those of us who went with him to Cairo and Jerusalem remember and smile.

IF THE MIDDLE EAST journey was the high point of those four years, the night of Desert One was the low point.

Five months into the Iran hostage crisis, on the night of Thursday, April 24, 1980, in conditions of absolute secrecy, eight helicopters and a number of C-130 transport planes took off for a site in the Iranian desert. The plan was to set up a staging area there, and then use the helicopters to fly into Tehran—first to the outskirts of town and then to the American Embassy itself in the heart of the city, where most of the fifty-three American hostages were being held by armed student militants. The militants, with tacit but increasingly open Iranian government support, had seized the building and the people in it the previous November, supposedly to protest the admission of the deposed Shah into the United States for medical treatment. Diplomatic efforts, though tirelessly pursued, had proved unavailing, and Carter had reluctantly given his approval for a rescue mission. The Desert One base was the tip of the iceberg. Men and materiel had also been infiltrated into Tehran itself over the preceding several months. It was an enormous, elaborate effort.

But three of the helicopters broke down or never made it to Desert One, because of sandstorms. There was still a chance to carry out the mission with the remaining five, but the margin of error was gone. The commander on the ground recommended that the mission be aborted. The choppers and C-130s would be flown out again, along with a busload of very surprised Iranians who had stumbled upon the scene and suddenly found themselves in the middle of a bewildering bustle of men and machines.

Then, horror descended upon the desert. In the darkness, a C-130 crashed into a helicopter as it was taking off. Eight commandos were killed. The mission ended in failure and chaos. There would be no second chance.

Like everyone in the White House who didn't have a "need to know," I had been kept in the dark about the mission. In fact, I took it for granted that a rescue mission was impossible. Many of us suspected that some kind of military action was imminent, but we thought it would involve the bombing or mining of Iranian ports and cities. I was against that kind of military action; I thought it would worsen the situation, perhaps start a war, and have no effect on the hostages except perhaps to get them killed. The week before, I had spoken out against an attack at a senior staff meeting, and word of the meeting had leaked to the press. I was worried that Carter would think I was the leaker, which I wasn't. Later, I realized that the leak was probably part of a deception to mislead the Iranians.

When the mission failed, I was at home asleep. I was awakened by a frantic phone call from Pat Caddell, Carter's pollster, who was in California and had heard the news on television. I immediately went to the White House to see if I could help out, and was put to work writing a statement for Carter to deliver in the morning. It was a night of shock and grief. Staff members moved about like zombies, or stood with faces stained by tears, or sat with their heads in their hands, or tried to distract themselves with work. Jody Powell, the President's press secretary, was a calm center, comforting the rest of us and bucking us up.

The Iran rescue mission became the ultimate symbol of what people considered Carter's incompetence and haplessness. The magazine I would later edit, *The New Republic*, cleverly but cruelly called it "The Jimmy Carter Desert Classic." Everyone complained that it was typical of Carter that he tried to scrimp on helicopters and didn't send enough. But in truth the number of helicopters had to be balanced between the requirements of sufficiency and the requirements of secrecy.

When the mission failed, we all realized that we would probably lose the election. But I've thought a lot about it over the years, and to me the disaster in the desert was one of Jimmy Carter's finest hours. This was not a careless or excessive or immoral use of force. The amount of force was calibrated to the goal: freeing the hostages, and freeing them directly, as opposed to raining down indiscriminate destruction on Iran in order to put pressure on an Iranian government that was probably too unstable and divided to respond. And the potential payoff was very high. As I wrote in my diary a few days later,

> What made us saddest was thinking of the historical moment we missed. If the mission had succeeded, the explosion of joy in this country would have been unlike anything anyone in our generation has ever seen. It would have been a catharsis that would have wiped away ten years of spiritual, yes, malaise. So it was worth trying. Paradoxically—despite the fact that this is on one level a metaphor for three years of Carter Administration screwups—it has made me feel better about the Administration. This was a rational, intelligent thing to have tried. It would have been a solution to the problem. There is all the difference in the world between this and a blockade or mining. I just wish it had worked. I just wish it had worked.

Carter said afterwards that the mission had been "an incomplete success"—a line I don't mind saying I didn't write. Naturally he was roundly ridiculed for saying that. But the funny thing is, he was right. The incomplete part I don't have to explain. But the mission *was* a success of sorts. It convinced the Iranians that we were ready to use force—and that they had better make sure the hostages did not come to any harm. Along with Carter's patient diplomacy—and, yes, along with the Iranians' fear that President Reagan would not be so patient—the rescue mission, for all its horror and disappointment, ultimately achieved its goal: the release of the hostages, and their safe return home on Ronald Reagan's inauguration day.

Jimmy Carter was an interesting experiment for the American presidency. Electing him to the job was as close as the American people have ever come to picking someone out of the phone book to be President. He was a man of faith and morality—a kind of Christian pacifist—a man whose quest was as much spiritual as political.

Here is how Orwell ends his essay on Gandhi:

> One may feel, as I do, a sort of aesthetic distaste for Gandhi, one may reject the claims for sainthood made on his behalf (he never made any such claims himself, by the way), one may also reject sainthood as an ideal and therefore feel that Gandhi's basic aims were anti-human and reactionary: but regarded simply as a politician, and compared with the other leading political figures of our time, how clean a smell he has managed to leave behind!

Is Carter a saint? On second thought, I'll leave God to be the judge of that. Were his aims anti-human and reactionary? Of course not. But I do think we can say of Jimmy Carter, as Orwell said of Gandhi, "how clean a smell he has managed to leave behind!"

RONALD REAGAN
1981–1989

by
Peggy Noonan

IN A PRESIDENT, character is everything. A president doesn't have to be brilliant; Harry Truman wasn't brilliant, and he helped save Western Europe from Stalin. He doesn't have to be clever; you can hire clever. White Houses are always full of quick-witted people with ready advice on how to flip a senator or implement a strategy. You can hire pragmatic, and you can buy and bring in policy wonks.

But you can't buy courage and decency, you can't rent a strong moral sense. A president must bring those things with him. If he does, they will give meaning and animation to the great practical requirement of the presidency: He must know why he's there and what he wants to do. *He has to have thought it through*. He needs to have, in that much maligned word, but a good one nonetheless, a *vision* of the future he wishes to create. This is a function of thinking, of the mind, the brain.

But a vision is worth little if a president doesn't have the character—the courage and heart—to see it through.

•

RICHARD NIXON said there are two kinds of men who run for the presidency, those who want to do big things, and those who want to be big. Those who merely want to be big—to fulfill some sense of personal destiny, to receive self-validation through the hurrahs of the people—have a tendency to act as if their particular talents (and they have talent—they became President, after all) will help them know what their presidency is about once they're there. They are doomed to failure, because the presidency is one office you can't go into assuming it will guide you; you must know what you desire and attempt to guide it.

Ronald Reagan was the first kind of man in the Nixon formulation. He didn't want to be big; he already thought he *was* big. He was secure. He didn't go into politics to fill up some empty hole inside him. He was reluctant to run for the governorship of California in 1966. He still loved show business, and thought he had a future in it. He didn't need politics to feel good about himself.

Reagan was in it for big reasons. Life is mixed and nothing's pure, but he had a purpose beyond the need to fill up an empty suit. And there were things bigger than *staying* in office for Reagan. He didn't need power, which contributed to his power with the people —they could tell he didn't need it, and so felt free to give it to him.

Reagan wanted to do big things. His vision was of a freer and more peaceful world, and of an America in full and vibrant possession of its economic freedoms. When I asked him a while back to sum up his legacy, he responded with words that were blunt and simple. He wrote of himself, "He tried to expand the frontiers of freedom, in a world at peace with itself."

To get a freer and more peaceful world he'd have to confront the world's great troublemaker and trouble-spreader, the Soviet Union. To restore America's economic vitality he'd have to confront the American government, which was sapping that vitality.

He was clear about his intentions. His views were no secret. He spoke of them in the speech he gave in 1964, before he entered politics, a speech so famous that it is still referred to, in political lore, as "The Speech," the one broadcast the week before the voting in the 1964 Goldwater-Johnson race. He wanted to beat back and delegitimize imperialistic communism; he wanted to reduce the size of our own American government; he wanted to reduce the tax burden on the American people, and on American businesses; he wanted to unleash the economy.

He knew what he wanted. He'd thought it through.

He had the vision. Did he have the courage without which it would be nothing but a poignant dream? Yes. At the core of Reagan's character was courage, a courage that was, simply, natural to him, a courage that was ultimately contagious. When people say President Reagan brought back our spirit and our sense of optimism, I think what they are saying in part is, the whole country caught his courage.

There are many policy examples, but I believe when people think of his courage, they think first of what happened that day in March 1981 when he was shot. He tried to walk into the hospital himself but his knees buckled and he had to be helped. They put him on a gurney, and soon he started with the one-liners. Quoting Churchill, he reminded everyone that there's nothing so exhilarating as to be shot at without effect. To Mrs. Reagan, it was, "Honey, I forgot to duck." To the doctors, "I just hope you're Republicans." To which one doctor replied, "Today Mr. President we're all Republicans." Maybe he caught Reagan's courage too.

But Reagan the political figure had a form of courage that I think is the hardest and most demanding kind. A general will tell you that anyone can be brave for five minutes; the adrenaline pumps, you do things of which you wouldn't have thought yourself capable.

But Reagan had that harder and more exhausting courage, the courage to swim against the tide. And we all forget it now because he changed the tide. Looking back, we forget that the political mood of today, in which he might find himself quite comfortable, is quite different from the political mood the day he walked into politics.

But he had no choice, he couldn't *not* swim against the tide. In the fifties and sixties all of his thoughts and observations led him to believe that Americans were slowly but surely losing their freedoms.

When he got to Hollywood as a young man in his twenties, he shared and was impressed by the general thinking of the good and sophisticated people of New York and Hollywood with regard to politics. He was a liberal Democrat, as his father was, and he felt a great attachment to the party. He was proud that his father had refused to take him and his older brother Moon to the movie, *Birth of a Nation*, with its racial stereotypes. And he bragged that his father, Jack, a salesman, had, back long ago when Reagan was a kid, once spent the night in his car rather than sleep in a hotel that wouldn't take Jews. Ronald Reagan as a young man was a Roosevelt supporter, he was all for FDR, and when he took part in his first presidential campaign he made speeches for Harry Truman in 1948.

When Reagan changed, it was against the tide. It might be said that the heyday of modern political liberalism, in its American manifestation, was the 1960s, when the Great Society began and the Kennedys were secular saints and the costs of enforced liberalism were not yet apparent. And that is precisely when Reagan came down hard right, all for Goldwater in 1964. This was very much the wrong side of the fashionable argument to be on; it wasn't a way to gain friends in influential quarters, it wasn't exactly a career-enhancing move. But Reagan thought the conservatives were right. So he joined them, at the least advantageous moment, the whole country going this way on a twenty-year experiment, and Reagan going that way, thinking he was right and thinking that sooner or later he and the country were going to meet in a historic rendezvous.

His courage was composed in part of intellectual conviction, and in part of sheer toughness.

When we think of Reagan, we think so immediately of his presidency that we tend to forget what came before. What came before 1980 was 1976—and Reagan's insurgent presidential bid against the incumbent Republican President, Gerald Ford. Ford was riding pretty high, he was the good man who followed Nixon after the disgrace of Watergate; but Ford was a moderate liberal Republican, and Reagan thought he was part of the problem, so he declared against him.

He ran hard. And by March 1976 he had lost five straight primaries in a row. He was in deep trouble—eleven of twelve former chairmen of the Republican National Committee called on him to get out of the race, the Republican Conference of Mayors told him to get out, on March 18 the *Los Angeles Times* told him to get out, on March 20 the Republican Governors Association told him to quit. The Reagan campaign was $2 million to $3 million in debt, and they were forced to give up their campaign plane for a small leased jet, painted yellow, that they called "The Flying Banana." On March 23, they were in Wisconsin, where Reagan was to address a bunch of duck hunters. Before the speech, Reagan and his aides gathered in his room at a dreary hotel to debate getting out of the race. The next day there would be another primary, in North Carolina, and they knew they'd lose. Most of the people in the room said, It's over, we have no money, no support, we lost five so far and tomorrow we lose six.

John Sears, the head of the campaign, told the governor, You know, one of your supporters down in Texas says he'll lend us a hundred thousand dollars if you'll rebroadcast that speech where you give Ford and Kissinger hell on defense. The talk went back and forth. Marty Anderson, the wonderful longtime Reagan aide who told me this story, said he sat there thinking, This is crazy, another hundred grand in debt. . . .

The talk went back and forth and then Reagan spoke. He said Okay, we'll do it. Get the hundred thousand, we'll run the national defense speech. He said, I am taking this all the way to the convention at Kansas City, and I don't care if I lose every damn primary along the way. And poor Marty thought to himself, Oh Lord, there are twenty-one. . . .

The next night at a speech, Marty was standing in the back and Frank Reynolds of ABC News came up all excited with a piece of paper in his hand that said 55–45. Marty thought, Oh, we're losing by ten. And Reynolds said, You're winning by ten! Reagan was told, but he wouldn't react or celebrate until he was back on the plane and the pilot got the latest results. Then, with half the vote in and a solid lead, he finally acknowledged victory in North Carolina with a plastic glass of champagne and a bowl of ice cream.

Ronald Reagan, twenty-four hours before, had been no-money-no-support-gonna-lose-dead—but he made the decision he would not quit, and at the end he came within a whisker of taking the nomination from Ford.

He lost with 47.4 percent of the delegates behind him. And when it was over he met with friends and staff, and he talked to them in words that were as beautiful a tribute to the system, and to democracy, as ever have been uttered.

He said: "The cause goes on. It's just one battle in a long war, and it will go on as long as we all live. Nancy and I, we aren't going to go back and sit in a rocking chair on the front porch and say that's all for us.

"You just stay in there with the same beliefs and the same faith that made you do what you're doing here. The individuals on the stage may change. The cause is there and the cause will prevail because it's right.

"Don't give up your ideals. Don't compromise. Don't run to expediency. And don't for heaven's sake, having seen the inner workings of the watch, don't get cynical.

"No, don't get cynical. Don't get cynical because look at yourselves and what you were willing to do, and recognize that there are millions and millions of Americans out there who want what you want. Who want it to be that way. Who want it to be a shining city on a hill."

That was nineteen years ago. Needless to say, there weren't many dry eyes in that room, and that was the beginning of the 1980 campaign, which was the beginning of the Reagan presidency, which was the beginning of the revolution currently ongoing in Washington.

•

WE HAVE ALL noticed in life that big people with big virtues not infrequently have big flaws, too. Reagan's great flaw it seemed to me, and seems to me, was not one of character but personality. That was his famous detachment, which was painful for his children and disorienting for his staff. No one around him quite understood it, the deep and emotional engagement in public events and public affairs, and the slight and seemingly formal interest in the lives of those around him. James Baker III called him the kindest and most impersonal man he'd ever known, and there was truth in that. And it caused frustration in his aides, who suspected they were pretty much interchangeable, and were I think pretty much right. That, of course, in the scheme of things, goes under the heading, "Tough." They were lucky to be there. I was lucky to be there.

I wrote in my first book that Reagan's detachment caused a kind of psychic disorientation in those around him. I remember once, shortly after I had left the White House, I had gone back to visit a friend, and Reagan started coming down the hall in one of his big suits. And he saw me, and waved so nicely, and called out, "Hi . . . Patti." His children, particularly Michael, have written movingly about how hard it was to love a man who seemed so removed. As I say, I didn't understand it then and I don't understand it now. Patti Davis recently said that she'd had a kind of epiphany a few years ago. Talking about the old days with her father, she looked in his eyes and realized: He's shy. When it comes to the serious, personal things, he's shy.

There were other flaws, but I kind of liked them.

People said he was lazy. I don't think that was true. I worked for him in 1984, when he was seventy-three, and left when he was seventy-five. And as a seventy-five-year-old man he worked a nine to five day and dinner and speeches in the evening. They said he was uninterested in details, and that was true. He became a conservative in part because he didn't love government, and so, unlike the incumbent President, he wasn't inclined to find its arcana interesting. They said he fell asleep at cabinet meetings. I never saw this, but I hope he did. I only went to one. They were pretty boring because they weren't where the action was; the action was in his office and in the halls and on the phone.

He had a temper. He didn't get mad lightly, but when he did it was real and hit like lightning. House Democratic leader Tip O'Neill tried to instruct him on the finer points of political morality one day in the Oval Office and Reagan took it for a while and then he did some instructing right back, and there's a picture of the two of them, sitting next to each other with their fingers pointing and their faces stern.

Reagan is always described as genial and easygoing, but Marty Anderson used to call him "warmly ruthless." He would do in the nicest possible way what had to be done. He was as nice as he could be about it, but he knew where he was going, and if you were in the way you were gone. And you might argue his ruthlessness made everything possible.

An example: In 1980, when he was again running for President, on the afternoon of the New Hampshire primary, there was terrible staff warfare going on. John Sears, who had helped Reagan come within an inch of Ford just four years before, was the campaign manager. A brilliant man—but he'd forced out some Reagan aides and made some decisions Reagan didn't like, and here they were just hours from what they knew would be a triumphant New Hampshire primary . . . and Reagan pulled the plug, flipped the switch, and fired Sears and his team. In spite of old affection and old loyalty. They weren't cutting it anymore, and they were out.

He was blunt, too. He was a gracious person, at great pains to put people at their ease, but he was not a great respecter of diplomatic niceties and politesse.

This was something new.

You remember when Jimmy Carter kissed Brezhnev at their big summit. This was considered a step forward by the American and European foreign affairs establishments. And the American delegation was full of talk about how the two leaders, Carter and Brezhnev, "dreamed the same dreams and hold the same aspirations for the world."

Well, Ronald Reagan didn't think that was true.

At the Geneva Summit in which President Reagan first met with Mikhail Gorbachev, they talked about Afghanistan. Reagan was given State Department talking points that said things like "Afghanistan is a matter of deep concern to the United States." Reagan didn't think much of the talking points, and instead he told Gorbachev, "What you're doing is perpetuating genocide!" Well, it wasn't genocide, but it was evil, and the point was made. The arms controller Ken Adelman was there and read the notes, and told me the other day he thought the State Department note taker's pants would never dry. . . .

Reagan also told Gorbachev, Look, we can continue to disarm or we can continue the arms race, and I tell you you can't win the arms race, there is no way. . . .

This of course is the President who early in his presidency called the Soviet Union the focus of evil in the modern world. Asked a few years later why, at such a delicate moment and so new in his presidency, he would say such a thing, he replied, "When I called them the evil empire in a public speech, I did it on purpose. I wanted 'em to know that we saw them for what they were."

Some saw in Reagan's words the dawn of a new age of bellicosity. But Reagan thought it was, simply, progress: We were being honest for a change. That speech by the way was not an isolated incident, but part of a strategy.

Two weeks after the speech, Reagan announced that the United States planned to build a protective missile defense system. Now, Reagan for years, since the seventies, had been decrying and criticizing the MAD doctrine, the doctrine of mutual assured destruction that held that neither the Soviets nor America would ever start a nuclear war because both countries would be destroyed. He had long insisted that MAD was mad—he said it's like two guys with guns pointed at each other's heads, sooner or later one will shoot. He had been for decades a great reader of books on military history, and he often thought about how every weapon that had ever been invented was followed by a defensive system to respond to it. The sword was followed by the shield, the invention of the bomb was followed by the bomb shelter.

In 1979, just after leaving the governorship of California, he went to the NORAD defense command in the mountains of Colorado. Huge three-story rooms, monitors, screens, top brass. Reagan got a VIP tour, and the general showing him around was asked at the end what would happen if a Soviet SS-18 hit a few hundred yards outside the big metal doors. The general said, It would blow us away. The NORAD center was built before missiles that size existed. The general told Reagan that in fact, if the Soviet fired a big missile at an American city, what NORAD could do, essentially, was warn the city about fifteen minutes before it hit.

Reagan was aghast. After he left, he said to his aides, We've spent all this money all these years and we can't stop a missile from hitting us. And he said a president having that kind of power, any individual having that kind of power, was unacceptable.

He talked to everyone he could about a missile shield, he got it written into the Republican platform in 1980, and he did everything he could to have it developed. And after the Joint Chiefs and the scientist Edward Teller started working on it, he announced its development and told Gorbachev we're going ahead with it, and it's not a negotiating device, and if we succeed we'll share it with you.

Naturally, it made the Soviets furious. They felt forced to the wall, they couldn't keep up with Reagan's defense buildup—literally, a *defense* buildup—because their economy couldn't sustain it, and they knew they couldn't catch up with what became the Strategic Defense Initiative (SDI). And it was for them—as many of them have admitted since 1983—the beginning of the end for their system.

Gorbachev and everyone else, by the way, badly underestimated Reagan's sophistication on this issue. He wasn't about to trade it away. Since SDI threatened no one, he pointed out again and again, there was nothing belligerent in maintaining it. And he pointed out again he'd share it with anyone.

Tom Clancy said Reagan had a guardian angel, but it wasn't at his side, it was off whispering in the ears of his enemies, "He's just an actor . . . don't take him seriously . . . he's not very bright. . . ."

Reagan was truly castigated for all this, though, in the American press, in Europe, among the intellectuals. They pounded him, they kept saying it's destabilizing. They were correct, but not as they intended: It was destabilizing all right. It destabilized the Soviet Union right off the map.

So HE WAS DARING. He was also steadfast. Ronald Reagan opposed abortion, as you know. But he was the only one in his top staff who did so; he was surrounded by people who told him, Don't talk about it, don't get involved, leave it alone, it's an 80–20. That was their mantra, It's 80 to 20 in the polls, only 20 percent fully oppose it, it's not an issue that helps your popularity, so forget it.

Mrs. Reagan was pro-choice, his children were pro-choice. He was surrounded. But it was Reagan's willingness to veto the appropriations bill for the Department of Health and Human Services during his first term that saved the Hyde amendment. Henry Hyde told me recently, It was Reagan who did it, Reagan alone.

The Hyde amendment forbade the use of federal taxpayer funds to pay for abortion. And Reagan said he would veto the entire appropriations bill for HHS in order to save that amendment when it was first put forward.

It would be a tough veto. There were billions of dollars in the appropriation, which included funding for popular programs, the entire National Institutes of Health, cancer research. Hyde told me it was the third biggest budget in the *world*. To veto that over an unpopular and controversial question like abortion was unheard of. It was the opposite of politically astute—it enraged and further empowered the pro-choice movement and its allies; and as for Reagan's allies, he didn't have to do it to please his pro-life constituency because, ultimately, where were they going to go? He was all they had. They'd stick with him anyway if he backed other parts of their agenda.

But that wasn't the way he looked at it. It wasn't politics. The way he looked at it, when something is as controversial as abortion, the last thing you want to do is make taxpayer funds go to providing it.

And so he stuck to his guns, and waited the Democratic majority in Congress out, and Congress blinked and sent over a new HHS budget with the Hyde amendment attached—and Ronald Reagan signed it. Taxpayer funds would not be paid to provide for abortions unless the mother's life was in danger.

Henry Hyde told me recently, "He was strong. And I have always thought the world of him for standing tall on that issue."

PART OF COURAGE, one of the least noticed forms of courage, is simple consistency. And one way to judge consistency in a president is to look at what he promises when he runs for office, and what he later fights for and delivers.

Reagan in 1980 castigated the inflation rate under Carter, said that inflation robs the old of their savings and the young of their wages. Inflation was running at 12.5 percent in 1979, Jimmy Carter's last year. Reagan promised to cut it in half. By 1983, Reagan had it down to less than 4 percent, and it remained at 3–4 percent throughout his presidency.

He promised to cut taxes. He delivered dramatic cuts in tax rates for individuals and businesses.

He said he'd reduce unemployment. The day he came into office, it was 7.4 percent. When he left, it was 5.4 percent.

He said he'd back a tighter monetary policy. He did. The Fed applied the brakes in '81, he backed them, took a recession, absorbed a huge political cost, but it worked.

He said he'd lower interest rates, and he did—by 1986 they were less than half what they were when he took office. He said he'd fight off protectionism, and he did. He said he'd reduce federal regulation, and he did. The *Federal Register*, which grew to 87,000 pages of rules and regulations under Carter, sank to a low of 47,000 by 1986. One of Reagan's first official acts was to freeze all new federal regulations for sixty days, and many were later amended or killed.

He said he'd cut the bureaucracy, and he did, the number of federal workers actually declining slightly during his eight years in office.

He said he'd name a woman to the Supreme Court, he said he'd oppose racial quotas, he said he'd appoint conservatives for once to the federal bench, he said he'd oppose abortion. Done, done, done, and done.

He said he'd balance the budget. He didn't. It is said by his liberal critics—most of whom, it must be added, never decried a deficit until they could pin one on Reagan—that the reason behind the growth of the deficit was increased defense spending. But this is not true, and they know it. Reagan did increase defense spending, but only after Carter had cut it seriously, and Reagan's increases were very modest as a proportion of the budget. Then the liberals charged the budget deficit went up because Reagan's pets, those wild and woolly supply-side economists, convinced him, wrongly, that if taxes were cut, tax revenues would increase as a result of increased economic growth and action. According to liberal lore, Reagan cut taxes, and tax receipts went down, and thus the deficit soared.

But this too is untrue. When Reagan cut taxes, the amount of tax money going to the government *did* increase—just as the supply-siders predicted. Only not enough to keep up with increased government spending.

Which gets us to the cause of the deficit, and Reagan's part in it. It is not exactly a secret that the growth in the power and cost of government in the past thirty years has been the work and desire not of conservatives, but of liberals whose programs, embodied in the Great Society and after, were huge, costly, fully national. For thirty years, when Reagan took office, an entrenched Democratic Congress had been on what might fairly be called a taxing and spending binge. (A Reagan standby: "What's the difference between a liberal and a drunken sailor on leave? The sailor spends his own money.") And, sadly—for the nation and, even now, I would say for the Republican Party—many Republicans won and kept power in those years by accepting and becoming part of what the Democrats were doing.

By the time Reagan came in in 1980, the Democrats of Congress were still spending, entitlement spending was entering its out-of-control stage—and every time Reagan tried to cut the budget, he was damned in the media as an insensitive rich man.

The liberals devised a strategy as brilliant as it was, I would argue, wicked: If Reagan tried to cut spending, they'd call him cruel and use big media to get the message pounded home. If Reagan didn't try to cut spending, the deficit would grow, in which case they'd call him irresponsible and use big media to pound the message home. Either way he lost, they won.

Reagan didn't cut. He tried and often succeeded in winning modest decreases in the size of various programs' yearly increase. But he did not effectively day by day make a priority of attempting to cut the cost of the federal government. There were reasons. I think it comes down to this: His priorities were reigniting the economy and defeating communism; he never got to the war he would have had to fight with Congress to cut spending. And it would have taken a war.

Am I making excuses for him? Yes, but I think they're valid. I'm not sure anyone could have, in that climate and in those days, fought three wars at the same time. He won on communism and won on taxes but didn't fight hard on spending—and that is his failure.

IN FOREIGN AFFAIRS, he said he wouldn't bow to the Soviet Communist state, he'd call 'em what they were and convince them to come to the bargaining table, not through plaintive pleas but through strength. He went to Westminster and made a speech in which he said the Soviet Union was over, done for, finished, and would soon be consigned to the ash heap of history.

The Soviets walked out of arms talks in 1982, hoping to humiliate him and put him on the defensive in the eyes of the world. He built up the military, began the development of SDI, and they came to the bargaining table. And they made a deal.

He said he'd restore our neglected defenses. He did. He modernized forces, restored the Navy to 580 major ships. He walked into office saying he wanted real arms control: he didn't want to control the growth, he wanted to cut the arsenals, and he wanted to develop a space shield to protect America from ballistic missiles. Well, he finally got the Soviets to the bargaining table, and he got Gorbachev to eliminate intermediate-range nuclear missiles in Europe, and, by sticking with the Strategic Defense Initiative, he helped roll the Soviets aside. He supported the Afghan rebels, spurring the Soviets to start withdrawing from Afghanistan; he toppled a Marxist regime in Grenada; he helped keep alive the Contras who ultimately, by not disappearing, helped do in the Sandanistas.

As the *National Journal* conceded when he left office,

> Reagan has thrived on taking bold risks, has been thick-skinned in the face of criticism . . . he will exit the Oval Office with head held high and accomplishments that the history books will record. . . . With infectious optimism and an insouciant refusal to be dragged down by the burdens of age or office, he has rekindled national pride and exuded a sense of assurance that the country's problems could be managed.

And he accomplished all that while enduring a few personal dramas of his own. He was shot in 1981 and, we now know, almost died. He endured two cancer operations.

You look at those eight years—the first two-term presidency since Eisenhower—and they are breathtaking.

That is why I think that as we get around, as the century turns, to pondering the great presidents of this century, it will come down to two men: Mr. Roosevelt, FDR, of New York, and Mr. Reagan of California. Both changed the realities of government in America, both changed the map of the world.

Reagan of course is not yet celebrated as one of our greatest presidents. In fact there is an extraordinary disjunction between what he did and how he is viewed by modern historians, between his accomplishments and his historical reputation.

Some of this is inevitable. Big men, when they leave the presidency, are often dismissed and derided for years before we see their true dimensions. As I say, this is inevitable. You need distance before you can see how big the mountain is. Up close, a mountain's just a mass; but take some time and travel away from it, and you can turn back and see how big it was, and how it changed the landscape.

Reagan changed the landscape.

But critics are ever busy, and as Reagan was ideologically vivid his enemies were ideological, and vivid, too.

Back in the winter of 1994 I got to thinking about all this, and wrote Reagan, asking how he felt about it.

And he replied, "I'm not the sort to lose sleep over what a few revisionists say about my record. I'm more than willing to submit my actions to the judgment of time. Let history decide; it usually does."

A very Reagan reply. He thinks justice will happen the same way he thought the Berlin Wall would fall.

His critics continue to say he was just lucky, an affable dunce controlled by his staff, who lucked out in history's Lotto.

I happen to think the first thing to remember is that historians are intellectuals; some writers are intellectuals; and many journalists view themselves as intellectuals. And intellectuals have always thought Ronald Reagan dumb, for one essential reason: He thought the wrong things. He thought like a conservative; they thought like liberals. Ergo, Reagan must be dumb.

Also, intellectuals tend to be most comfortable in the realm of abstractions, and that wasn't Reagan's kind of mind at all. He wasn't really drawn to abstractions, didn't love them. His mind was drawn to the concrete, to the lessons of history and the truths to be found in experience. This is a form of intelligence the elites put down, but it is in its way as subtle as that of the intellectuals. Reagan believed in what he had experienced in life. When he first met with Gorbachev and had to negotiate arms control, he had no great anxiety because, as he put it, he'd been president of the Screen Actors Guild, he'd negotiated with Sam Goldwyn and Jack Warner, and Gorbachev was nothing compared to those guys.

His mind was commonsensical and grounded in reality, in what he'd seen and heard and witnessed over the years—and in what he'd read. His friend Ed Meese recently reminded me that Reagan was a loner, an affable loner. He liked to read, he was happy to be by himself or with Nancy and just read. Ed remembered him always carrying a book and magazines and newspapers with him.

Also, Reagan never protected his intellectual flank. When he first ran against Pat Brown for governor of California, Brown said, Reagan is nothing but a dumb actor who reads scripts. Reagan could have gone into full erudition overdrive and impressed everyone with his reading—"As Milton Friedman said," "As Hayek observed"—but instead he laughed and told people how much he liked to read the comics. (This is a man who, when he was accused of being lazy, answered, "I know hard work never killed anyone but I figure, why take a chance?")

He had no intellectual vanity, and part of the reason was that he had no great respect for intellectuals, not just because they seemed so wrong on so much but because Reagan believed in God. Reagan was schooled, by his mother, in the Bible. And so Reagan believed that God made the foolish things of the world to confound the wise, God created the common sense of the gas station attendant to outshine and outweigh the cerebral contortions of the Marxist professor from Yale. Reagan was as impressed as anyone else by brains, but he didn't think that just because you were smart you were right. (He liked to say an economist was a guy with a Phi Beta Kappa key on one end of the chain, and nothing on the other.) He didn't assume you had anything interesting to say just because you had a high IQ.

Young John Kennedy made it a point to pepper his conversation and his speeches with historical references and quotes that underscored, sometimes subtly, the idea of his erudition. And that was a smart thing to do: just because it was calculated doesn't mean it wasn't genuine. He *was* well read, and an accomplished author. But he knew that as the handsome young heir of a great fortune, he ran the risk of being dismissed early on as a dilettante and a playboy.

Reagan, himself dismissed early on as a pretty-boy actor, never made it a point to broadcast his intellectual interests. It would have been high hat, showoffey, very non-midwestern, even non-Hollywood, those being the days when stars were loathe to chatter on about their thoughts for fear of being obnoxious. Also, why would he waste time trying to impress reporters and writers, most of whom opposed his politics and most of whom were invested in Reagan as idiot, not Reagan as wise man? It's good to remember that there was no conservative counterestablishment in the fifties and sixties to counter the liberal establishment, no real corps of conservative columnists and commentators. George Will was in college in the sixties, Bill Safire was in public relations and about to become a speechwriter, Pat Buchanan was a young editorial writer, the young masters of the editorial page of the *Wall Street Journal* were some of them literally babies when Reagan started out in politics. He had no media to do his work for him, to play Boswell for him.

I WILL END with a story about kindness, the almost Lincolnian kindness that was another part of Reagan's character, and that always seemed to me to balance out the famous detachment.

Everyone who worked with Reagan has a story about his kindness. One that is unknown is the story of Frances Green. She was eighty-three years old and lived by herself on Social Security in a rough neighborhood in a town called Daley City, in California. She had very little money, but for eight years she'd been sending one dollar a year to the Republican National Committee.

And one day she got in the mail an RNC fund-raising letter as only the Republicans would do it—beautiful, thick cream-colored invitation, black and gold writing—to come to the White House to meet President Reagan. She didn't notice the little RSVP card, and she didn't notice the suggestion that a positive reply be accompanied by a donation. She thought she'd been invited because they appreciated her dollar a year.

So she took every cent she had, and she took a four-day train trip across America. She couldn't afford a sleeper, so she slept sitting up in coach. And she showed up at the appointed time at the White House gate: a little old lady with white hair, white powder all over her face, an old white suit that was now yellow with age, white shoes, white stockings, an old hat with netting. She gets to the guard, and there's an executive with Ford Motor Company standing behind her. He's watching her and he knows there's something wrong here, this extraordinary old woman all by herself who looks like Mary Pickford.

She gives her name to the guard, and he goes down the list, and he says, brusquely, Your name isn't here, you're not cleared in. She says, Oh, I was invited. But he won't let her in. She's heartbroken. The Ford executive takes all this in, takes Frances Green aside, and gets her story. He says, Stay here. He goes into the White House, he can't get anyone to help him, he goes back out to her. Mrs. Green is standing there, looking through the gate at the White House. He says, Can you stay in Washington a day or two? She says yes, she plans to. He says, Good, go to your hotel and meet me here at nine in the morning on Tuesday. He knows by then he'll be able to do something.

She's heartbroken but she leaves. The Ford executive goes to Anne Higgins, a presidential aide, Anne goes to the President's secretary and tells her the story, she goes to President Reagan, he says, Bring her in here when she comes. Tuesday arrives, and it's what you might call a heavy news day—Ed Meese resigns, there has been some military action abroad. The executive knows Reagan won't be able to take any time.

But he meets Frances Green at the gate and he gives her a

wonderful personal tour of the White House, and then he goes by the Oval Office at the appointed time, thinking maybe she can get a glimpse of the President. They're waiting outside the Oval Office, the National Security Council comes out, generals come out, the Ford executive peeks in, Reagan gestures to him. Frances Green walks in.

This is why Reagan is Reagan. He knows Mrs. Green is a little old lady all by herself in the world, she's no one, with nothing to give him, and Reagan is behind his desk, and he rises and calls out, "Frances!" He says, "Those darn computers, they fouled up again! If I'd known you were coming I would have come out there to get you myself." He asked her to sit down and they talked about California, and he gave her a lot of time, and if you say on a day like that it was time wasted, there are a lot of people who'd say, Oh no it wasn't. No it wasn't.

So that was Reagan. There are a million such stories, and they're part of why those who loved Reagan loved Reagan.

So HE WAS very kind, very brave, had many flaws, and stuck to his guns. And his legacy is this: He unleashed the greatest peacetime economic expansion in all of U.S. history. And within a year of his leaving the White House, the Berlin Wall fell . . . and Soviet communism, which at its height held millions of people in its grip and the whole world its nuclear hostage, collapsed.

Not too bad for Jack Reagan's son, Pat Brown's hapless opponent, Jerry Ford's losing adversary, and the intellectuals' favorite affable dunce.

Ronald Reagan loved to quote Tom Paine to the effect that we have it within us to remake the world. He was occasionally castigated for this and told, no we don't, grow up.

But the leading practitioner in our time of the least romantic political philosophy was, I think, something of a romantic: a man who saw in the sweep of history the constant attempts of men and women to find lives of decency and freedom, to win and protect their rights from inevitable oppressors, to move toward the good, to walk awkwardly toward grace. And so I will, in tribute to him, end on a romantic note.

We live, still, though we all forget it, in a time of giants. Our music is banal, our culture is not elevated, our movies sweep the globe leaving us thinking: poor globe.

But when it is evening in America, dawn is breaking over Rome; and the Pope who helped Reagan bring down communism is likely, at this moment, preparing for morning mass. And, wherever she is, Margaret Thatcher is perhaps thinking about or dreaming about her next big speech on Chechnya or Bosnia; or perhaps she is reminding her American friends, as she did a short while ago, that Ronald Reagan was elected President at the age of sixty-nine, and she is sixty-nine and not currently occupied.

And in the city of Los Angeles, in the suburb of Bel Air, on a street called St. Cloud Way, sleeps a grand old warrior, too worn by time to fully apprehend the drama now in Washington.

For there a freshman class of seventy-three Republican men and women in the Congress of the United States are in day 61 of their "Contract with America." They believe they are part of a great effort to save a country by beating back a government. And they are Reagan's children.

I spend my days covering the new Congress. And I walk the halls of that spectacular old Capitol building with the high windows and the high rays of light and the shined stone floors, and through the Rotunda, and Statuary Hall. And I see the congressmen rushing out of the subcommittee meeting and running to vote, and right above them, unnoticed, will be the statue of old Ben Franklin, and Thomas Jefferson, and Andy Jackson, and Father Damien who lived with the lepers, and schoolmarms who broke through the Northwest Territory and tamed a savage wilderness . . .

They are shiny, bronze and heroic, these statues, and they were made by people who knew that no one becomes perfect but some become great, and just as some of us are very bad, some of us are actually very good, and some of us have helped our country.

In *John Brown's Body*, Stephen Vincent Benét wrote of the old agitator, and of his times:

Sometimes there comes a crack in Time itself.
Sometimes the earth is torn by something blind.
Sometimes an image that has stood so long
It seems implanted as the polar star
Is moved against an unfathomed force
That suddenly will not have it any more.
Call it the *mores*, call it God or Fate,
Call it Mansoul or economic law,
That force exists and moves.
                    And when it moves
It will employ a hard and actual stone
To batter into bits an actual wall
And change the actual scheme of things.

Ronald Reagan was the kindest, sweetest man ever to be a hard and actual stone who changed the actual scheme of things. And that is what they could say on his statue, if they put it up in Statuary Hall, where it belongs.

GEORGE BUSH
1989–1993

by

Michael R. Beschloss

RAISED WITHIN the pre–World War II Republican Party of the eastern seaboard and Wall Street, of Theodore Roosevelt and Wendell Willkie, George Herbert Walker Bush had the misfortune of spending his political career trying to quash the suspicions of a party that was rushing toward the South, West, and right. More than any other leader portrayed in this book save Eisenhower, Bush based his campaigns for the presidency less on issues and ideology than on his persona as a leader of experience and character.

Born in Milton, Massachusetts, in 1924, Bush matured in Greenwich, Connecticut, a setting that gave him little inkling of the political culture in which he would spend his adulthood. The boy was surrounded mainly by Anglophile, moderate Republicans, for whom politics was Good Government and the town meeting, who minimized partisan confrontation and overstatement. As Bush's mother, Dorothy, admonished, one did not brag about oneself. Extremism, even in the defense of liberty, was a vice.

Into young adulthood, Bush was influenced by three political leaders who would have served as splendid models had the Republican Party remained frozen in amber after World War II. The first was his father, Prescott S. Bush, a New York investment banker, founder of Planned Parenthood, and board member of CBS. As George recalled, "Dad was a Republican and was active in state party fundraising, but the subject of politics seldom came up at family gatherings. Once a week, he would sit in as moderator of the Greenwich town meeting, but that was more of a civic than a political commitment."

In 1950, Prescott Bush ran for the U.S. Senate from Connecticut. "I knew what motivated him," his son later wrote. "He'd made his mark in the business world. Now he felt he had a debt to pay." Like most Republicans of his state and class, the elder Bush was an internationalist who felt that the Roosevelt-Truman domestic programs had done the country some good but had gone too far. He wished to craft a "responsible Republican alternative," revising and editing the excesses of the Democratic majority.

After a hairbreadth loss in 1950, Prescott Bush was elected in 1952 to the unexpired term of the late Brien McMahon. He served in the Senate for a decade. It was the kind of fit between a leader, his state, and his party that his son George never enjoyed. The elder Bush's moderate politics were eminently suited to the Connecticut of the 1950s. These were the years that Dwight Eisenhower was trying to recast the Republican Party at the center of American politics, promoting "modern Republicanism."

As the best Republican golfer in the Senate, Prescott Bush was often sought by Eisenhower to join him on the course at Burning Tree Club. In the Senate, he was admired for his congenial rectitude and good fellowship. Even though he voted to censure Senator Joseph McCarthy in 1954, he was one of the few senators to visit the Wisconsin demagogue in the hospital when he fell ill. Like his son later, he was a stickler for responding to every letter and telegram.

In 1962, Senator Bush's final year in office, Yale gave an honorary degree to him and to President John F. Kennedy, in a ceremony that brought JFK and George Bush together for the only time of their lives. On that occasion, Kennedy said that in the mid-twentieth century, "political labels and ideological approaches" were "irrelevant" to "solutions." What was needed was "not labels and cliches, but more basic discussion of the sophisticated and technical questions" of government. Although the language was Kennedy's, this was, almost word for word, the political credo of the senior Bush. Privately the son could not have disagreed, but had he used such rhetoric at any Republican Convention from 1976, when his party began its lurch to the right, through 1992, when he was nominated the second time for President, he would have been heckled.

A second political model for George Bush was Franklin Roosevelt's legendary Secretary of War, Henry L. Stimson, who spoke at Bush's graduation from Andover in 1942. Stimson was what a later generation would have called the chairman of the American establishment. During the world crisis that followed the fall of France in 1940, he had joined FDR's cabinet—an act of particular boldness for a Republican during a presidential election year. Stimson was the embodiment of the notion that foreign policy should be set above partisan wrangling. Republican interventionists loath to honor Roosevelt for anything at all looked on Stimson with hero worship.

Stimson told the Andover Class of 1942 that while America would need fighting men for the long war, the students would serve their country better by acquiring more education before donning a uniform. George Bush was unconvinced. That summer, at the age of eighteen, he had himself sworn into the Navy. But Stimson lingered in Bush's mind as a supremely honored leader for whom foreign policy provided refuge from domestic partisanship. Stimson was at the center of the great moral struggle of the twentieth century, the fight against fascism in Europe and Asia, which was the formative political experience of Bush's generation. In August 1990, after Saddam Hussein's invasion of Kuwait, the forty-first President repeated almost verbatim the words Stimson spoke at Andover, vowing "to stand up for what's right and condemn what's wrong."

For Bush, perhaps the most serious political model of all was the thirty-fourth President. Dwight Eisenhower was the first president Bush ever met, the first he voted for, and the first who knew him by name. Prescott Bush was among those who had called on the Supreme Commander of NATO to return from Paris and save America from the isolationism of the Republican presidential front-runner, Senator Robert Taft. When Eisenhower once scrawled out a list of possible presidential successors, Senator Bush's name ranked high. George Bush was the kind of fine young man whom Eisenhower hoped to bring into politics. In 1968, although Bush was merely a freshman congressman from Houston, Eisenhower urged Richard Nixon to consider him for Vice President: George was a "comer."

During the Eisenhower era, Prescott Bush once introduced his son to a French diplomat in Washington by saying, "One day George is going to be President." For a young Republican of the 1950s imagining a career that might lead to the White House, Eisenhower, the most beloved American leader of the time, would have seemed a superb example. Would not future Republican presidents resemble Ike, the instinctively moderate, apartisan leader, who considered domestic politics tawdry, who was venerated for his command of foreign and military affairs? As late as 1979, when Bush announced his first candidacy for President, he approvingly quoted Eisenhower's demand for moderation—"a middle way between the untrammelled freedom of the individual and the demands for welfare of the whole nation." As Vice President and President in the 1980s and 1990s, struck by the full strength of the Republican right, Bush would not have dared use such rhetoric.

HAD BUSH in 1948 stayed in Connecticut after his heroism in the Pacific War and graduation from Yale, he would have been well poised to succeed his father in politics. As senator from Connecticut, George Bush would have been temperamentally and ideologically in tune with his state and party. Instead, eager to hack out his own business career, the young man took his wife, Barbara, and son, George, to the oilfields of Texas. This meant that from the day he entered politics, he would have to submerge many of his views and instincts to please an electorate that was notably more conservative than he. Politics was easier for Ronald Reagan: for every minute of his political career, he had the luxury of being in natural harmony with his party.

Not Bush. The first harbinger of this was in the spring of 1962, when Houston friends persuaded him to run for chairman of the Harris County Republican Party, whose slogan was "Conservatives Unite!" The local party was in imminent danger of takeover by the John Birch Society. During a speech near Houston, Bush was asked where he stood on the "Liberty Amendments." This referred to planks in the John Birch program such as "get the U.S. out of the U.N." and "abolish the Federal Reserve." Baffled, Bush turned to his wife, working on her needlepoint, who could offer no help. Bluffing, he told the questioner he needed time to study "these important amendments." Like a Puritan in Babylon, Bush tried both to broaden his party and mollify the Birchers, telling a colleague, "There's some good in everybody." The reply: "George, you don't know these people. They mean to kill you!"

Having learned that lesson, Bush swung to the opposite extreme when he ran for the Senate in 1964. He opposed the Civil Rights Act and the Nuclear Test Ban Treaty. He wished to arm Cuban exiles to go after Fidel Castro. He denounced the United Nations. The Democrats were "too soft" on Vietnam: if the generals asked for nuclear weapons against the North, they should not be ignored. Back in Connecticut, Prescott Bush was hoping that someone like Nelson Rockefeller, Henry Cabot Lodge, or William Scranton would save the Republican Party from Barry Goldwater. His son implored him not to say a word about this in public. He was for "Mr. Conservative."

Since Texas Republicans were scarce, Bush hoped to win by exploiting a split among the Democrats. His Democratic opponent,

Senator Ralph Yarborough, was a liberal and a sworn enemy of Lyndon Johnson, whom he called a "power-mad politician." Bush hoped to attract enough conservative Democrats to slip through. One reason John Kennedy came to Texas in November 1963 was to heal the cleavage: he worried that if Bush ran ahead of Yarborough in 1964, it would jeopardize his own chance to win Texas.

After Kennedy's murder, Johnson flew to Houston and threw an arm around Yarborough's shoulder in front of photographers. When Johnson's limousine passed by Republican headquarters, Bush, ever the gentleman, told his campaign workers to go downstairs and wave at the President. The campaign went downhill from there. Bush charged Yarborough with dangerous left-wing radicalism. His opponent retorted that Prescott Bush should not have sent his "carpetbagger" son, "little Georgie," darling of the Birchers, down to Texas to "buy" a Senate seat. Amid the national Johnson landslide, Bush lost the election with 44 percent of the vote. He told his Houston minister, "I took some of the far-right positions to get elected. I hope I never do it again. I regret it."

Never again during his career did George Bush wage a campaign so unrelievedly conservative, or so oriented toward issues. When he ran for Congress from Houston in 1966, he created the archetype of the Bush campaigns of the future: the candidate's personal qualities were emphasized over stark ideological commitments. Bush told a reporter, "Labels are for cans." Opposed by a conservative Democrat, he assembled a coalition of Republicans and moderate Democrats to win with 58 percent. As if to suggest that he had turned his back on the 1964 experience, one of Bush's first congressional actions was for aid to birth control, his father's old interest, which moved the chairman of the Ways and Means Committee, Wilbur Mills, to refer to the young freshman as "Rubbers."

Another sign of Bush's new moderation was his vote in April 1968 for Lyndon Johnson's Fair Housing Act, which banned discrimination in the sale and rental of housing. In his district, Bush told a town meeting that it seemed "fundamental that a man should not have a door slammed in his face because he is a Negro or speaks with a Latin American accent." He was jeered. Bush wrote a friend, "I never dreamed the reaction would be so violent. Seething hatred —the epithets. . . . The country club crowd disowning me and denouncing me. . . . Tonight [I was on] this plane and this older lady came up to me. She said, 'I'm a conservative Democrat from this district, but I . . . will always vote for you now.' . . . Her accent was Texan (not Connecticut) and suddenly somehow I felt that maybe it would all be OK—and I started to cry—with the poor lady embarrassed to death—I couldn't say a word to her."

Although he suffered for his support of the Voting Rights Act, Bush's House seat was probably safe for as long as he wished. Nor did the vote seem likely to harm him when he decided to run for the Senate in 1970. Presuming that his foe would again be Yarborough, Bush knew that this time the Democrat would not benefit from an incumbent President's patronage or the wave of sympathy that followed the Kennedy assassination. In a straight contest of liberal versus moderate conservative, right-wing Texans would have nowhere to go but Bush. The congressman from Houston grandly hoped that 1970 might even mark a realignment in Texas politics, which was still Democratic by more than four to one. Retaining their conservative base, Republicans might somehow make inroads into the black and Hispanic electorate.

These hopes collapsed when former Democratic Congressman Lloyd Bentsen defeated Yarborough in the primary. Like Bush, Bentsen was a World War II veteran with experience in business and politics. No less conservative than Bush, he was able to mobilize the Democratic majority that might have fled a renominated Yarborough in large numbers. This encouraged Bush all the more to avoid ideology. Contriving to cast the election in terms of a Republican future versus a Democratic past, he said, in his patrician Connecticut accent, "We're on the threshold of a new de-*cade*." (Knowing how hard Bush was working, his handlers could not bring themselves to remind him that Texans did not accent the second syllable.) Nor did Bush have the stomach to resort to low tactics.

After Bush's defeat with 46 percent, President Nixon's aide Charles Colson complained to his boss that the Texan had "refused to allow us to use some very derogatory information about Bentsen. . . . We probably should have forced him to do more."

WITH HIS SECOND DEFEAT for the Senate, Bush had come to the end of his tether in Texas politics. The next six years he spent in the very different world of the bureaucracy—as Nixon's Ambassador to the United Nations that he had once denounced; as Republican national chairman; as President Gerald Ford's envoy to China; and as Director of Central Intelligence. Working in foreign policy for the first time, Bush seemed to find his calling. Diplomacy drew on his natural talents as an extrovert. He was impressed that the Chinese Foreign Service assigned some of its best people not to substance, but protocol. The Chinese believed that a congenial negotiating atmosphere could compel foreigners to relax pursuit of their own interests. Nixon and Henry Kissinger would have thought this absurd. Bush thought it ingenious. Twenty years later, as President, he could cite the relationships he had built through informal visits, handwritten letters, and telephone calls with such leaders as Hosni Mubarak of Egypt and François Mitterrand of France as crucial in building the international coalition that fought the Persian Gulf War.

Dealing with issues free of partisanship, that crossed party lines, at a time of national Cold War consensus, liberated Bush from the kind of demeaning struggle and compromises he felt he had had to make in electoral politics. More than ever, he was drawn to distinguish high statesmanship from the grubbing for votes required to put statesmen in office. Cultivating presidents nurtured his innate qualities of fidelity—not coincidentally, the name he later gave the cigarette boat kept at his summer home in Kennebunkport, Maine.

Bush as appointee showed few of the kind of independent views that made Franklin Roosevelt a restless and unpredictable member of Woodrow Wilson's under-cabinet. At the United Nations in 1971, even after he discovered with horror that Nixon had compelled him to use his good name to fight Taiwan's expulsion from the United Nations while the President and Kissinger had been quietly doing the opposite, Bush did not complain.

As Nixon's party chairman during Watergate, Bush defended the President across the country until it was absolutely plain to him that Nixon had lied to him in denying involvement in the scandal. At the cabinet meeting in August 1974 which turned out to be Nixon's last, Bush infuriated Nixon by counseling him to resign. For Nixon, the problem was not so much the message—others closer to the President were giving him the same advice—as Nixon's expectation of nothing but loyalty from Bush. After Nixon quit, Gerald Ford came close to choosing Bush for Vice President but changed his mind after his trusted friend Bryce Harlow advised him that "many top leaders" regarded Bush as "intellectually 'light,' " and that selecting him would be viewed as "a weak and depressingly conventional act."

By the end of 1975, Bush's presidential chances were dying. When Ford nominated him to head the CIA, Democrats considering Bush's confirmation, who worried about the Agency's politicization, persuaded the President to promise not to consider Bush for his 1976 ticket. After Jimmy Carter's election, Bush quietly told the President-elect that he would be willing to stay on as his CIA director in order to encourage later presidents to remove the job from politics. This offer showed how far Bush had gravitated from partisan struggle. Had Carter accepted, it would have crippled Bush's future in national politics. With his notion of proper behavior, it would have been almost unimaginable for him to quit Carter's administration in mid-term and then run against the man.

DURING HIS FIRST presidential campaign in 1980, Bush bowed to no one in denouncing Carter's softness toward the Russians. But like his father and Eisenhower, he grounded his appeal for votes on his own persona. Bush strategists gushed about "the best résumé in America" and hoped that, although Bush was more conservative than a Rockefeller or Lodge, his family links would draw the support of the still sizable northeastern wing of his party. To show their man more vital than the sixty-nine-year-old Reagan, they had him jog before photographers, insisting that, unlike some people, he was "up for the eighties." Television commercials heralded "A President We Won't Have to Train." Asked how he could seek the presidency without a traditional base, Bush said, "I've got a big family and lots of friends." What was he proudest of? "The fact that our children still come home."

This approach brought Bush victory in the Iowa caucuses, where Reagan scarcely campaigned. With the national spotlight shining on him, the weeks before the crucial New Hampshire primary gave him the opportunity to explain with Reaganesque clarity what he would do if elected. Instead, Bush prattled away that he had the big momentum—the "Big Mo"—which suggested to conservatives that this was not a leader who took their causes with due gravity. Bush later confessed that such "preppy phrases" gave "an impression that my campaign lacked substance." In New Hampshire, Reagan turned the tide, besting him by more than two to one.

Bush said later that he should have spent more time on "the vision thing." Even allowing for the late-1960s slang, this was not a term that many other leaders in American history would have used. Not driven in any case by deep ideological passions, especially in domestic affairs, Bush knew that extensive public discussion of his general instincts (civility and moderation, Planned Parenthood, gun control, civil rights, the natural right to rule of the eastern establishment) was not likely to help him in the new Republican Party. Thus vision, which stood at the core of the greatness of such presidents as Washington, Jefferson, Lincoln, and the two Roosevelts, became for the campaigning Bush almost a set of disagreeable passwords which, if uttered, would open the gates of the presidency. Did he understand the damage that conservative Republicans could do to him after he became President if they concluded that he had not meant what he said?

At the Republican Convention in Detroit, Ronald Reagan worried about the depth of Bush's convictions. At first he resisted advice to choose for Vice President the man who had gotten the second most votes in the primaries. He privately disparaged Bush's ability to "stand up to the pressure of being President": "I'm concerned about turning the country over to him." He worried about the depth of Bush's convictions. But after former President Ford withdrew his name from consideration, Reagan swallowed his doubts, made the call, and asked Bush whether he could support the party platform, the most conservative in forty years.

This was no small question. During the primaries, Bush had derided Reagan's hallmark pledge to cut taxes while hugely increasing the defense budget as "voodoo economics." He had supported abortion rights. But, willing to pay the price for political rebirth, Bush immediately told Reagan that he could support the platform "wholeheartedly." Deprecating "the vision thing," he underestimated how much this somersault would annoy many of his old moderate supporters, who began viewing him as a trimmer, and raise the suspicions of conservatives, who were unconvinced by his nomination-eve conversion and suspected that Bush could just as easily betray commitments he made to them. Senator Jesse Helms of North Carolina and others on the right were persuaded to retract their threat to oppose Bush's nomination, but they kept a wary eye on the new Vice President.

Bush's eight years as Reagan's number two were made miserable by his ostentatious effort to convince what he privately called the "extra-chromosome" conservatives that he was not some kind of closet one-world liberal. Bush's vice-presidential predecessor, Walter Mondale, had warned him after the 1980 election that "a President does not want and the public does not respect a Vice President who does nothing but deliver fulsome praise of a President." But Bush felt that his only chance for President in 1988 lay in winning over Reagan and his increasingly dominant wing of the party. On the simple level of private character, he showed admirable loyalty. More than any other vice president of the postwar era,

Bush refused to allow sunlight between himself and his President. He eschewed background interviews with reporters designed to make himself look good at the boss's expense and used all public opportunities to demonstrate himself as a Reaganite, at one moment incautiously saying, "I'm for Mr. Reagan, blindly!" He defended himself by saying that in his family, loyalty was "not considered a character flaw."

It was the unrelenting ardor of that loyalty, from a Vice President who had once so disagreed with the Reaganites, that critics considered a character flaw. The political philosopher Garry Trudeau, in his cartoon strip "Doonesbury," wondered whether the Vice President had put his "manhood in a blind trust." The conservative columnist George Will wrote that Bush had become a Reagan "lapdog," emitting "a tinny 'arf.' " Richard Nixon privately recalled that Prescott Bush had been "tough as nails, with that ramrod, erect posture, but I just don't know what's happened to George."

IN NOVEMBER 1986, the Iran-Contra scandal, almost like a practical joke, threatened to turn Bush's closeness to Reagan into a brutal liability. For some of those with the greatest doubts about Bush, the episode seemed to expose the problem with his manner of being number two. A Vice President of more independent mien, willing to tell his President when he thought he was wrong, might have kept Reagan from being drawn into an affair that had his administration accused of violating the President's vow not to trade arms for hostages and of breaking the law to funnel money to the Nicaraguan Contra rebels, which put Reagan in some danger of impeachment. Bush carefully devised a strategy for surviving the scandal which had him sticking by his President but claiming that he had been "out of the loop" of the decision making. Dictating an entry into his private diary, he said, "I think in the long run . . . it will be O.K., and then we can have stories out there [saying] 'Didn't panic, didn't run, didn't duck away from the President.' " Over the short term, this strategy worked, helping Bush to withstand the scandal along with Reagan. But as the Iran-Contra investigations dragged on, it left Bush vulnerable to the possibility that some piece of evidence might suggest that he was indeed in the loop.

In 1988, Bush's loyalty to Reagan did not move the President to scrap his longtime refusal to choose sides in Republican primaries. But eight years of courting the Moral Majority, the right-to-life movement, and other conservative groups had sufficiently disarmed the right that Bush won the nomination. Bush's two terms as Vice President had not changed his tendency to value, more than most national leaders do, personal virtues such as congeniality and deference over public virtues like political courage and commitment. If anything, they made him more hungry for the kind of filial loyalty he had offered Reagan. From among twelve vice-presidential finalists, including incontestably greater leaders such as Senator Bob Dole of Kansas and Congressman Jack Kemp of New York, Bush chose Senator Dan Quayle of Indiana, who seemed to offer Bush that kind of obeisance.*

NOT EVEN BUSH would argue that his fall campaign against Massachusetts governor Michael Dukakis was a lofty moment of his political life. Designed by the no-holds-barred operative Lee Atwater of South Carolina, whom Bush had groomed during his party chairman days, it demonstrated Bush's old emphasis on character and personality over divisive issues, and illuminated the stark distinction Bush had come to draw between high statesmanship and base politics. Some Bush television commercials showed the candidate as family man and statesman, embracing his granddaughter and hobnobbing with world leaders like Margaret Thatcher ("Ready from Day One to Be a Great President"). Others evoked the race card by denouncing Dukakis's support for a program (actually inherited from his Republican predecessor) of weekend furloughs for life

---

* But if this was Bush's assumption, he was wrong. As Vice President, Quayle spoke up against Bush's views during official meetings and made a quiet effort among activists and the press to suggest that, unlike the President he served, he was a genuine conservative.

prisoners without parole, such as the convicted black murderer Willie Horton, who used his weekend off to stab a white man and rape a white woman in Maryland.

In the tradition of the southern candidate who denounced his opponent's wife as a "thespian," Bush called Dukakis, a first-generation Greek-American, "a card-carrying member of the A-C-L-U [American Civil Liberties Union]," which subliminally raised the specter of un-Americanism. This was reinforced when Bush castigated Dukakis for having vetoed a measure to require recitation of the Pledge of Allegiance in Massachusetts schools. In case some voters did not get the point, Bush made certain to be photographed visiting a flag factory and pledging support for a constitutional amendment to prohibit burning of the American flag. More than anything else, Bush's campaign would be remembered for his New Orleans convention promise: "Read my lips—No new taxes!"

After winning the presidency with 54 percent of the vote, Bush immediately dismissed the pyrotechnics of his campaign as irrelevant: "The American people are wonderful when it comes to understanding when a campaign ends and the world of business begins." But even if Americans were willing to forget Willie Horton and the flag factory, Bush's way of winning the presidency had deprived him of a clear mandate for a set of actions. When Reagan was elected in 1980, he could claim large national support not just for himself as a personality in juxtaposition to the unpopular Jimmy Carter, but for a wide array of specific positions, starting with tax cuts, a balanced budget, and a large defense buildup.

Bush could not, even on the issue that fired his imagination more than any other—foreign affairs. During the campaign, with an eye to impressing the right, he had staked out a position on the Soviet Union more hard-line than Reagan's, declaring himself more skeptical of Mikhail Gorbachev's reforms. But even on this issue, Bush had been ambiguous enough that on taking office in January 1989, he felt compelled to order a four-month "policy review" to decide what approach to take with Moscow.

The new President did enjoy a moment of good feeling that enveloped the nation and the world. The year 1989 was a time of almost eerie, happy quiet. The U.S. economy was still booming. Eastern Europe was hurtling out of the Soviet orbit. Bush was content to keep a remarkably low profile, proposing to Congress one of the most modest first-year domestic programs of the postwar era. Despite his campaign rhetoric, he made no serious effort to cut federal spending or the Washington bureaucracy. In the spirit of the President and the time, some intellectuals repeated the arguments of Francis Fukiyama and other scholars that with the Cold War ending, they were witnessing the "end of history." This was just as some had once predicted, at the time John Kennedy gave his Yale speech, "the end of ideology."

Bush had enough sense to recognize that he was the beneficiary of an unnatural calm before some kind of historical torrent. In September 1989, during a television interview in the White House family quarters, he gestured at George P. A. Healy's 1868 portrait of Abraham Lincoln and his generals, *The Peacemakers*, and said that, unlike Lincoln, he had not been "tested" yet. During those early months, Bush did little to exploit the instant of goodwill by enlisting the public behind a series of vital domestic issues, as Reagan had. This might have deepened Bush's national support so that it might better survive the moments of crisis and setback that befall every president.

Instead the Reaganites began to feel seduced and abandoned. During the campaign, Bush had encouraged the impression that his first years in office might be tantamount to Reagan's third term, with many Reagan appointees held over and the former President perhaps flown in from California from time to time as a kind of political godfather. That did not happen. Few high officials survived from the era of Reagan into that of Bush. During the Bush presidency, the forty-first President, who still held the hearts of most Republicans and to whom Bush owed his office, appeared in the White House exactly twice. Many conservatives suspected that by thumbing his nose at Reaganism, the new President, intoxicated by victory, was paying them back for all the years of humiliations while courting the right.

If they were correct, Bush was showing dangerous hubris and self-indulgence. The Republican Party, if anything, was growing more conservative than ever. If Bush did not wish to expend the effort to try moving his party to the center, as Eisenhower had attempted and failed to do, it would have been more sensible for the President to show that he understood the balance of forces within his party. But, buoyed by his high approval ratings, Bush gave signs of allowing himself to believe that he was unsinkable. His "what-me-worry?" attitude culminated in July 1990, when he reneged on his supreme campaign promise not to raise taxes. This told conservatives once and for all that Bush was not really one of them. It stripped the President of an essential layer of political support just as the nation was dropping into a grave recession for which many Americans were likely to blame him.

Still, it was during that same period of strange quiet that Bush worked toward the two achievements for which his presidency will probably be best remembered: his contribution to the end of the Cold War, and the U.S. victory over Saddam Hussein in the Persian Gulf. Had someone other than Bush been President during those years it is conceivable that the Cold War could have ended under terms less favorable to the West than it did. Bush's gift for building relationships with other leaders was put to excellent use with Gorbachev. Like Bush, Gorbachev had spent his political career concealing his private views from superiors and a party that did not share them. Like Bush, he was uncomfortable with the intense emotion and the unpredictability unleashed by ideological true political believers like Boris Yeltsin. The two men felt that they spoke the same language.

Through their summits and other means, Bush succeeded in putting the Soviet leader at ease that if he made dangerous concessions, such as allowing his Eastern European satellites to go free, he could expect Bush not to exploit them or embarrass him for domestic political gain. When Gorbachev allowed the Berlin Wall to collapse, Bush denied himself considerable domestic capital by refusing to go to Berlin and capitalize on the victory. The best example of Bush's diplomatic talent was the swift unification of Germany within NATO. After the Wall fell, almost immediately Bush asked Gorbachev to set aside Russia's historical fear of the German nation and accept its inclusion in the Western alliance that for forty-one years had been devoted to containment of the Soviet Union. Bush's strategic vision had told him that if the Cold War were truly to end, Germany must be unified and the division of Europe ended fast.

This required a gamble. Since the time of Adolf Hitler, whatever they said in public, American leaders had been anxious that a unified Germany might resume its authoritarian, militaristic, and expansionist history. Adlai Stevenson said privately in the 1950s that the one truth an American politician could never tell the voters was that America would never tolerate German unification. Thanks largely to Bush's diplomacy, Gorbachev agreed to a unified Germany within NATO in July 1990, only eight months after the Wall fell. Had the process taken a fortnight longer, German unification might have languished while the Soviet Union and the West struggled with a more urgent danger—Saddam Hussein's invasion of Kuwait.

AFTER THE IRAQI ARMY struck in August 1990, few others who might have been President would have seen the threat as sharply as Bush did. Notwithstanding whatever role the Reagan and Bush administrations had in bolstering Saddam's military might, Bush's history in the oil industry and his international experience enabled him to instantly understand the danger of Saddam in domination of the Middle East with weapons of mass destruction.

The President took on serious hazards by declaring that the Iraqis' act would not stand. The routing of the Iraqi army by an international coalition seemed anything but foreordained. Bush knew how difficult it would be to prod Americans and Congress, in the post-Vietnam age, to support what might be an extended conflict with tens of thousands of casualties. No one could foresee that Bush and his Secretary of State, James Baker III, would succeed in building an international coalition to fight such a war, establishing a standard for the post–Cold War era. A President of lesser mettle might have convinced himself that Operation Desert Storm fought by a coalition was not worth the trouble or the domestic political danger. The Persian Gulf War displayed Bush's best political self: a President of stature, willing to take risks and exert himself to educate the public in international relations, in ways that he was never willing to do in domestic affairs or party politics.

Bush emerged from the Gulf War in March 1991 with a public approval rating of 91 percent, but with the recession in earnest. Some political advisers proposed that he wage an "Operation Domestic Storm" to strengthen the economy and address other domestic problems ignored during Bush's first two years. The President refused. He saw his Gulf victory, the approaching end of the Cold War, and his commanding popularity as a vindication of his decision to concentrate on world affairs. Calling attention to the weak economy would merely damage public confidence and prolong the recession. And who could unhorse a President so clearly indispensable in foreign policy? Rather than respond to increasing signs of public discomfort, he looked the other way.

RUNNING FOR REELECTION in 1992, Bush was faced with what he later called the "most bizarre" political year he had ever seen, "the worst year of my life." Required to prove himself all over again to Reagan Republicans, admonished to describe his domestic vision for a second term, Bush was playing to his weaknesses. It was only as the year wore on that the President fully realized that voters were no longer absorbed with world affairs and, with the recession still on, demanding to know what kind of leadership he would exercise to relieve their misery. The President and his aides tried one speech, television commercial, and slogan after another to describe "the Bush agenda" to the public. They failed because voters perceived that the President's heart was not in it.

Before the Republican Convention at Houston, pollsters advised Bush that substituting a new running mate for Dan Quayle might help him win a close race. Franklin Roosevelt would never have been fazed by such a prospect; in 1944, he pushed Henry Wallace over the side without batting an eyelash. As the New Dealer Thomas Corcoran once said, "A great man cannot always be a good man." But Bush displayed the same fealty to private virtues that had led to Quayle's selection in the first place. While briefly tempted, he refused to dump a Vice President who, he thought, had been so loyal to him—even if it meant reelection.

Of Bush's eight political campaigns, in none did the issue of character figure so prominently as in the last. In the fall of 1992, running consistently behind Bill Clinton, threatened also by the independent candidate Ross Perot, Bush found the voters obsessed by the economy and domestic problems. In this atmosphere, he sought to build a fire wall for himself on the issue of character. He could not bring himself to believe that Americans would oust him in favor of someone like Clinton, who had avoided the draft and confessed problems in his marriage. In the Oval Office, while flipping through a memorably illustrated article on Clinton's self-described paramour Gennifer Flowers, Bush told an aide, "Can you imagine other world leaders reading that before he's even inaugurated? I worry about what this means for the country!"

Thus the President's final campaign took refuge in Bush's public persona as a man of character. Underlying this was the notion that a president's principal role was chief of state, who had to have sterling personal qualities and an unblemished background for schoolchildren to look up to him and other national leaders to respect him. In her convention speech nominating Bush, Secretary of Labor Lynn Martin repeatedly cried, "You can't be one kind of man and another kind of President!" On the hustings, Bush quoted Horace Greeley: "Fame is a vapor, popularity an accident, riches take wing, and only character endures." For those who did not get the point, Bush added, "I believe that is especially true in the Presidency."

Clinton's campaign tacitly argued, in contrast, that in the modern age, character should not be defined in terms of traditional private virtues. By now, so the argument ran, Americans were sophisticated enough to no longer require a parent in the White House. Especially during a crisis like a recession, they wanted a tough, informed, responsive political manager who could make difficult decisions on domestic issues, whatever his personal history. Bush and his handlers cast aspersions on Clinton's draft history, his protest against the Vietnam War, and his student trip to Moscow. Clinton replied in their first presidential debate by circling back to the start of Bush's life and career. He implied that the President had grown so desperate for reelection that he had become the kind of American that Prescott Bush had once opposed: "Your father was right to stand up to Joe McCarthy. You were wrong to attack my patriotism."

By the last week before the election, Bush had aroused enough doubts about his opponent that, according to one poll, he had drawn dead even with Clinton. Then came the indictment of Reagan's Defense Secretary, Caspar Weinberger, with the release of evidence suggesting that Bush may have been more involved in the Iran arms-for-hostages decision making than he had insisted. Clinton seized the opportunity to argue that Bush had no business taking the high road on character. Bush's gains fell away almost overnight, destroying the last chance that he might eke out reelection.

It is not without irony that, after convincing Americans that he was better equipped than Bush to handle the sagging economy, Clinton thus cinched the election on, of all things, the issue of character. During the 1992 campaign and afterwards, he had presumed that if he proved a canny enough leader, Americans would be content to overlook his personal defects and ignore the President's need to be a unifying national emblem. As if to dispense with that role, Clinton in his early months gave up many of the ceremonial trappings of the presidency in order to impress the public with his relentlessness and devotion to getting his program passed. But, like a low-grade fever, public doubts about the new President's character and personal qualities kept his popularity from rising to a point commensurate with his presidential performance. This suggested that Americans had in no way surrendered the notion that a president must be a unifying figure of personal character and virtue, an example to their children—the task that George Bush filled so successfully.

The chief-of-state and commander-in-chief role conformed perfectly to Bush's instinctive desire to avoid partisanship and ideology. This manifested itself in Bush's high public approval ratings of 1989, when the President was so publicly quiescent, and of 1991, during the Persian Gulf crisis, when he was operating as war leader. But by requiring that a president be politician as well as monarch, the Founders had asked for more. Bush showed boldness in foreign policy, but not where it counted for the voters of 1992.

GREATNESS SOMETIMES requires a synthesis between leaders and their times. Had Franklin Roosevelt to preside over the status quo prosperity of the 1920s or the 1950s, he would probably have been a frustrated and mediocre President. Had Dwight Eisenhower, the ineffective public educator, been President in the teens or the late 1930s, he probably would have failed to convince Americans that they should enter wars in Europe and Asia. If the Republican Party of the 1980s had remained the moderate preserve of Wall Street and Main Street, if the Americans of the 1990s had remained absorbed by foreign affairs, Bush's historical reputation would probably be assured.

Greatness can also emerge when leaders try to remake the political setting in which they find themselves. Had Bush been less willing to ignore his natural instincts, he might have fought to move his party closer to the center or to show Americans why, even in the absence of a Soviet threat, they must maintain their interest in foreign affairs. Instead, alongside the brief shining moment of the Persian Gulf conflict and the end of the Cold War, Bush is likely to be viewed by future generations as a leader who tried but ultimately failed to synthesize a political personality that would allow him to thrive in a party and political culture in which the Prescott Bushes, Henry L. Stimsons, and Dwight Eisenhowers were rapidly becoming extinct.

About the Authors

DORIS KEARNS GOODWIN is the author of the *New York Times* bestseller and Pulitzer prize winner *No Ordinary Time: Franklin and Eleanor Roosevelt: The Home Front in World War II*, as well as *The Fitzgeralds and the Kennedys* and *Lyndon Johnson and the American Dream*. She lives in Concord, Massachusetts, with her husband, Richard Goodwin, and their three sons.

DAVID MCCULLOUGH is the author of six widely acclaimed books, including *The Johnstown Flood*, *The Path Between the Seas*, *Mornings on Horseback*, and, most recently, the *New York Times* bestseller and Pulitzer prize winner *Truman*. He is host of *The American Experience* and was narrator of Ken Burns's *The Civil War* and other PBS documentaries.

STEPHEN E. AMBROSE is the author of the *New York Times* bestseller *D-Day*, as well as a two-volume biography of Dwight D. Eisenhower and a three-volume biography of Richard Nixon. He lives in Bay St. Louis, Mississippi, and Helena, Montana.

RICHARD REEVES is the author of eight books, including the national best-seller *President Kennedy: Profile of Power* and *An American Journey: Tocqueville in Search of Democracy in America.* He lives in Los Angeles with his wife, Catherine O'Neill.

ROBERT DALLEK is a professor of history and public policy at UCLA. He is the author of several books, including *Franklin D. Roosevelt and American Foreign Policy, 1932–1945,* which won a Bancroft Prize, *The American Style of Foreign Policy: Cultural Politics and Foreign Affairs,* and *Lone Star Rising: Lyndon Johnson and His Times, 1908–1960,* the first part of a two-volume biography.

TOM WICKER, who lives in New York City and Vermont, retired in 1991 after twenty-five years as a political columnist for the *New York Times.* He is the author of nine novels and five works of nonfiction, including *One of Us: Richard Nixon and the American Dream.*

JAMES CANNON is a writer and a politician. He has written for *The Baltimore Sun, Time,* and *Newsweek,* for whom he was chief political writer, national affairs editor, and chief of correspondents. He served as a political adviser to Governor Nelson Rockefeller of New York, Assistant to President Ford for Domestic Affairs, and Chief of Staff to Senate Majority Leader Howard Baker. His most recent publication is *Time and Chance: Gerald Ford's Appointment with History.*

HENDRIK HERTZBERG has been Executive Editor of *The New Yorker* since September 1992. Prior to that he worked for *The New Republic,* including two stints as its editor, was a staff writer for *The New Yorker,* and was a San Francisco correspondent for *Newsweek.* Mr. Hertzberg served on the White House staff during the whole of the Carter administration. He was President Carter's chief speechwriter from 1979 to 1981.

PEGGY NOONAN was special assistant to President Ronald Reagan and chief speechwriter to Vice President George Bush during the 1988 presidential campaign. She is the author of two books, *What I Saw at the Revolution:*

A Political Life in the Reagan Era and *Life, Liberty, and the Pursuit of Happiness.* She lives in New York.

MICHAEL R. BESCHLOSS is the author of five books on the American presidency, including *Kennedy and Roosevelt: the Uneasy Alliance, Mayday: Eisenhower, Khrushchev and the U-2 Affair,* and *The Crisis Years: Kennedy and Khrushchev, 1960–1963.* He has held appointments in history at St. Antony's College, University of Oxford; the Harvard University Russian Research Center; and the Smithsonian Institution.

ROBERT A. WILSON has his own communications company in Dallas and is a partner with David McCullough in their film and television production company. He and his wife, the photographer Laura Wilson, have three sons, Andrew, Owen, and Luke.

Index